ROBERT A. HEINLEIN

CITIZEN OF THE GALAXY

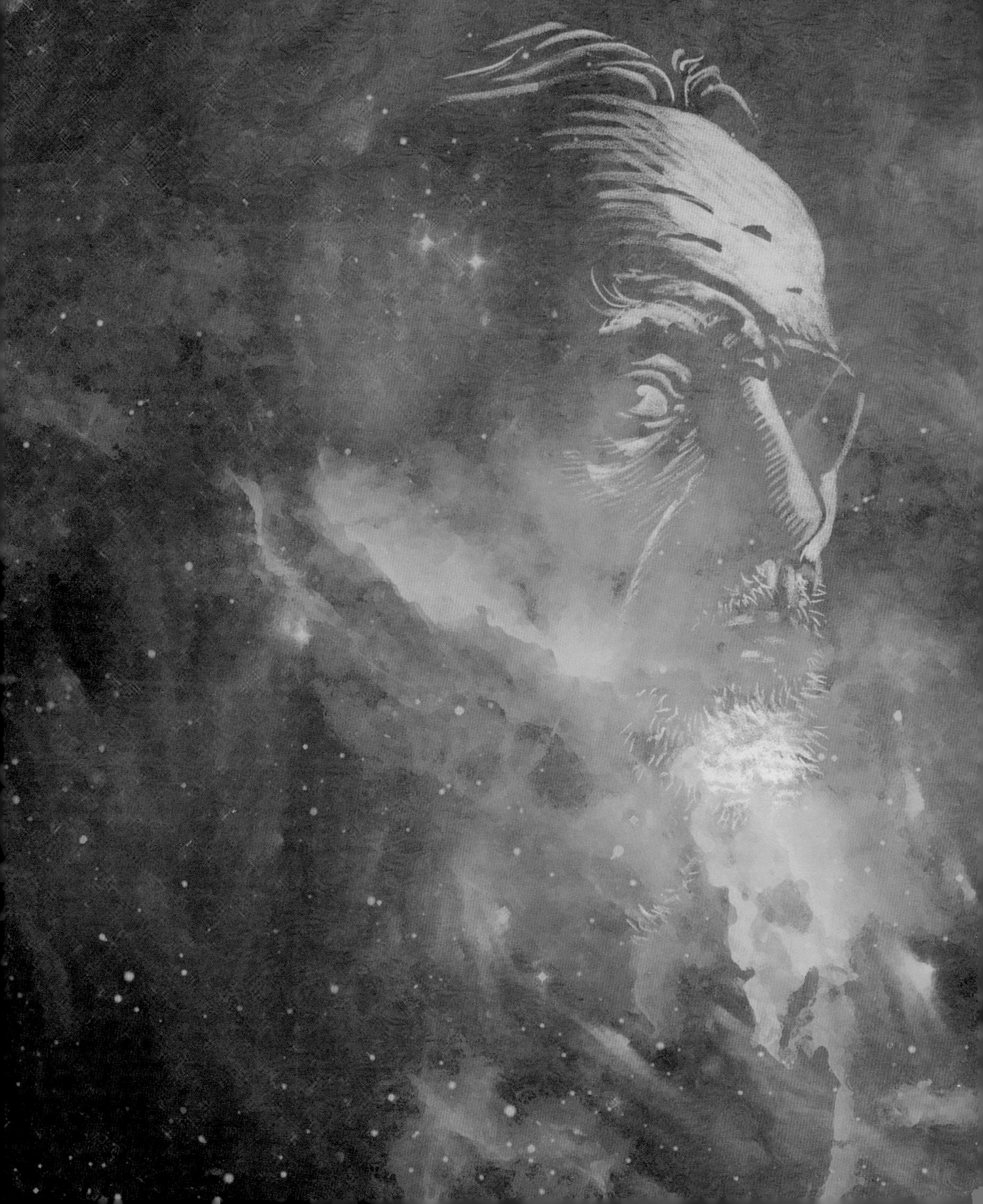

CITIZEN OF THE GALAXY

Adapted by
ROB LAZARO & ERIC GIGNAC

Art by
STEVE ERWIN

Inks & Colors by
ERIC GIGNAC

Letters by
ERIC GIGNAC & RICHARD SHEINAUS

Series Edits by
RED DULA & TOM WALTZ

ISBN: 978-1-63140-361-3

18 17 16 15   1 2 3 4

www.IDWPUBLISHING.com
IDW founded by Ted Adams, Alex Garner, Kris Oprisko, and Robbie Robbins

Ted Adams, CEO & Publisher
Greg Goldstein, President & COO
Robbie Robbins, EVP/Sr. Graphic Artist
Chris Ryall, Chief Creative Officer/Editor-in-Chief
Matthew Ruzicka, CPA, Chief Financial Officer
Alan Payne, VP of Sales
Dirk Wood, VP of Marketing
Lorelei Bunjes, VP of Digital Services
Jeff Webber, VP of Digital Publishing & Business Development

Facebook: **facebook.com/idwpublishing**
Twitter: **@idwpublishing**
YouTube: **youtube.com/idwpublishing**
Tumblr: **tumblr.idwpublishing.com**
Instagram: **instagram.com/idwpublishing**

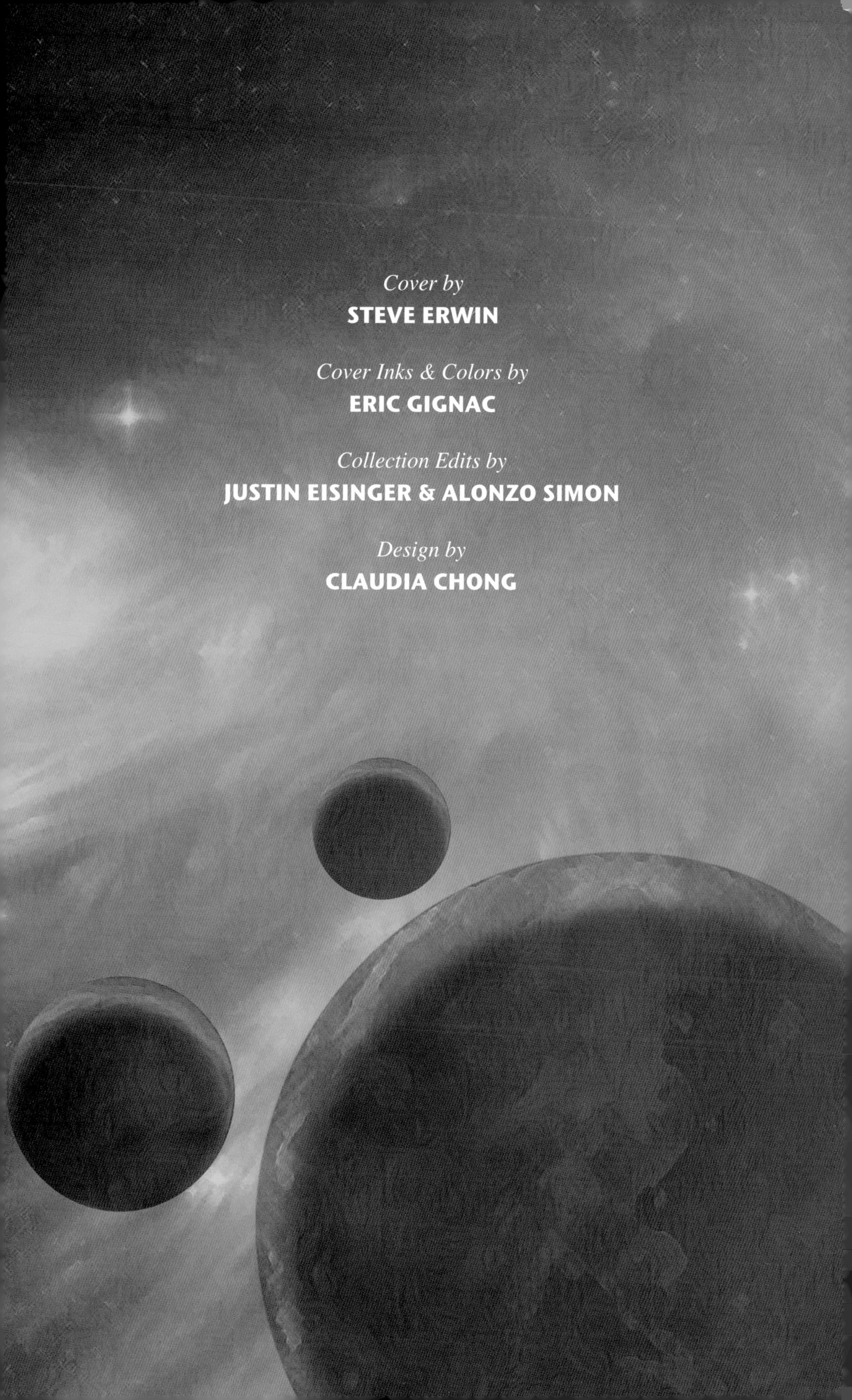

Cover by
STEVE ERWIN

Cover Inks & Colors by
ERIC GIGNAC

Collection Edits by
JUSTIN EISINGER & ALONZO SIMON

Design by
CLAUDIA CHONG

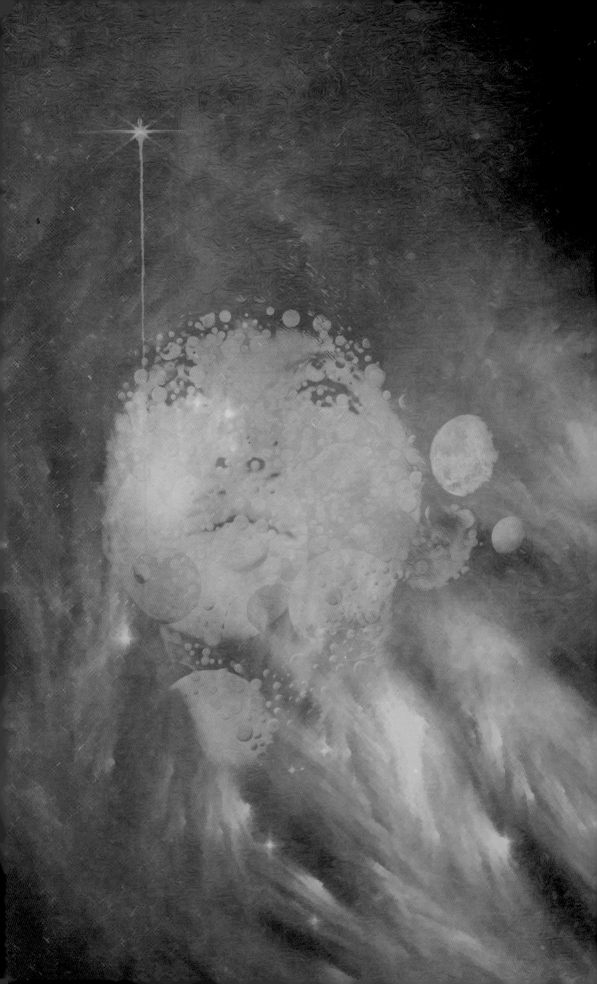

ABOUT CITIZEN OF THE GALAXY

(excerpt from the Virginia Edition Collection)

by

Robert James, Ph.D. and William H. Patterson, Jr.

IN THE AUTUMN of 1956, the privations and sacrifices of World War II were a fading memory. America was prosperous and complacent, self-satisfied with the way of life that had come about—except for that little "duck and cover" thing—and conformist. In a year that brought the U.S. into conflict with its former allies, England and France, over the Suez Canal, in which Nikita Khrushchev's Soviet Union bloodily crushed democratic revolutions in Poland and Hungary, the most-watched television event of the year was Lucy "Ricardo" having her baby on national television. By that point, Robert and Ginny Heinlein had been around the world twice in the last three years and knew at first hand that the progress which western liberal thought had achieved in America was not an established fact anywhere else in the world. Heinlein knew things could revert to the way things had been throughout most of human history, at any time.

All these matters were roiling in the back of his mind when the fall of the year came on, and it was time to write another book for Scribner's. Heinlein's ongoing struggle with his editor, Alice Dalgliesh, had settled into a working relationship, functioning if occasionally prickly. The conflicting advice Miss Dalgliesh offered about the age of the protagonist—and the confrontation she had forced on him with a children's librarian two years before—stymied his mental processes. "It isn't any one tabu; it is the total effect of all of them, until I feel mentally paralyzed—staked out with threads like Gulliver." The dilemma always put him in an emotional tailspin:

> *The kids' books worry me too much. Each one means four months of chronic insomnia and physical debilitation simply because I am so acutely conscious that so many censors stand between me and my readers.*

His best solution, he decided, was to avoid the problem altogether. This time, it would not be merely the growth of a boy into a man (the usual juvenile formula) but the growth of an individual from slave to free—"an adult story without a love interest," as Ginny Heinlein said of it.

Citizen of the Galaxy is a declaration of war against the enslavement of the human race, following in Thomas Jefferson's footsteps: "I have sworn upon the altar of God eternal hostility against every form of tyranny over the mind of man." Dangerous sentiments in a conformist era, when librarians and teachers wanted their charges orderly and well-behaved and quiet.

Heinlein once implied that the book was written without any preparation whatsoever:

> . . . *the brute force method was used on this one—no notes, no outline, just sit down at the typewriter and stare at the paper until something happened—and keep on staring, no letup.*

Nevertheless, there were at least two prior brainstorming sessions on paper. The first quite clearly laid out what became the basic plot of the beginning of the novel: "Our hero is a beggar-thief in a big city, an orphan . . ."

At all costs, though, ". . . it must be funny, adventurous, romantic." The second set of notes are for the Free Traders section. He considered Mark Twain's *The Prince and the Pauper* as a model, but it is Rudyard Kipling's seminal juvenile-for-adults, *Kim*, that gave him the basic framework for his story. Using models in this way can lead to rank imitation and copying—but as Pablo Picasso said, "Bad artists copy. Great artists steal." Ultimately, Heinlein followed his own best advice: "Or don't consider any of them and cut loose!" Whatever influence remained of those generative sources, Heinlein turned them into his own kind of art. The blank paper Heinlein stared at was first given the unfortunate title of "Uncle Tom's Cabin in the Sky." His focus had already settled on that "peculiar institution" that has been with mankind for most of its existence, persisting even today.

The book eventually became "The Chains and the Stars" and finally gained the title under which it was published: *Citizen of the Galaxy*. Thorby begins as a literal slave, in rags and on the auction block. With the help of a fiercely independent, loving mentor, he learns how to be free despite his slave condition— free inside, where it counts. That is the first step, on which all the rest are based. Thorby moves from example to example of how free men live, each conducting warfare against the slavery around them.

Continued...

As in *Time for the Stars*, the boy's family is itself an obstacle, but Thorby discovers that his own war shall take place on a different battlefield, freed from his family and from the tyranny of great wealth. The price of that freedom is eternal vigilance: every man, every woman, has to grow up, and having accepted his or her position freely, must do the right thing. Heinlein was tackling the most serious subject he had ever written about. The idea that slavery still exists, is not a dead issue, must still be fought over and over again, was serious enough, subversive enough, that the book did not need much of the between-the-lines subversion he had been crafting into these boys' books.

In choosing to attack slavery, at a time when the civil rights movement was facing stiff opposition, at a time when the free governments of the world were being challenged by the Cold War, Heinlein persisted in his chosen role as a teacher of the young. The lessons of freedom were crucial to his sense of purpose. Perhaps this is why he dedicated the book to Fritz Leiber, whose work was in a temporary eclipse following publication of *The Green Millennium* in 1953. As he said in one of the unpublished letters to Miss Dalgliesh, "The message [my work] carries—the message I try to put into my stories—is that all customs change, but that a free man with a free mind, a mind willing to study hard to learn the immutable truths, is at home anywhere, on any planet, in any culture." Regardless of the difficulties the market gave him, regardless of the struggles with his editor, these juveniles were Heinlein's personal battlefield, freely chosen. Heinlein, too, had sworn "eternal hostility against every form of tyranny over the mind of man." We were to be his recruits in that war—volunteers, of course. Every one of us.

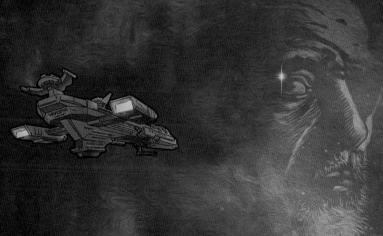

This work is dedicated to the memory of
William H. Patterson, Jr.
(1951 - 2014)

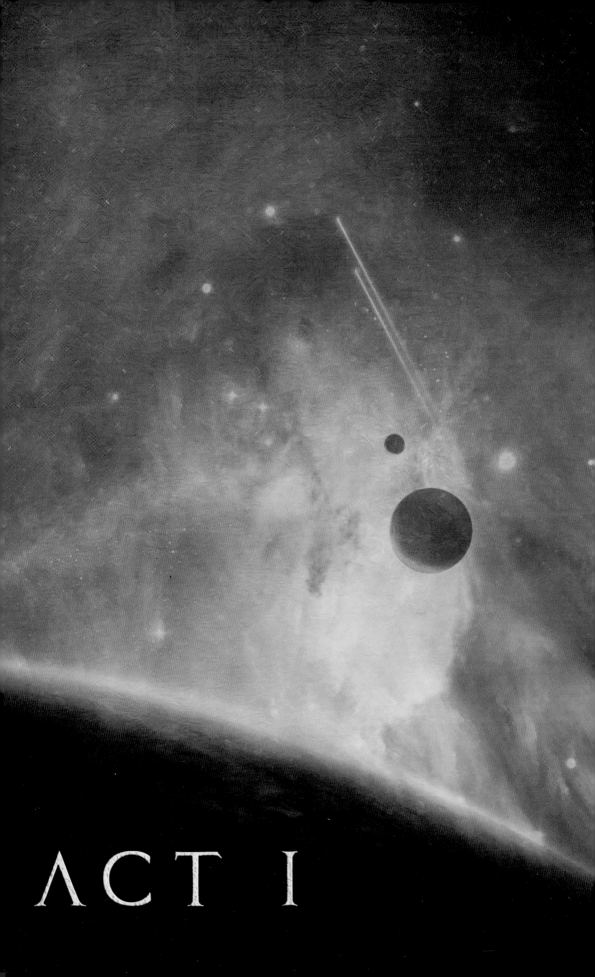

ΛCT I

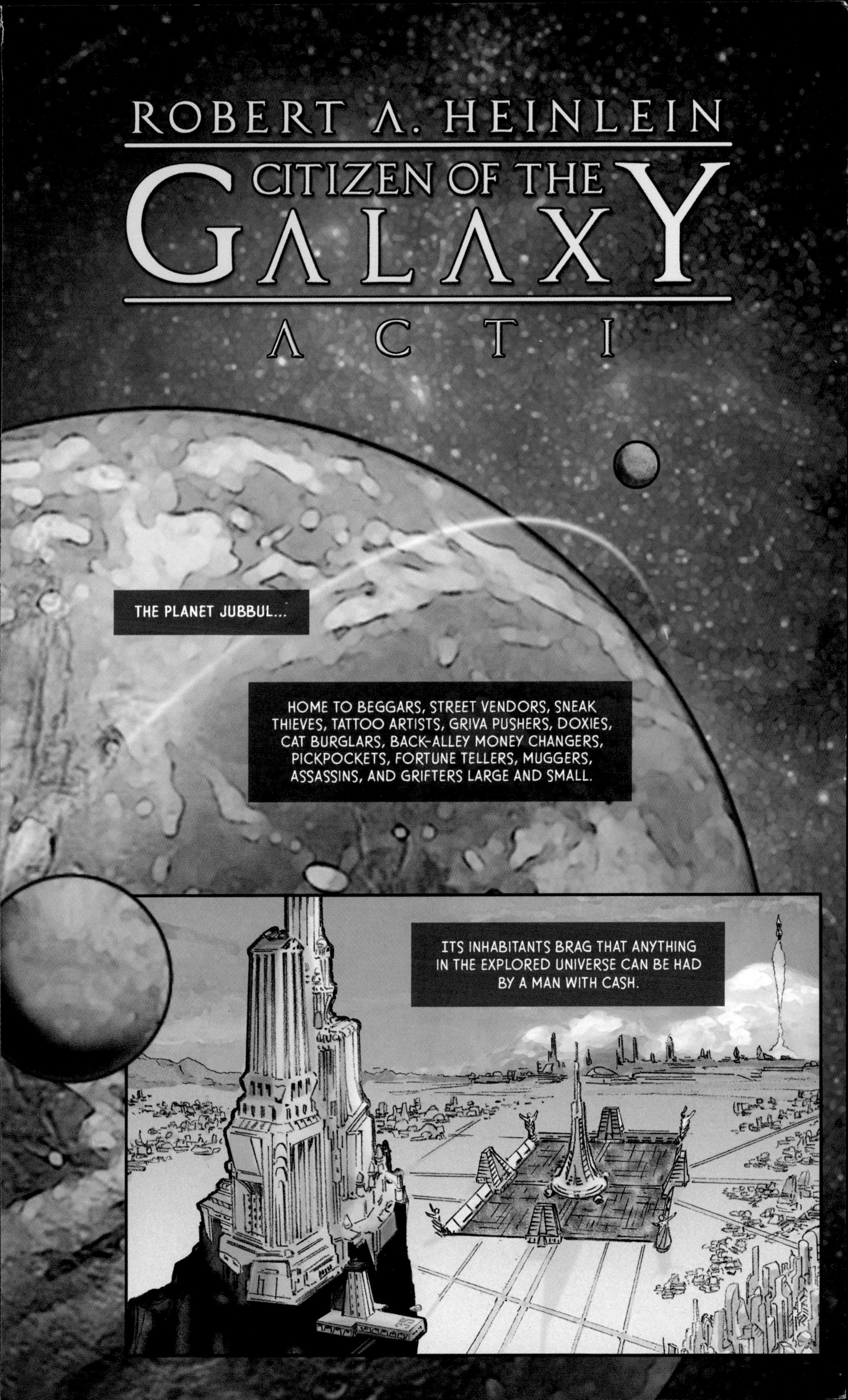
ROBERT A. HEINLEIN
CITIZEN OF THE GALAXY
ACT I
THE PLANET JUBBUL...
HOME TO BEGGARS, STREET VENDORS, SNEAK THIEVES, TATTOO ARTISTS, GRIVA PUSHERS, DOXIES, CAT BURGLARS, BACK-ALLEY MONEY CHANGERS, PICKPOCKETS, FORTUNE TELLERS, MUGGERS, ASSASSINS, AND GRIFTERS LARGE AND SMALL.
ITS INHABITANTS BRAG THAT ANYTHING IN THE EXPLORED UNIVERSE CAN BE HAD BY A MAN WITH CASH.

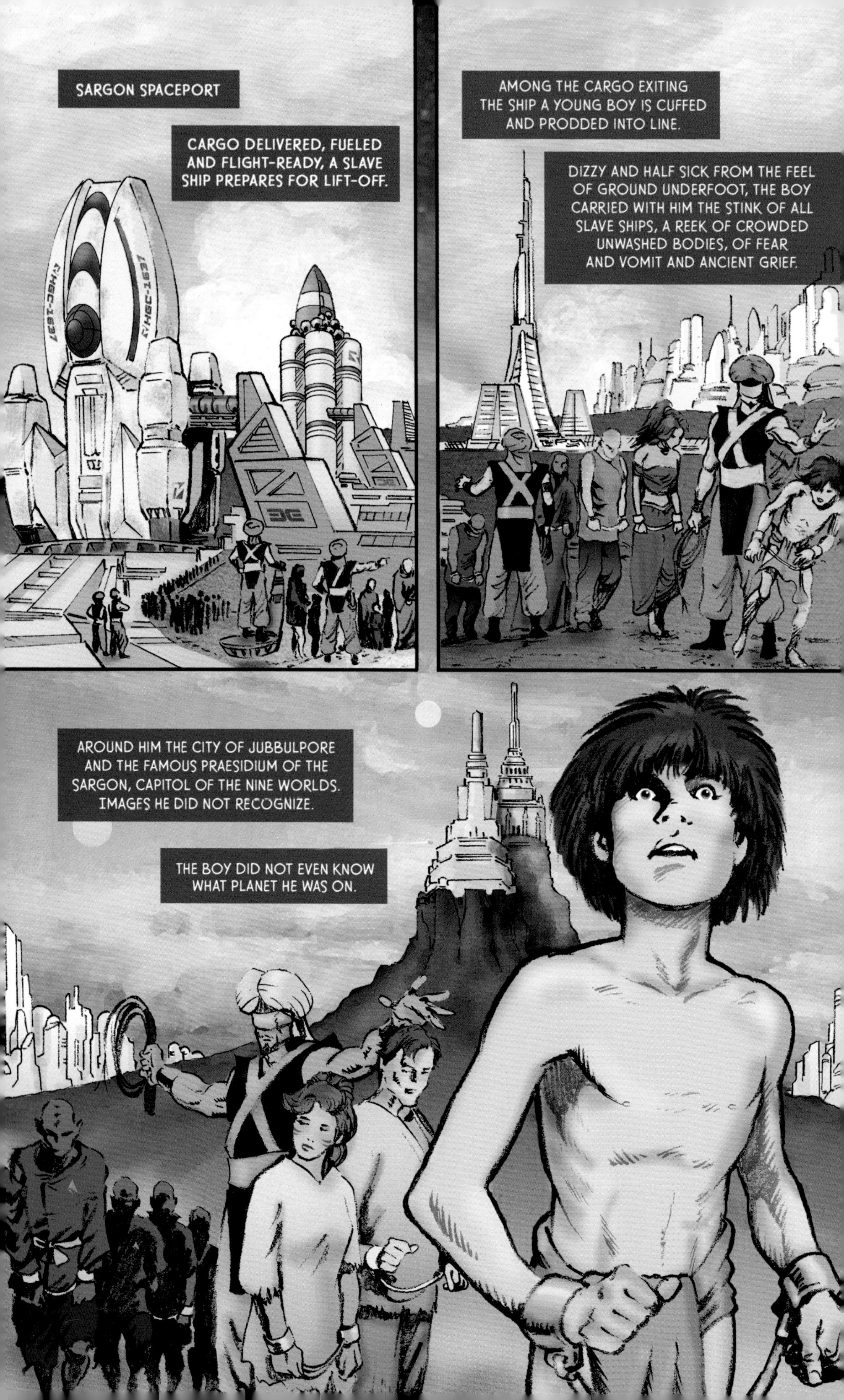
SARGON SPACEPORT
CARGO DELIVERED, FUELED AND FLIGHT-READY, A SLAVE SHIP PREPARES FOR LIFT-OFF.
AMONG THE CARGO EXITING THE SHIP A YOUNG BOY IS CUFFED AND PRODDED INTO LINE.
DIZZY AND HALF SICK FROM THE FEEL OF GROUND UNDERFOOT, THE BOY CARRIED WITH HIM THE STINK OF ALL SLAVE SHIPS, A REEK OF CROWDED UNWASHED BODIES, OF FEAR AND VOMIT AND ANCIENT GRIEF.
AROUND HIM THE CITY OF JUBBULPORE AND THE FAMOUS PRAESIDIUM OF THE SARGON, CAPITOL OF THE NINE WORLDS. IMAGES HE DID NOT RECOGNIZE.
THE BOY DID NOT EVEN KNOW WHAT PLANET HE WAS ON.

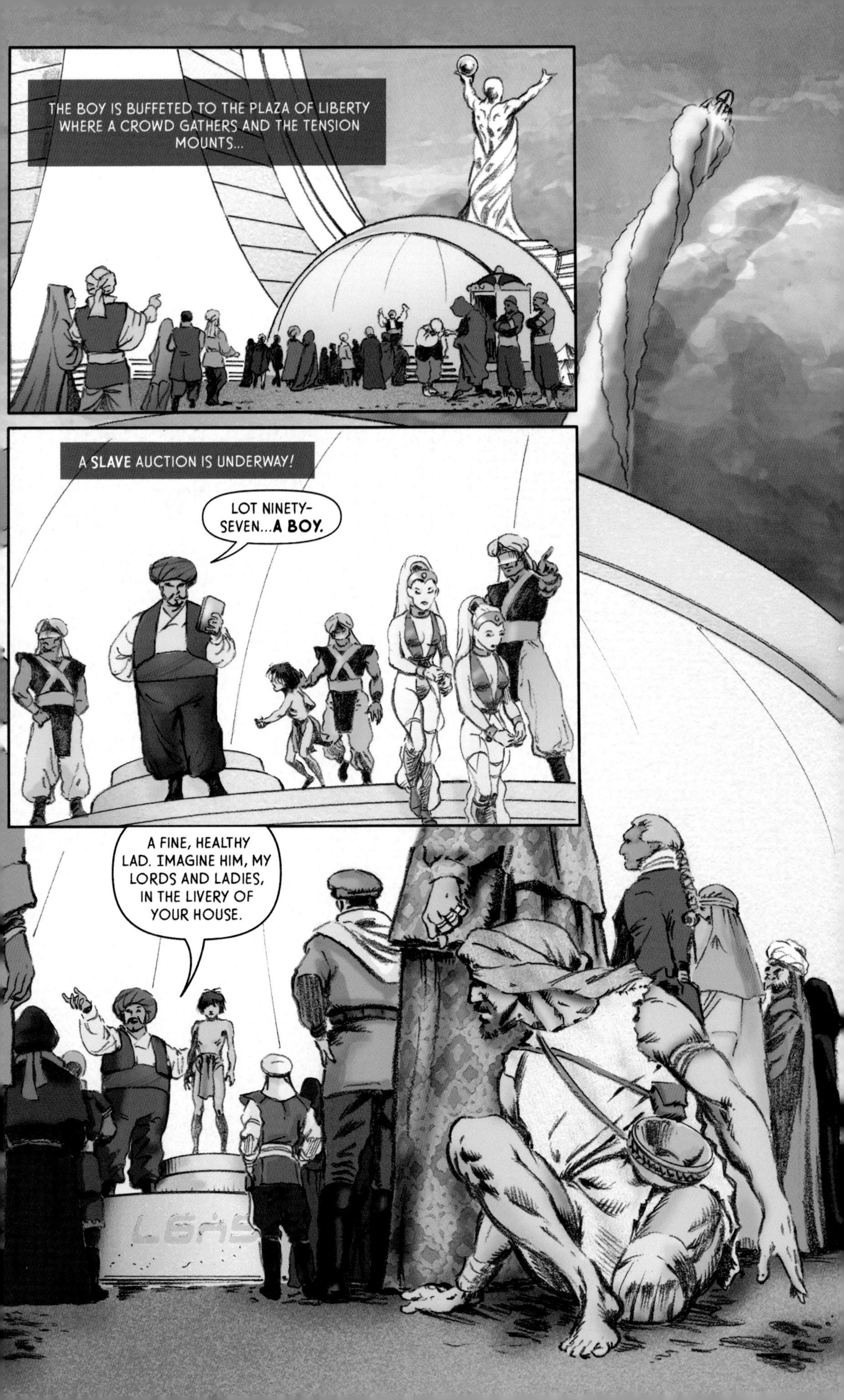
THE BOY IS BUFFETED TO THE PLAZA OF LIBERTY WHERE A CROWD GATHERS AND THE TENSION MOUNTS...
A SLAVE AUCTION IS UNDERWAY!
LOT NINETY-SEVEN...A BOY.
A FINE, HEALTHY LAD. IMAGINE HIM, MY LORDS AND LADIES, IN THE LIVERY OF YOUR HOUSE.

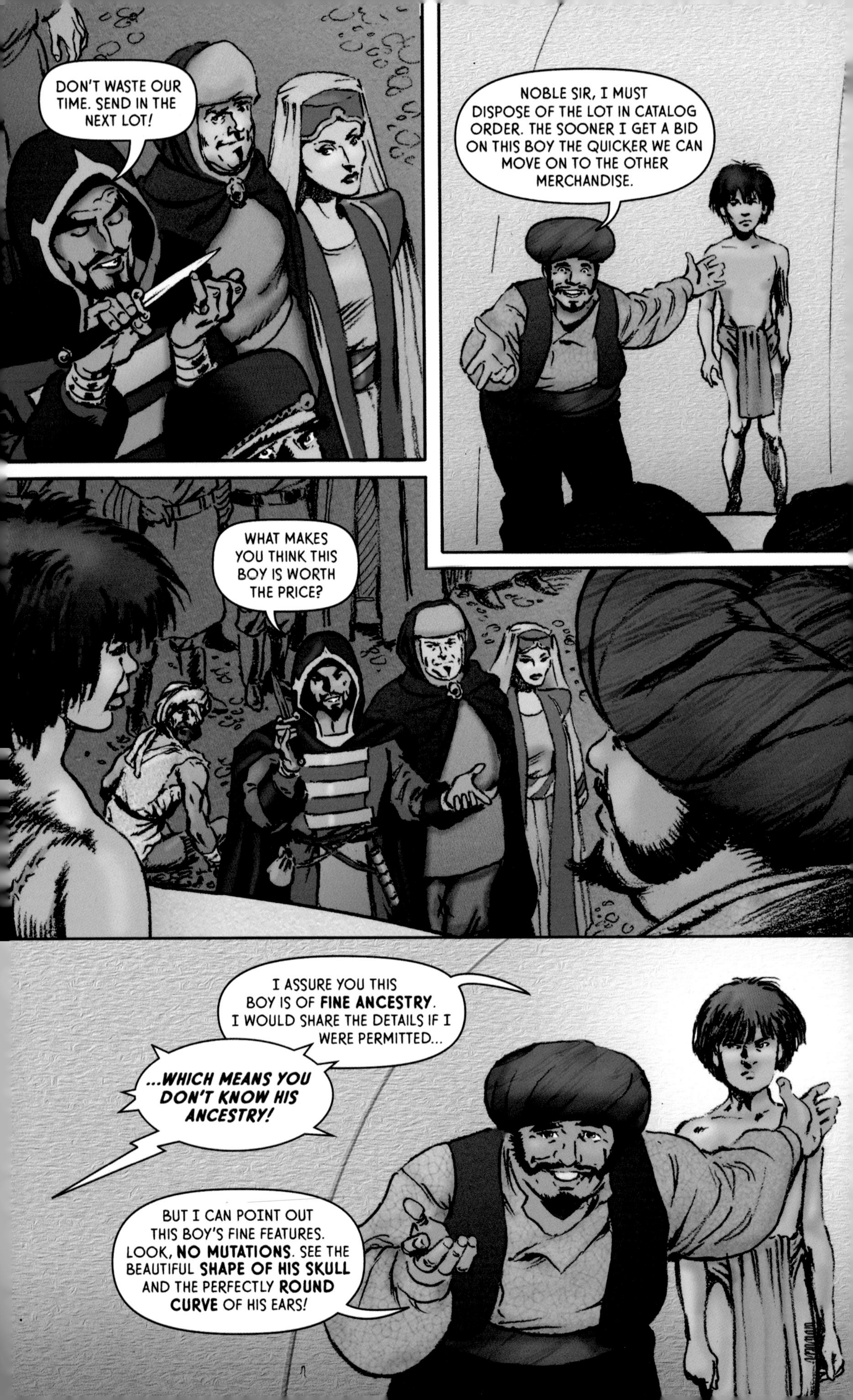
DON'T WASTE OUR TIME. SEND IN THE NEXT LOT!
NOBLE SIR, I MUST DISPOSE OF THE LOT IN CATALOG ORDER. THE SOONER I GET A BID ON THIS BOY THE QUICKER WE CAN MOVE ON TO THE OTHER MERCHANDISE.
WHAT MAKES YOU THINK THIS BOY IS WORTH THE PRICE?
I ASSURE YOU THIS BOY IS OF **FINE ANCESTRY**. I WOULD SHARE THE DETAILS IF I WERE PERMITTED...
...WHICH MEANS YOU DON'T KNOW HIS ANCESTRY!
BUT I CAN POINT OUT THIS BOY'S FINE FEATURES. LOOK, **NO MUTATIONS**. SEE THE BEAUTIFUL **SHAPE OF HIS SKULL** AND THE PERFECTLY **ROUND CURVE** OF HIS EARS!

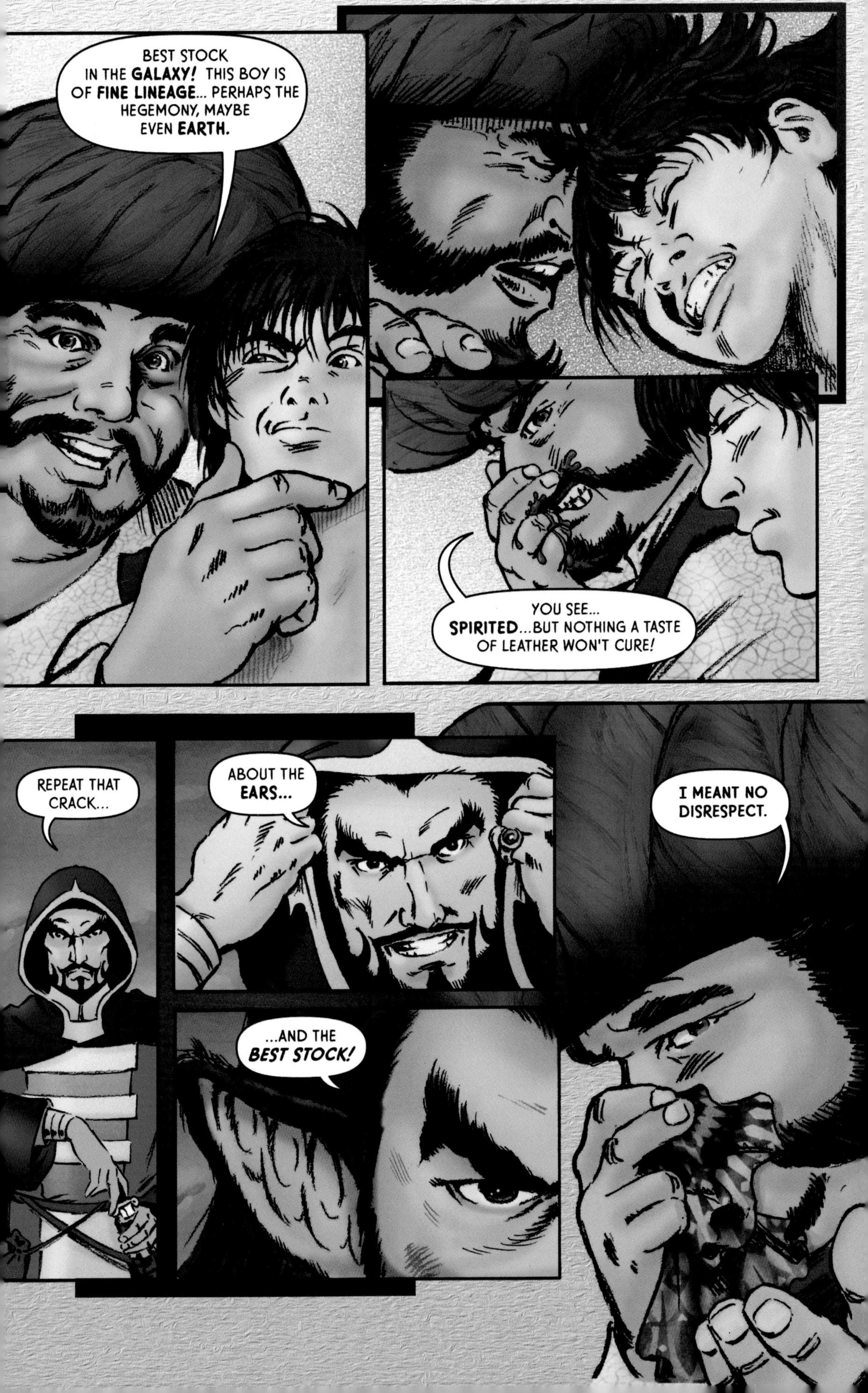
BEST STOCK IN THE GALAXY! THIS BOY IS OF FINE LINEAGE... PERHAPS THE HEGEMONY, MAYBE EVEN EARTH.
YOU SEE... SPIRITED...BUT NOTHING A TASTE OF LEATHER WON'T CURE!
REPEAT THAT CRACK...
ABOUT THE EARS...
...AND THE BEST STOCK!
I MEANT NO DISRESPECT.

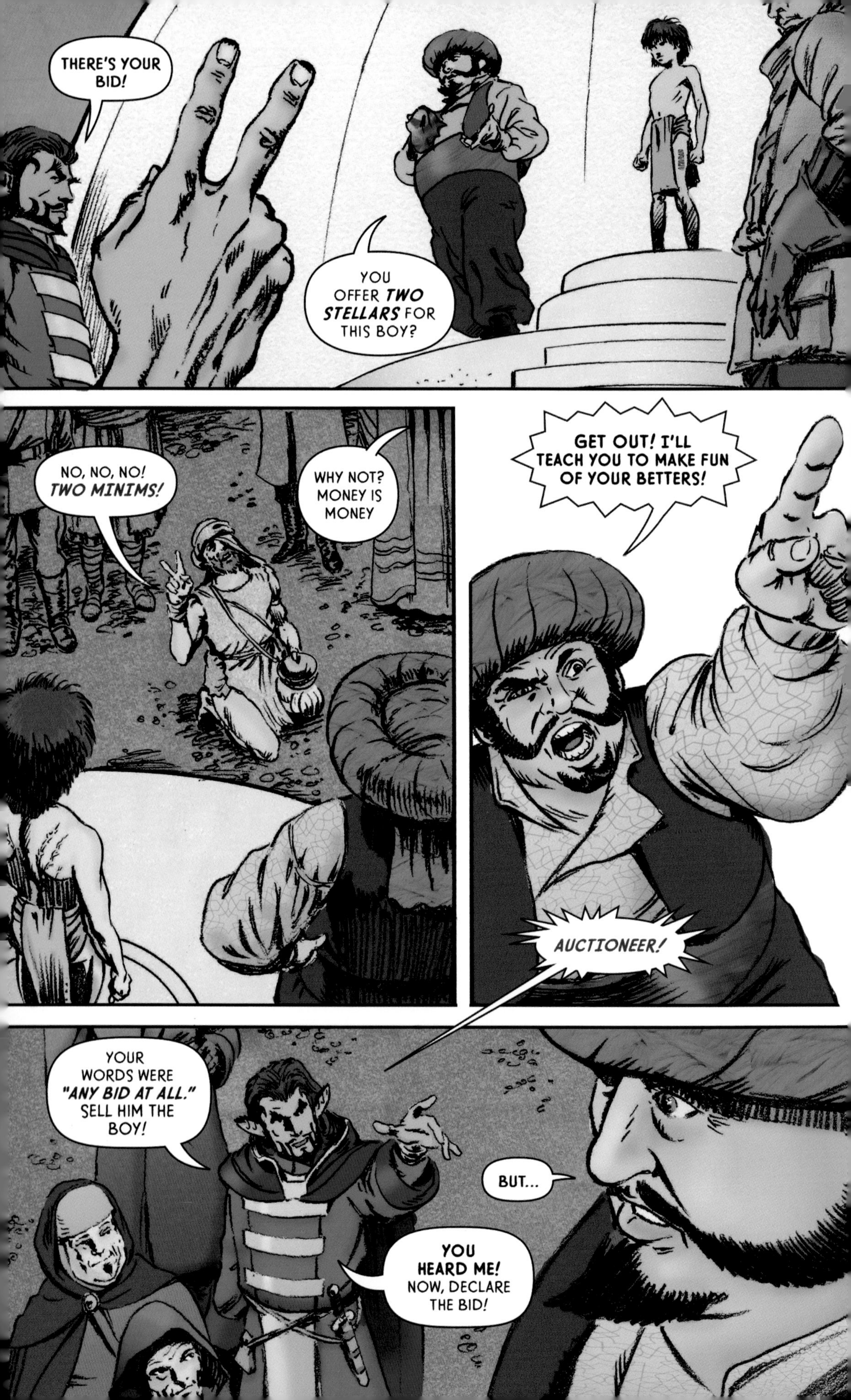
THERE'S YOUR BID!
YOU OFFER TWO STELLARS FOR THIS BOY?
NO, NO, NO! TWO MINIMS!
WHY NOT? MONEY IS MONEY
GET OUT! I'LL TEACH YOU TO MAKE FUN OF YOUR BETTERS!
AUCTIONEER!
YOUR WORDS WERE "ANY BID AT ALL." SELL HIM THE BOY!
BUT...
YOU HEARD ME! NOW, DECLARE THE BID!

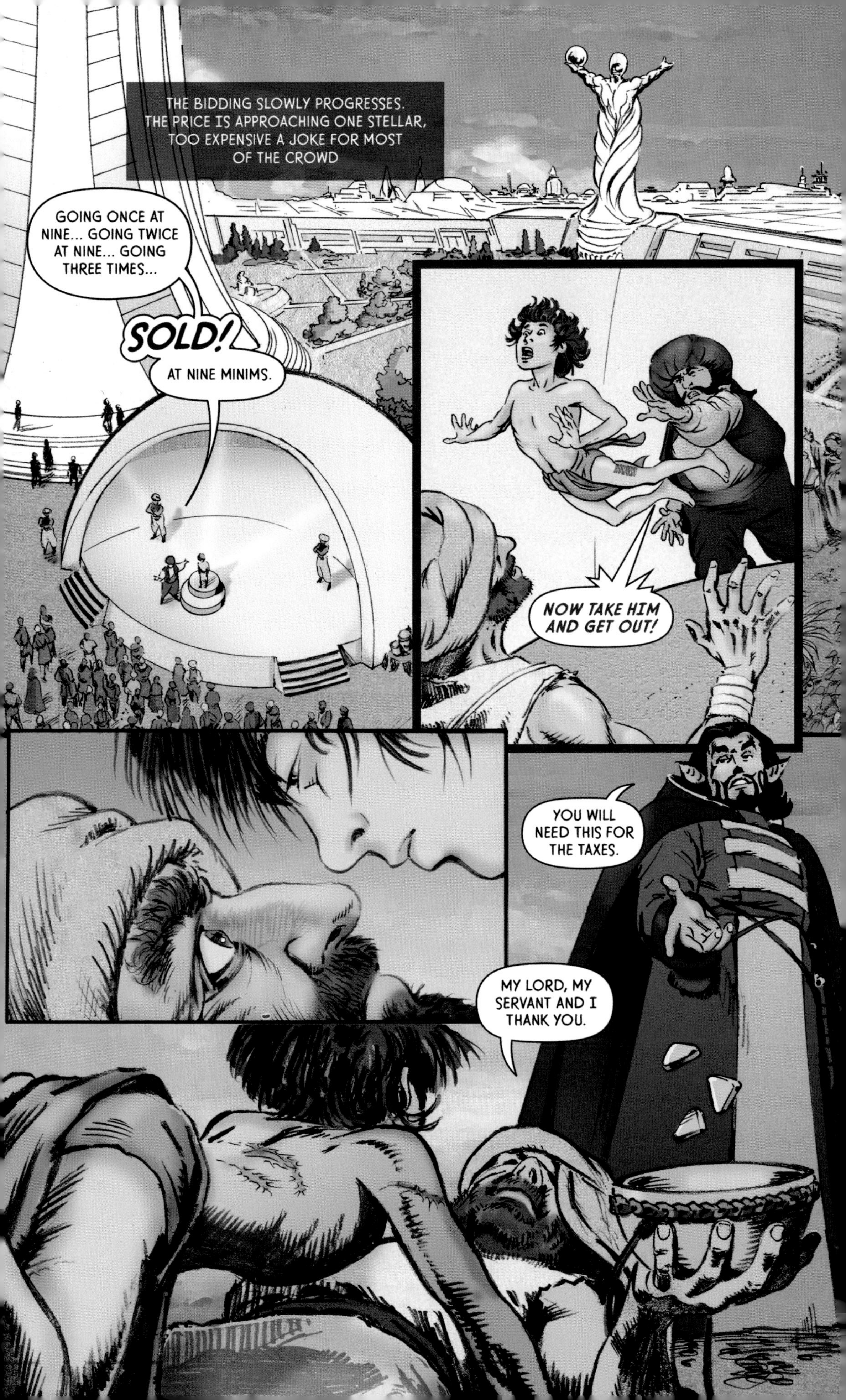
THE BIDDING SLOWLY PROGRESSES. THE PRICE IS APPROACHING ONE STELLAR, TOO EXPENSIVE A JOKE FOR MOST OF THE CROWD
GOING ONCE AT NINE... GOING TWICE AT NINE... GOING THREE TIMES...
SOLD!
AT NINE MINIMS.
NOW TAKE HIM AND GET OUT!
YOU WILL NEED THIS FOR THE TAXES.
MY LORD, MY SERVANT AND I THANK YOU.

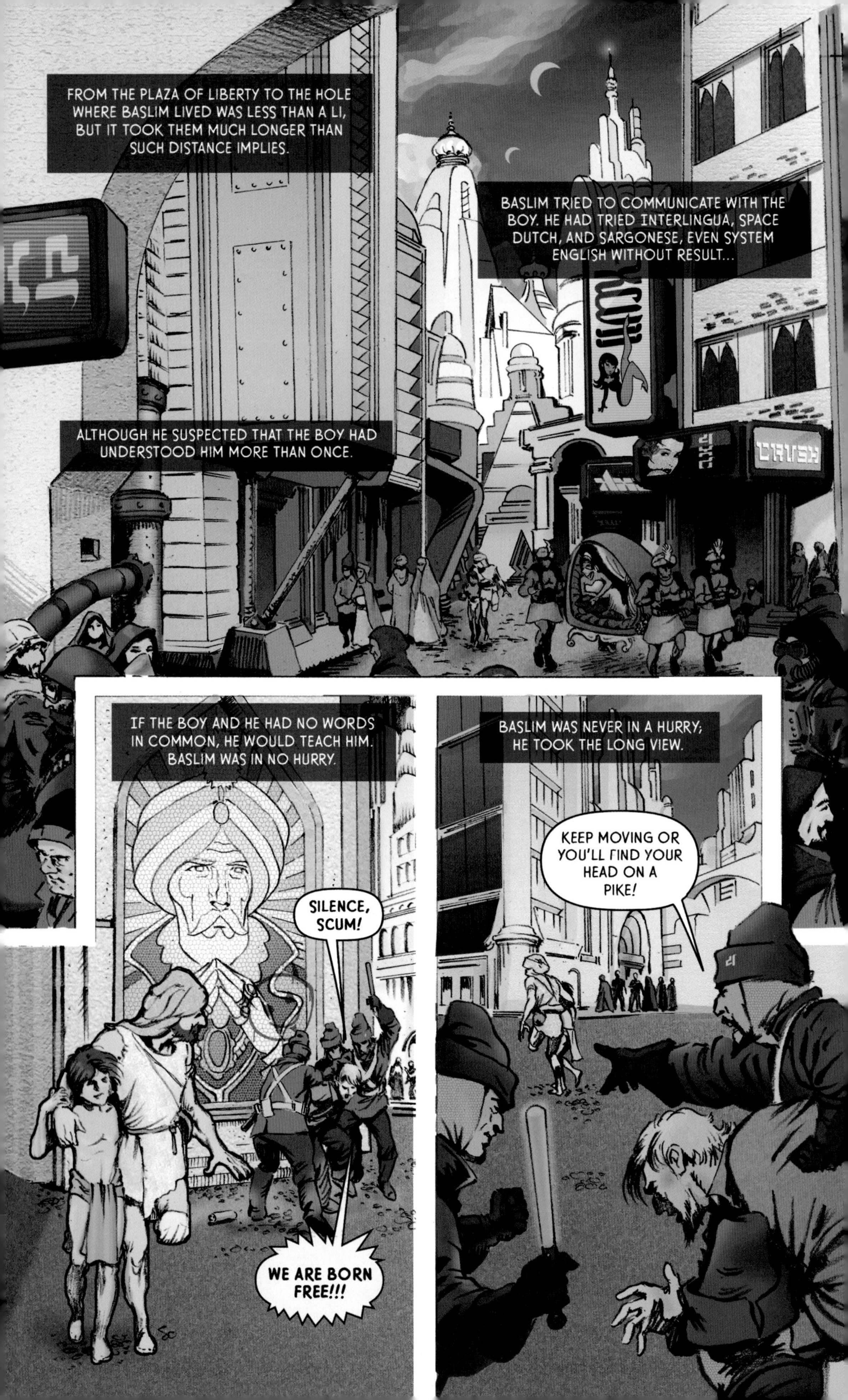
FROM THE PLAZA OF LIBERTY TO THE HOLE WHERE BASLIM LIVED WAS LESS THAN A LI, BUT IT TOOK THEM MUCH LONGER THAN SUCH DISTANCE IMPLIES.
BASLIM TRIED TO COMMUNICATE WITH THE BOY. HE HAD TRIED INTERLINGUA, SPACE DUTCH, AND SARGONESE, EVEN SYSTEM ENGLISH WITHOUT RESULT...
ALTHOUGH HE SUSPECTED THAT THE BOY HAD UNDERSTOOD HIM MORE THAN ONCE.
IF THE BOY AND HE HAD NO WORDS IN COMMON, HE WOULD TEACH HIM. BASLIM WAS IN NO HURRY.
SILENCE, SCUM!
WE ARE BORN FREE!!!
BASLIM WAS NEVER IN A HURRY; HE TOOK THE LONG VIEW.
KEEP MOVING OR YOU'LL FIND YOUR HEAD ON A PIKE!

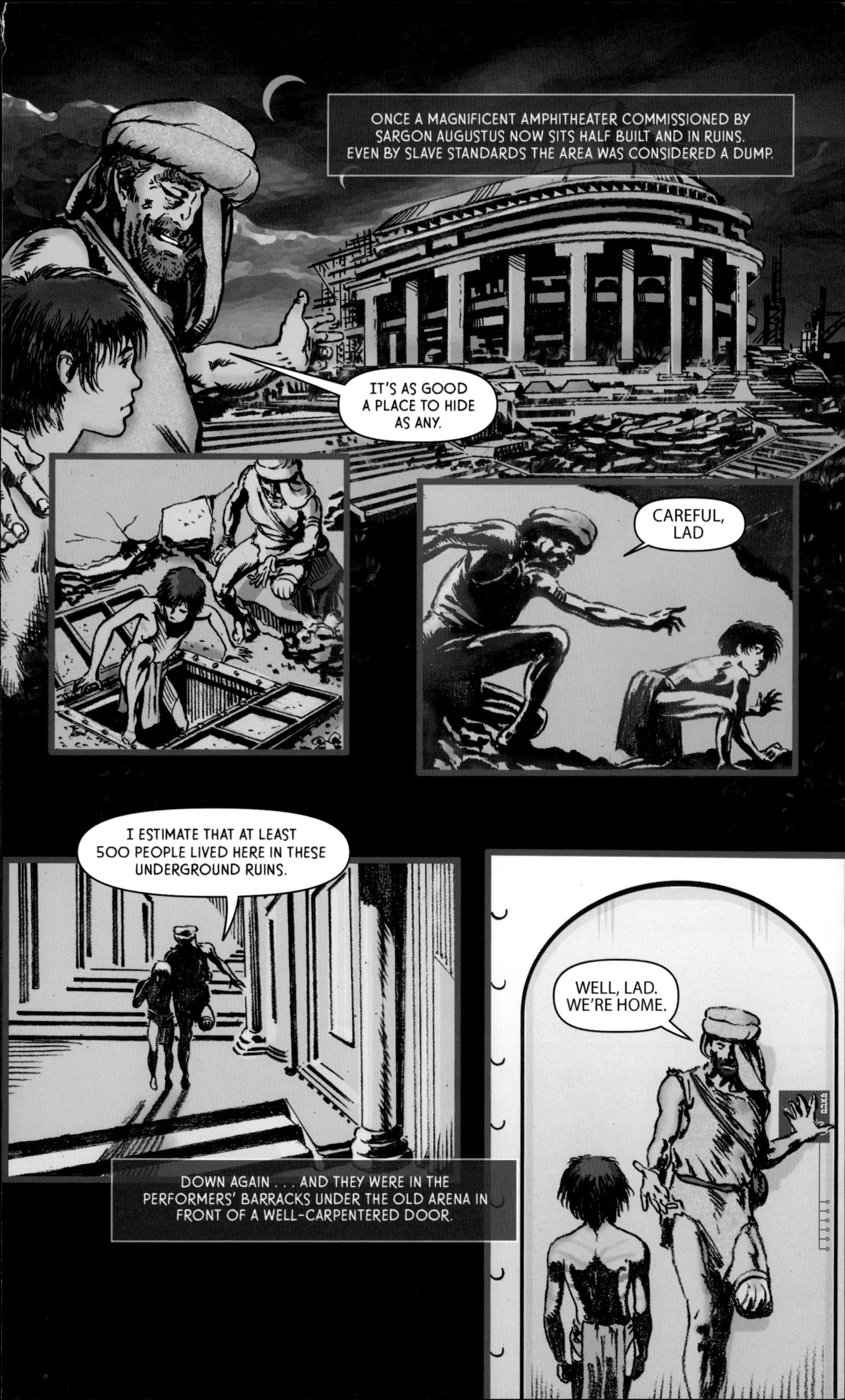
ONCE A MAGNIFICENT AMPHITHEATER COMMISSIONED BY SARGON AUGUSTUS NOW SITS HALF BUILT AND IN RUINS. EVEN BY SLAVE STANDARDS THE AREA WAS CONSIDERED A DUMP.
IT'S AS GOOD A PLACE TO HIDE AS ANY.
CAREFUL, LAD
I ESTIMATE THAT AT LEAST 500 PEOPLE LIVED HERE IN THESE UNDERGROUND RUINS.
DOWN AGAIN . . . AND THEY WERE IN THE PERFORMERS' BARRACKS UNDER THE OLD ARENA IN FRONT OF A WELL-CARPENTERED DOOR.
WELL, LAD. WE'RE HOME.

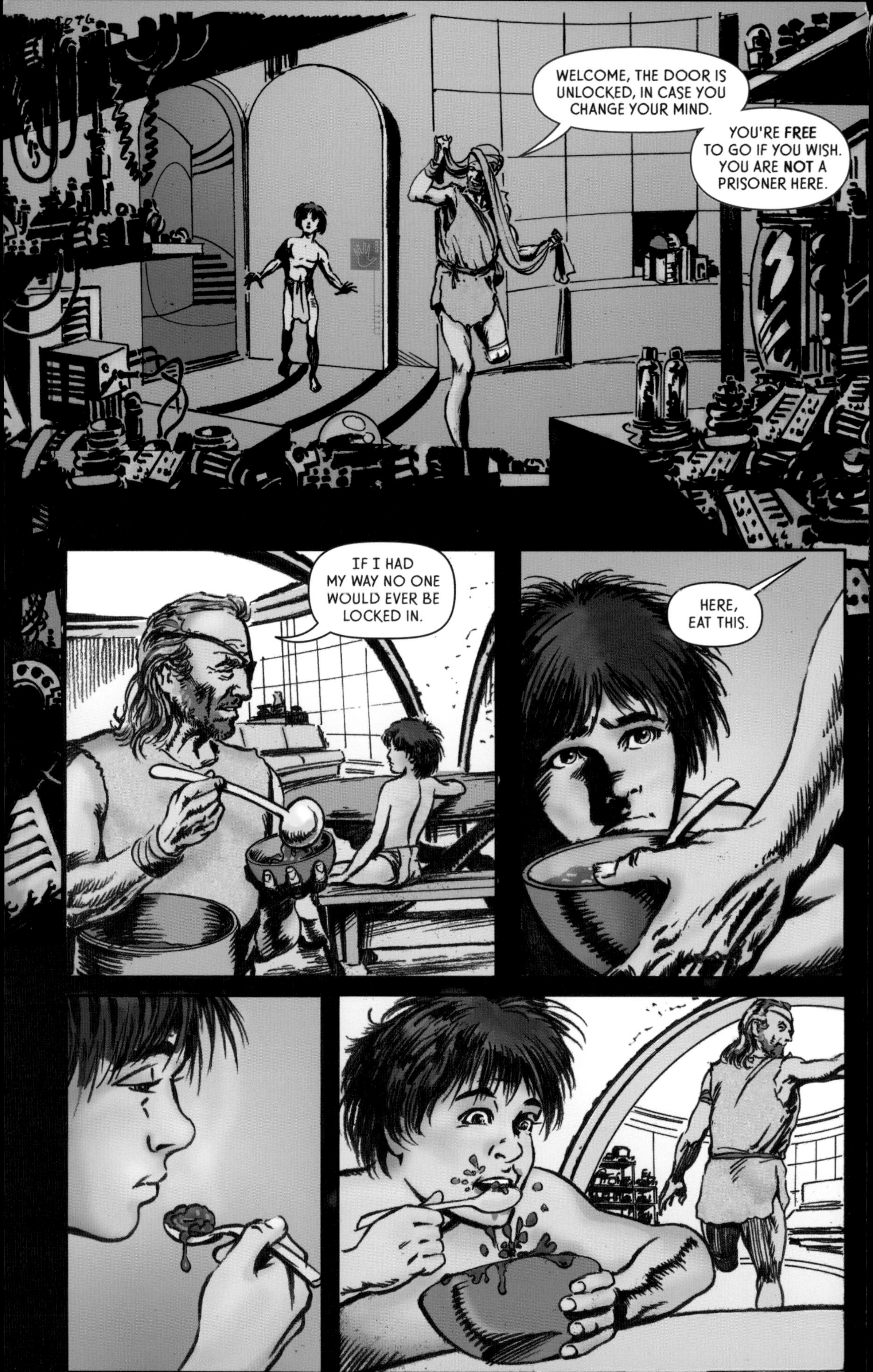
WELCOME, THE DOOR IS UNLOCKED, IN CASE YOU CHANGE YOUR MIND.
YOU'RE **FREE** TO GO IF YOU WISH. YOU ARE **NOT** A PRISONER HERE.
IF I HAD MY WAY NO ONE WOULD EVER BE LOCKED IN.
HERE, EAT THIS.

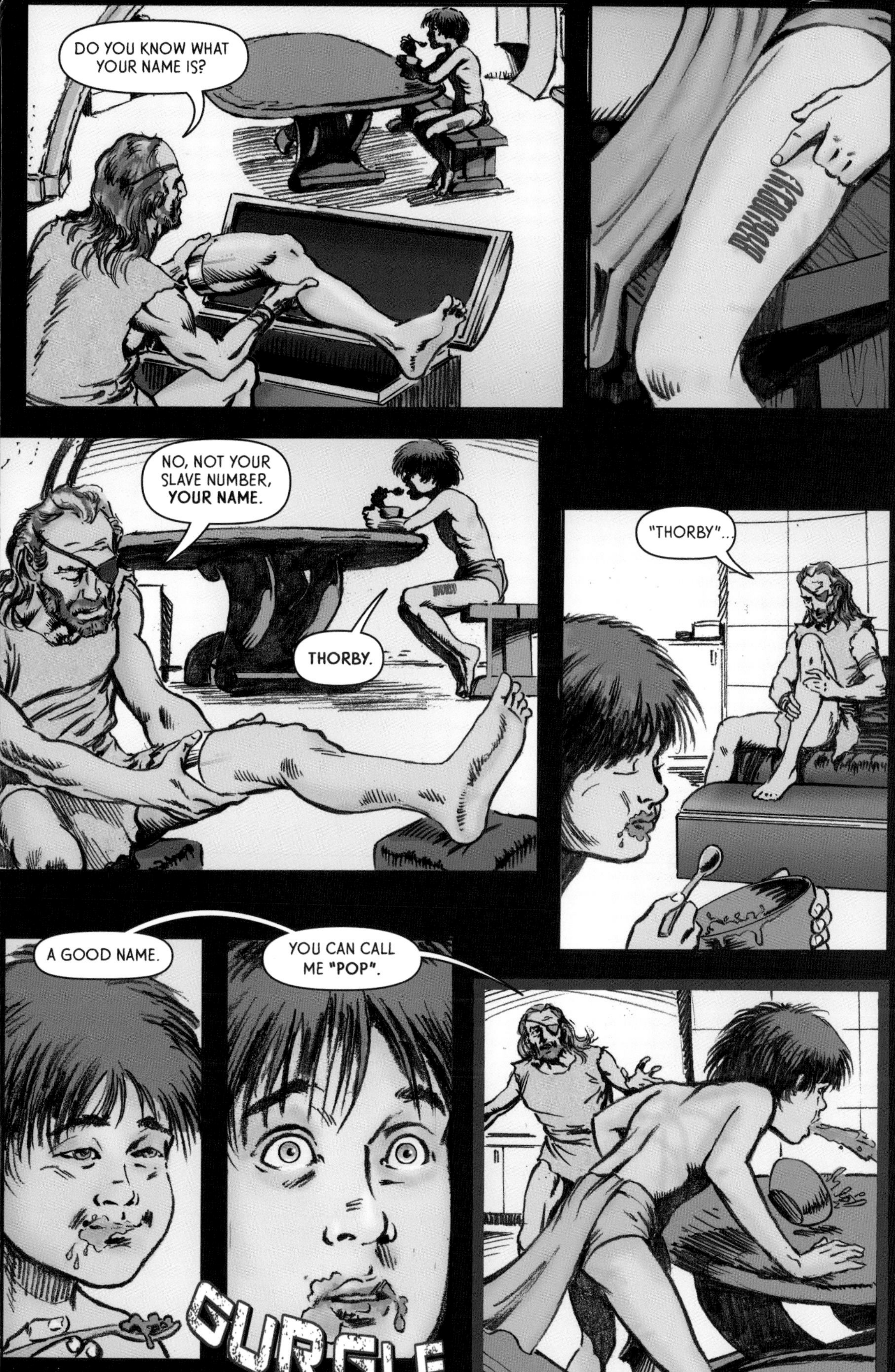
DO YOU KNOW WHAT YOUR NAME IS?
NO, NOT YOUR SLAVE NUMBER, **YOUR NAME.**
THORBY.
"THORBY"...
A GOOD NAME.
YOU CAN CALL ME **"POP"**.
GURGLE

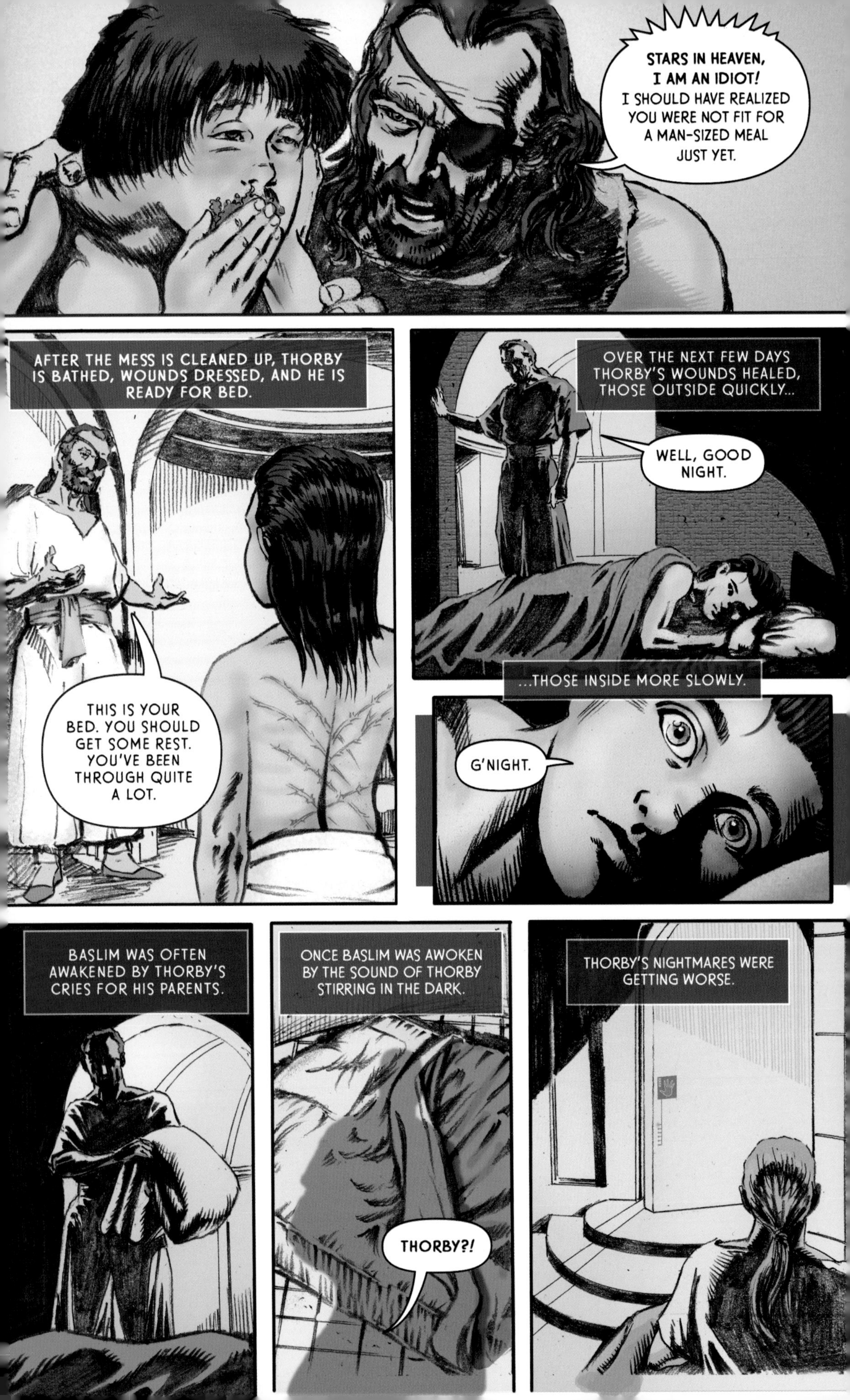
STARS IN HEAVEN, I AM AN IDIOT! I SHOULD HAVE REALIZED YOU WERE NOT FIT FOR A MAN-SIZED MEAL JUST YET.
AFTER THE MESS IS CLEANED UP, THORBY IS BATHED, WOUNDS DRESSED, AND HE IS READY FOR BED.
THIS IS YOUR BED. YOU SHOULD GET SOME REST. YOU'VE BEEN THROUGH QUITE A LOT.
OVER THE NEXT FEW DAYS THORBY'S WOUNDS HEALED, THOSE OUTSIDE QUICKLY...
WELL, GOOD NIGHT.
...THOSE INSIDE MORE SLOWLY.
G'NIGHT.
BASLIM WAS OFTEN AWAKENED BY THORBY'S CRIES FOR HIS PARENTS.
ONCE BASLIM WAS AWOKEN BY THE SOUND OF THORBY STIRRING IN THE DARK.
THORBY?!
THORBY'S NIGHTMARES WERE GETTING WORSE.

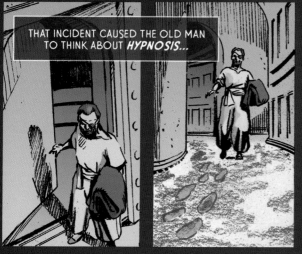

THAT INCIDENT CAUSED THE OLD MAN TO THINK ABOUT *HYPNOSIS...*

HE HAD NEVER LIKED HYPNOSIS, NOT EVEN FOR THERAPY.

I THOUGHT YOU MIGHT GET COLD.

BASLIM HAD AN ALMOST RELIGIOUS CONCEPT OF THE DIGNITY OF THE INDIVIDUAL; HYPNOTIZING ANOTHER PERSON *WAS A SIN.*

DO YOU KNOW WHICH ONE IS YOUR HOME STAR?

NO, POP. I CAN'T REMEMBER ANYTHING ABOUT MY HOME.

WHEN I'M DREAMING IT'S LIKE I'M STILL ON THE SLAVE SHIP...

AND WHEN I WAKE I CAN STILL SEE THOSE FACES AND HEAR THE CRIES! THE **SMELLS** AND THE **BURNINGS...**

BUT THIS, HE THOUGHT, WAS **AN EMERGENCY.**

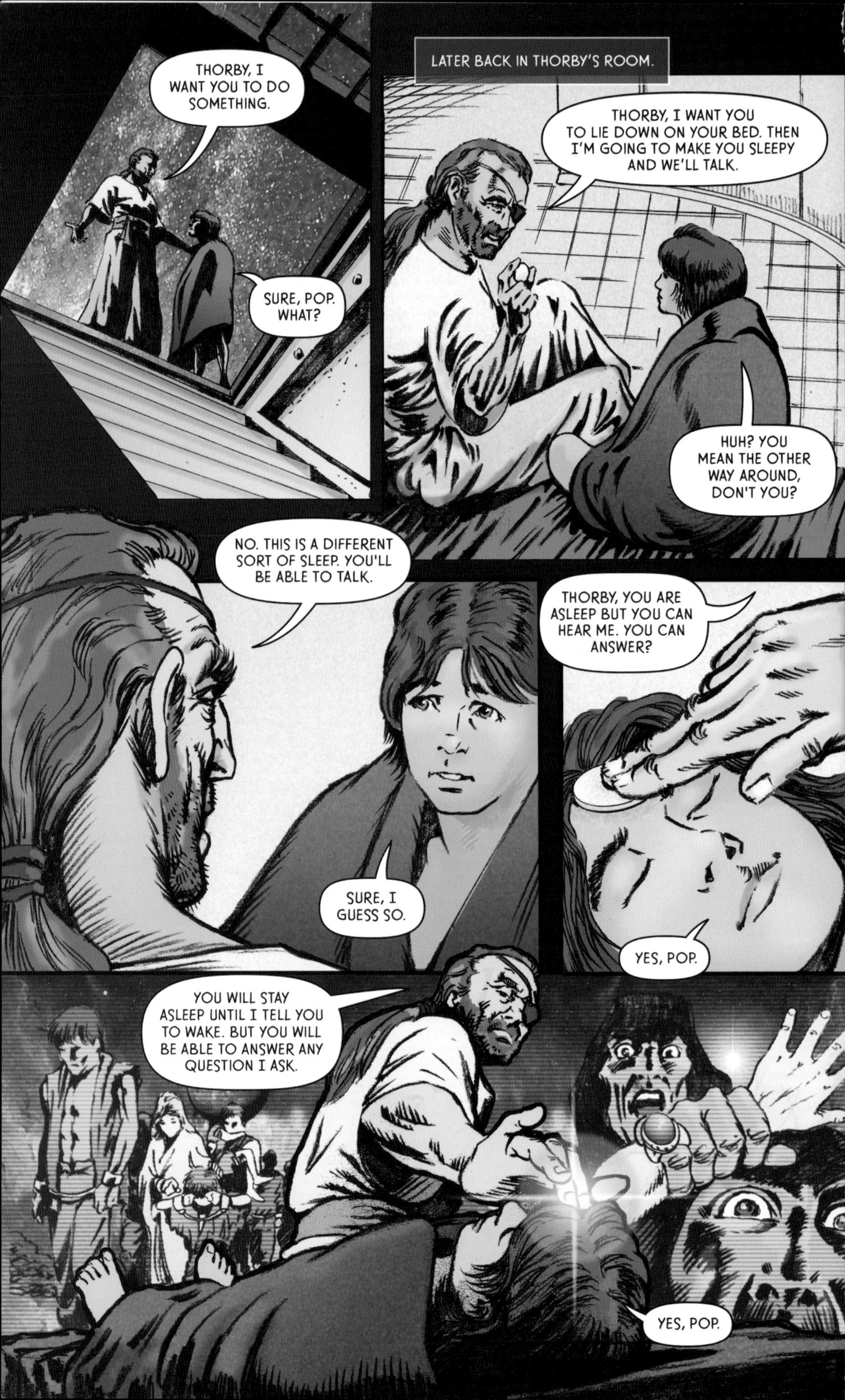
THORBY, I WANT YOU TO DO SOMETHING.
SURE, POP. WHAT?
LATER BACK IN THORBY'S ROOM.
THORBY, I WANT YOU TO LIE DOWN ON YOUR BED. THEN I'M GOING TO MAKE YOU SLEEPY AND WE'LL TALK.
HUH? YOU MEAN THE OTHER WAY AROUND, DON'T YOU?
NO. THIS IS A DIFFERENT SORT OF SLEEP. YOU'LL BE ABLE TO TALK.
SURE, I GUESS SO.
THORBY, YOU ARE ASLEEP BUT YOU CAN HEAR ME. YOU CAN ANSWER?
YES, POP.
YOU WILL STAY ASLEEP UNTIL I TELL YOU TO WAKE. BUT YOU WILL BE ABLE TO ANSWER ANY QUESTION I ASK.
YES, POP.

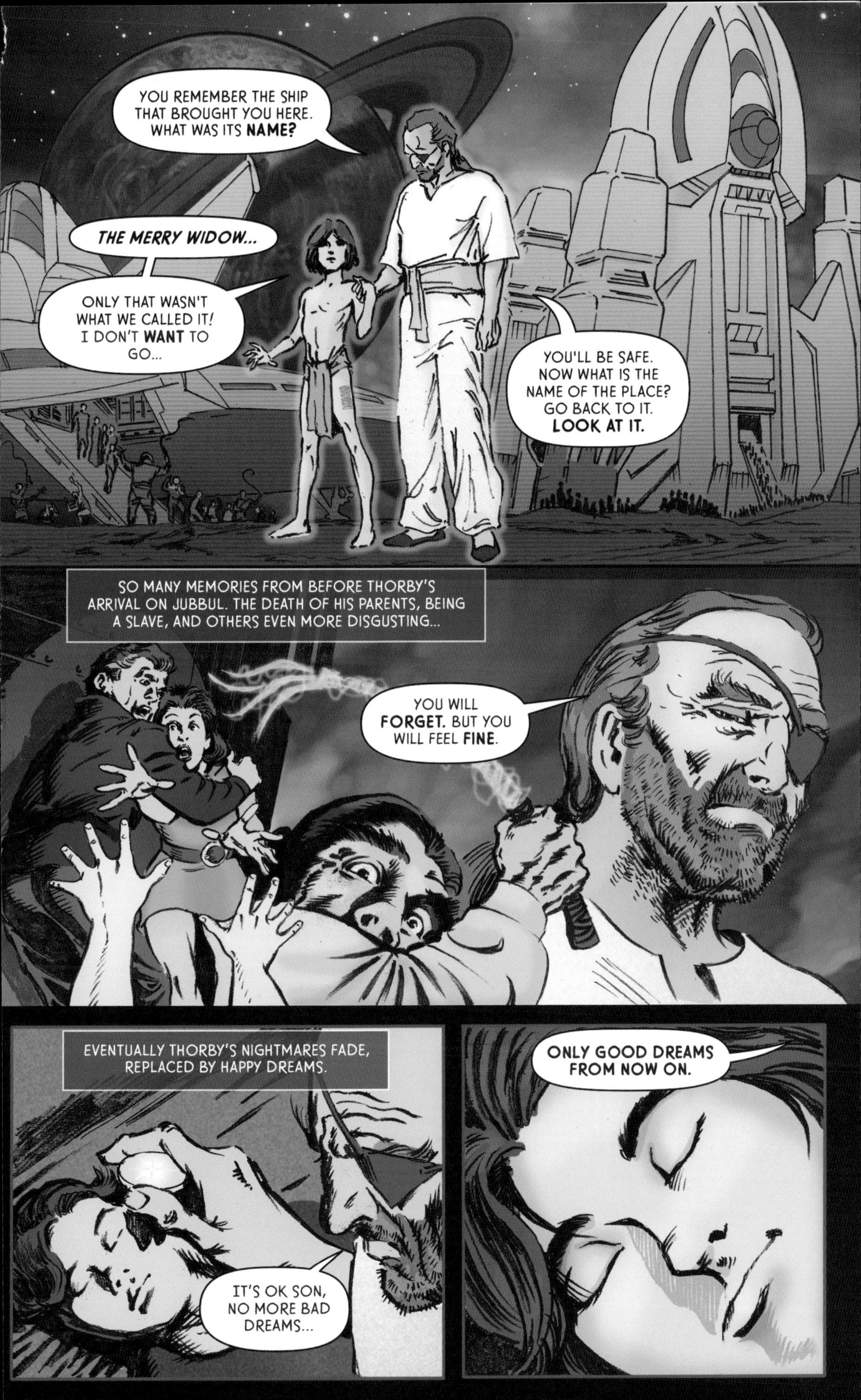
YOU REMEMBER THE SHIP THAT BROUGHT YOU HERE. WHAT WAS ITS **NAME?**
THE MERRY WIDOW...
ONLY THAT WASN'T WHAT WE CALLED IT! I DON'T **WANT** TO GO...
YOU'LL BE SAFE. NOW WHAT IS THE NAME OF THE PLACE? GO BACK TO IT. **LOOK AT IT.**
SO MANY MEMORIES FROM BEFORE THORBY'S ARRIVAL ON JUBBUL. THE DEATH OF HIS PARENTS, BEING A SLAVE, AND OTHERS EVEN MORE DISGUSTING...
YOU WILL **FORGET.** BUT YOU WILL FEEL **FINE**.
EVENTUALLY THORBY'S NIGHTMARES FADE, REPLACED BY HAPPY DREAMS.
IT'S OK SON, NO MORE BAD DREAMS...
ONLY GOOD DREAMS FROM NOW ON.

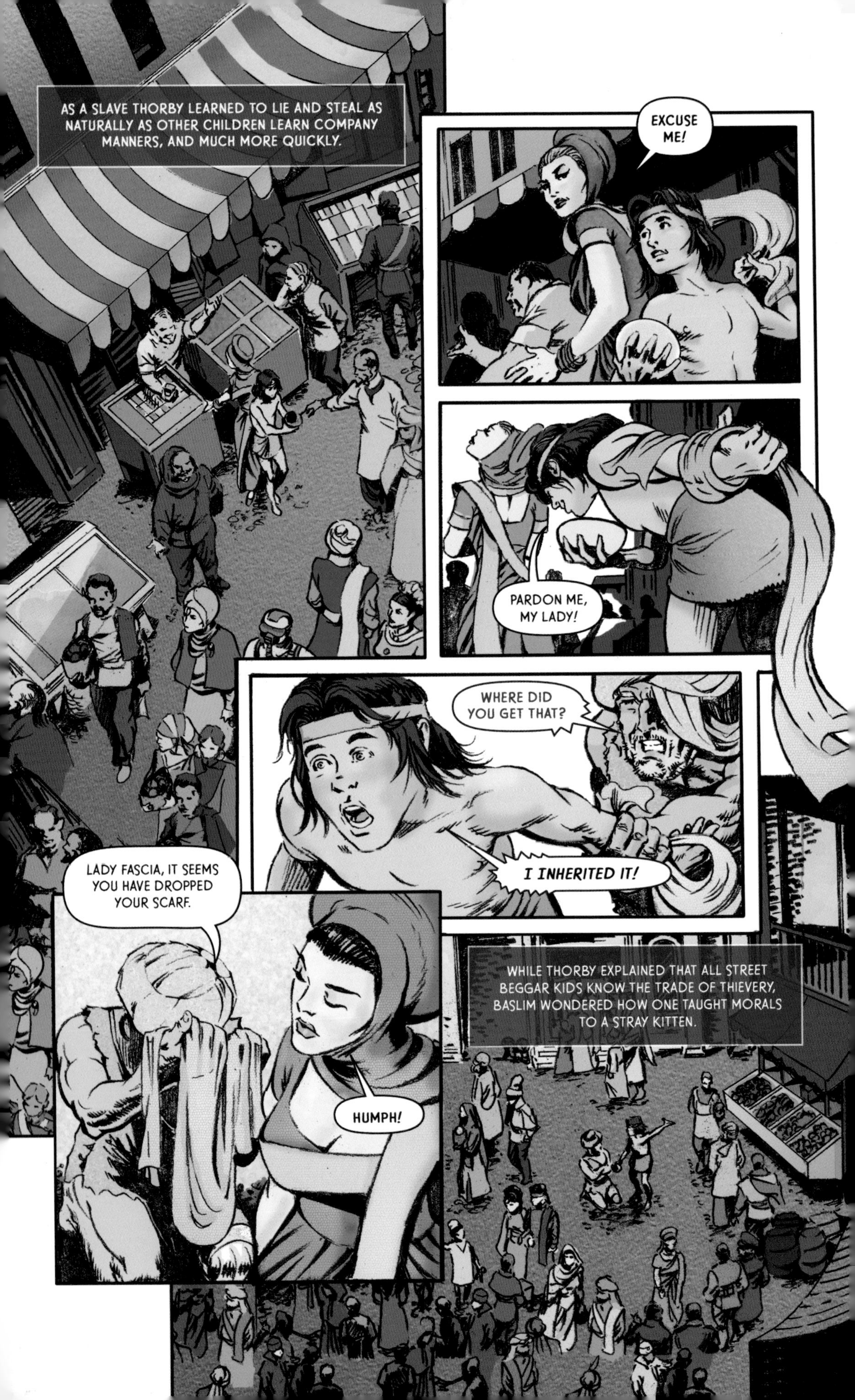

AS A SLAVE THORBY LEARNED TO LIE AND STEAL AS NATURALLY AS OTHER CHILDREN LEARN COMPANY MANNERS, AND MUCH MORE QUICKLY.
EXCUSE ME!
PARDON ME, MY LADY!
WHERE DID YOU GET THAT?
I INHERITED IT!
LADY FASCIA, IT SEEMS YOU HAVE DROPPED YOUR SCARF.
HUMPH!
WHILE THORBY EXPLAINED THAT ALL STREET BEGGAR KIDS KNOW THE TRADE OF THIEVERY, BASLIM WONDERED HOW ONE TAUGHT MORALS TO A STRAY KITTEN.

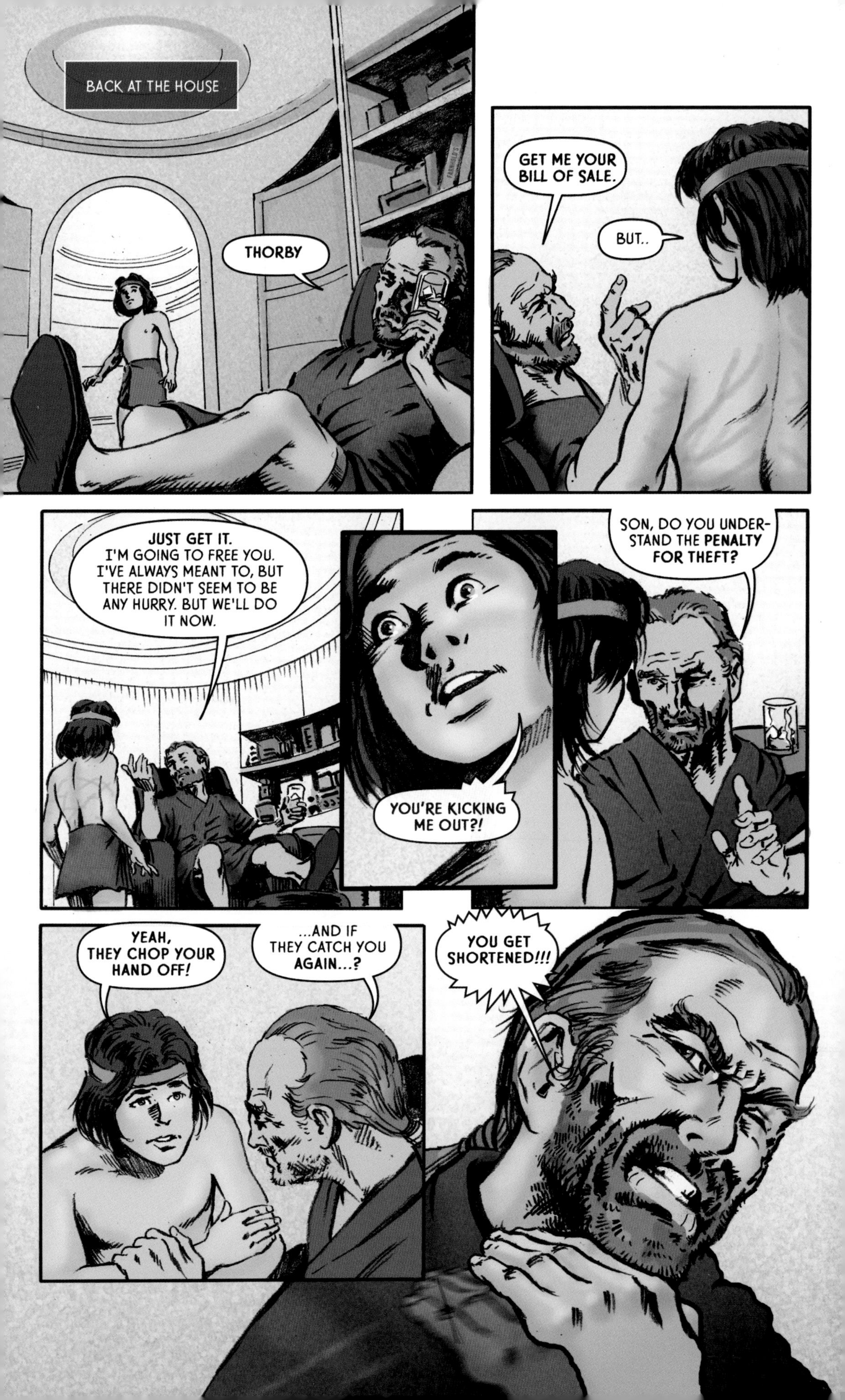
BACK AT THE HOUSE
THORBY
GET ME YOUR BILL OF SALE.
BUT..
JUST GET IT. I'M GOING TO FREE YOU. I'VE ALWAYS MEANT TO, BUT THERE DIDN'T SEEM TO BE ANY HURRY. BUT WE'LL DO IT NOW.
YOU'RE KICKING ME OUT?!
SON, DO YOU UNDERSTAND THE PENALTY FOR THEFT?
YEAH, THEY CHOP YOUR HAND OFF!
...AND IF THEY CATCH YOU AGAIN...?
YOU GET SHORTENED!!!

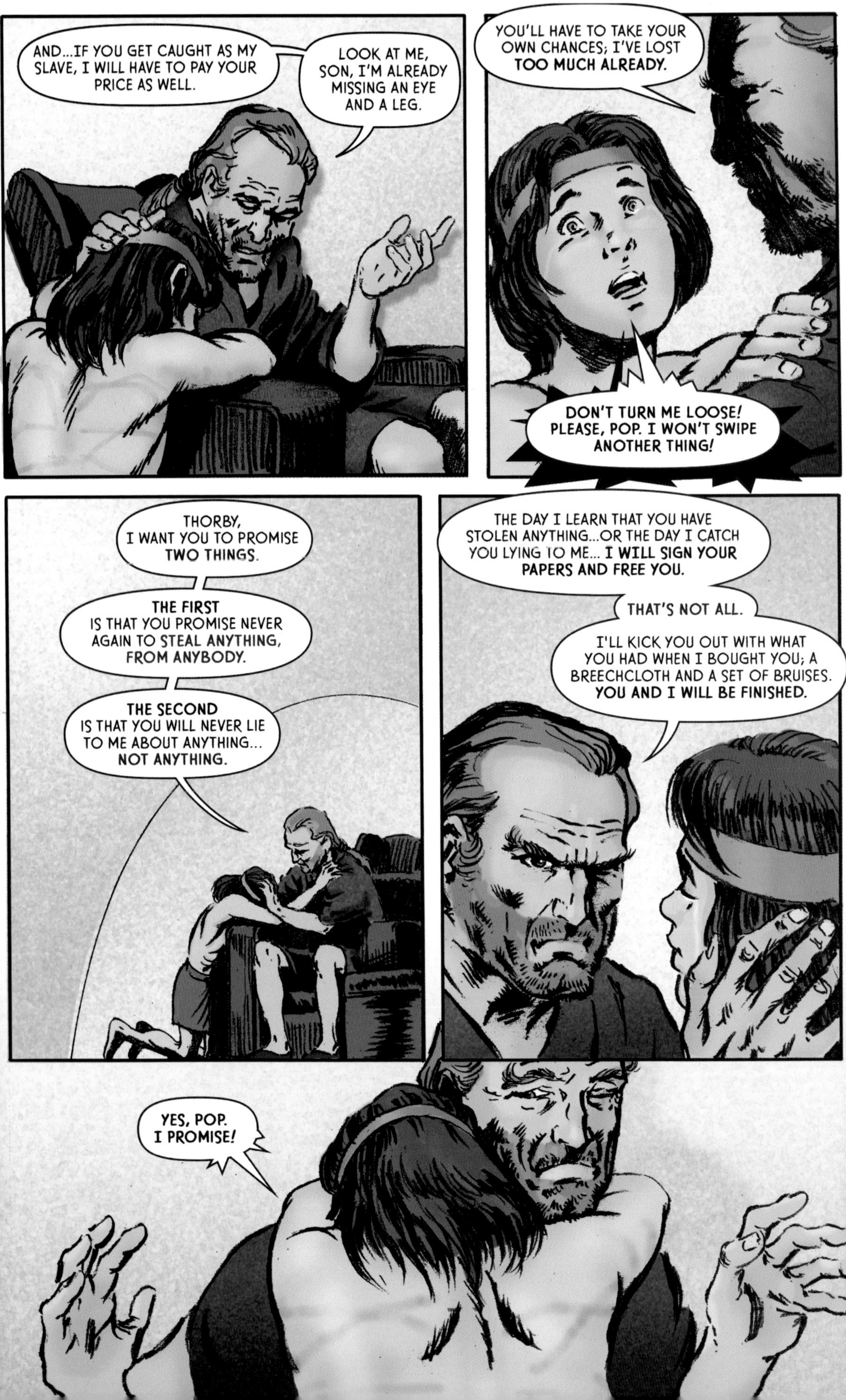
AND...IF YOU GET CAUGHT AS MY SLAVE, I WILL HAVE TO PAY YOUR PRICE AS WELL.
LOOK AT ME, SON, I'M ALREADY MISSING AN EYE AND A LEG.
YOU'LL HAVE TO TAKE YOUR OWN CHANCES; I'VE LOST TOO MUCH ALREADY.
DON'T TURN ME LOOSE! PLEASE, POP. I WON'T SWIPE ANOTHER THING!
THORBY, I WANT YOU TO PROMISE TWO THINGS.
THE FIRST IS THAT YOU PROMISE NEVER AGAIN TO STEAL ANYTHING, FROM ANYBODY.
THE SECOND IS THAT YOU WILL NEVER LIE TO ME ABOUT ANYTHING... NOT ANYTHING.
THE DAY I LEARN THAT YOU HAVE STOLEN ANYTHING...OR THE DAY I CATCH YOU LYING TO ME... I WILL SIGN YOUR PAPERS AND FREE YOU.
THAT'S NOT ALL.
I'LL KICK YOU OUT WITH WHAT YOU HAD WHEN I BOUGHT YOU; A BREECHCLOTH AND A SET OF BRUISES. YOU AND I WILL BE FINISHED.
YES, POP. I PROMISE!

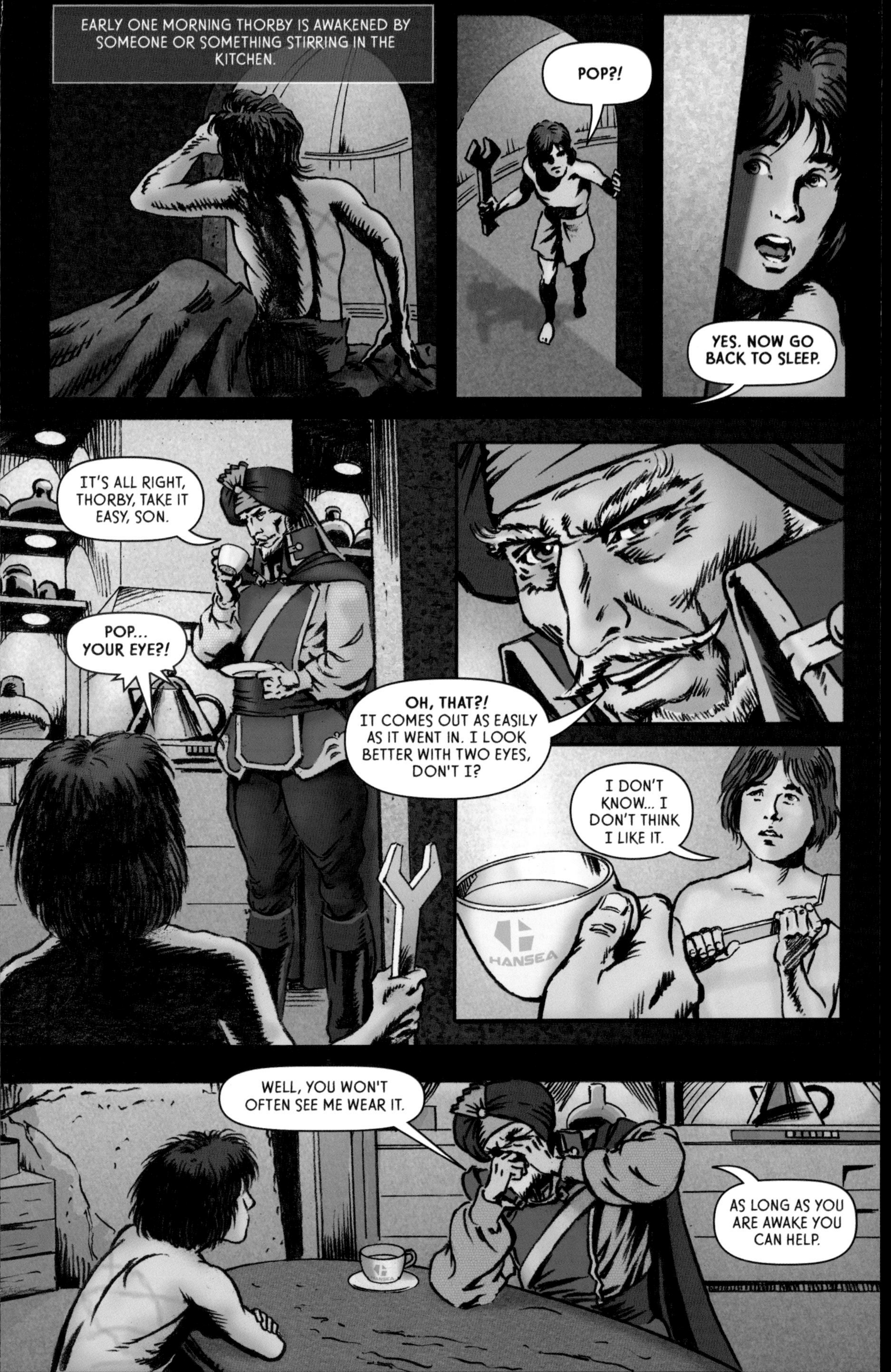
EARLY ONE MORNING THORBY IS AWAKENED BY SOMEONE OR SOMETHING STIRRING IN THE KITCHEN.
POP?!
YES. NOW GO BACK TO SLEEP.
IT'S ALL RIGHT, THORBY, TAKE IT EASY, SON.
POP... YOUR EYE?!
OH, THAT?! IT COMES OUT AS EASILY AS IT WENT IN. I LOOK BETTER WITH TWO EYES, DON'T I?
I DON'T KNOW... I DON'T THINK I LIKE IT.
HANSEA
WELL, YOU WON'T OFTEN SEE ME WEAR IT.
AS LONG AS YOU ARE AWAKE YOU CAN HELP.

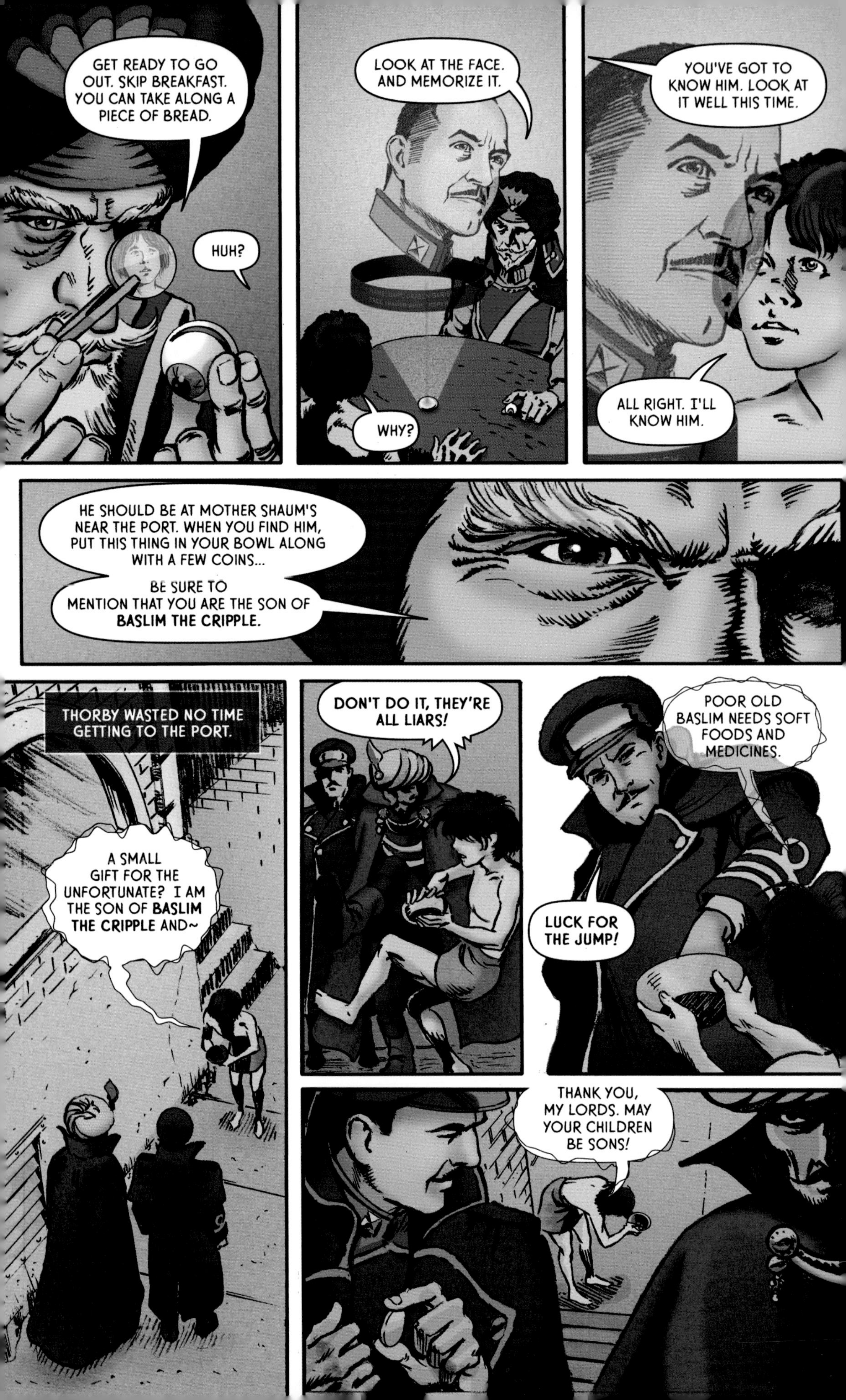
GET READY TO GO OUT. SKIP BREAKFAST. YOU CAN TAKE ALONG A PIECE OF BREAD.
HUH?
LOOK AT THE FACE. AND MEMORIZE IT.
WHY?
YOU'VE GOT TO KNOW HIM. LOOK AT IT WELL THIS TIME.
ALL RIGHT. I'LL KNOW HIM.
HE SHOULD BE AT MOTHER SHAUM'S NEAR THE PORT. WHEN YOU FIND HIM, PUT THIS THING IN YOUR BOWL ALONG WITH A FEW COINS...
BE SURE TO MENTION THAT YOU ARE THE SON OF **BASLIM THE CRIPPLE.**
THORBY WASTED NO TIME GETTING TO THE PORT.
A SMALL GIFT FOR THE UNFORTUNATE? I AM THE SON OF **BASLIM THE CRIPPLE** AND~
DON'T DO IT, THEY'RE ALL LIARS!
POOR OLD BASLIM NEEDS SOFT FOODS AND MEDICINES.
LUCK FOR THE JUMP!
THANK YOU, MY LORDS. MAY YOUR CHILDREN BE SONS!

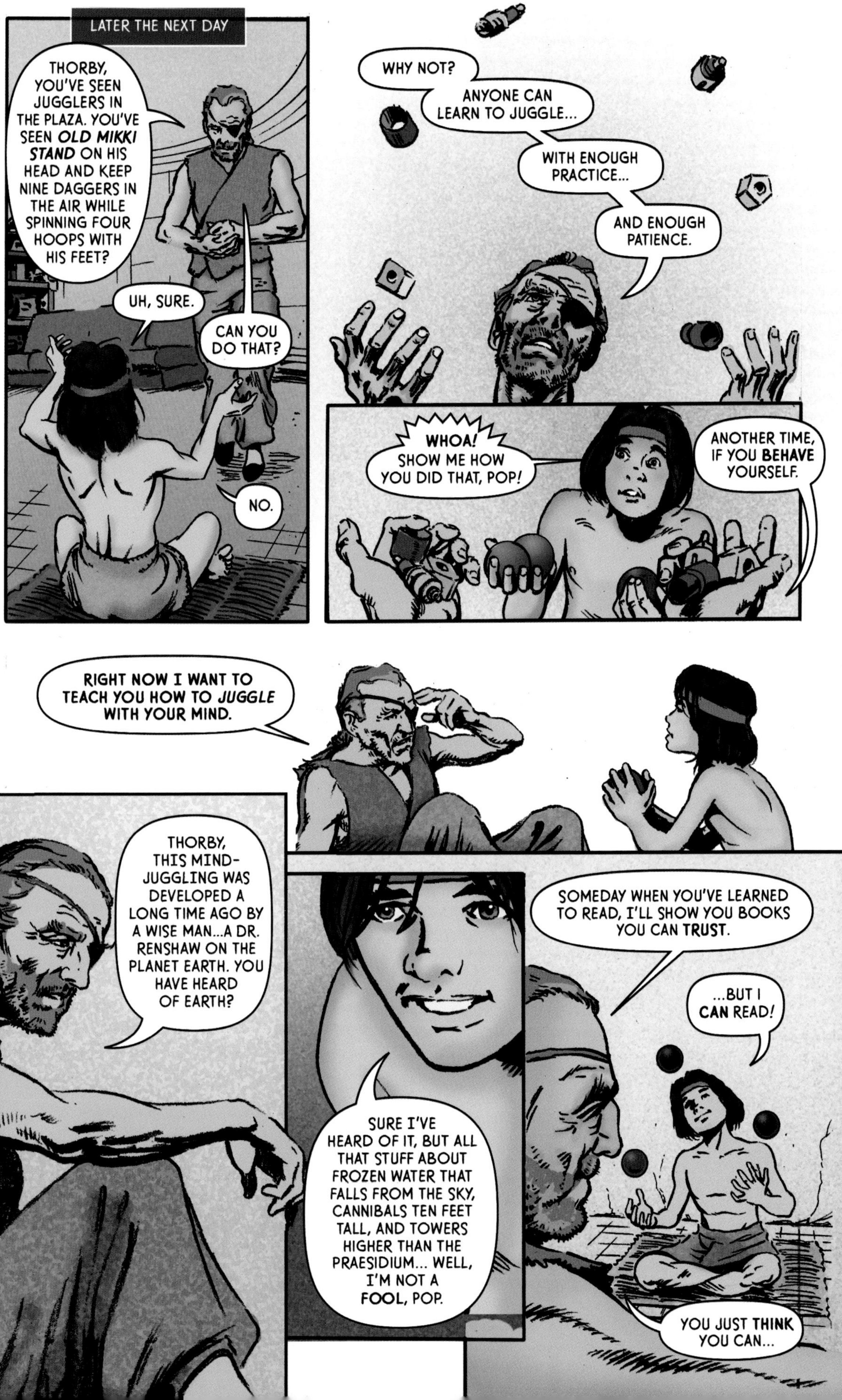

LATER THE NEXT DAY
THORBY, YOU'VE SEEN JUGGLERS IN THE PLAZA. YOU'VE SEEN OLD MIKKI STAND ON HIS HEAD AND KEEP NINE DAGGERS IN THE AIR WHILE SPINNING FOUR HOOPS WITH HIS FEET?
UH, SURE.
CAN YOU DO THAT?
NO.
WHY NOT?
ANYONE CAN LEARN TO JUGGLE...
WITH ENOUGH PRACTICE...
AND ENOUGH PATIENCE.
WHOA! SHOW ME HOW YOU DID THAT, POP!
ANOTHER TIME, IF YOU BEHAVE YOURSELF.
RIGHT NOW I WANT TO TEACH YOU HOW TO JUGGLE WITH YOUR MIND.
THORBY, THIS MIND-JUGGLING WAS DEVELOPED A LONG TIME AGO BY A WISE MAN...A DR. RENSHAW ON THE PLANET EARTH. YOU HAVE HEARD OF EARTH?
SURE I'VE HEARD OF IT, BUT ALL THAT STUFF ABOUT FROZEN WATER THAT FALLS FROM THE SKY, CANNIBALS TEN FEET TALL, AND TOWERS HIGHER THAN THE PRAESIDIUM... WELL, I'M NOT A FOOL, POP.
SOMEDAY WHEN YOU'VE LEARNED TO READ, I'LL SHOW YOU BOOKS YOU CAN TRUST.
...BUT I CAN READ!
YOU JUST THINK YOU CAN...

THORBY, THERE IS SUCH A PLACE AS *EARTH* AND IT TRULY IS STRANGE AND WONDERFUL. A MOST UNLIKELY PLANET. MANY WISE MEN HAVE LIVED AND DIED THERE ALONG WITH THE USUAL PROPORTION OF FOOLS AND VILLAINS AND SOME OF THEIR *WISDOM* HAS COME DOWN TO US.

SAMUEL RENSHAW WAS ONE SUCH WISE MAN. HE SHOWED HOW MAN COULD WAKE UP AND LIVE!

SEE WITH HIS EYES, HEAR WITH HIS EARS, TASTE WITH HIS TONGUE, THINK WITH HIS MIND, AND *REMEMBER PERFECTLY* WHAT HE SAW, HEARD, TASTED, AND THOUGHT.

DO YOU SEE THIS PATCH ON MY EYE? THIS DOESN'T MAKE ME A CRIPPLE. I SEE MORE WITH MY ONE EYE THAN YOU DO WITH *TWO*. BECAUSE *WHAT I SEE, I REMEMBER!*

SO WHICH ONE OF US IS *THE CRIPPLE?*

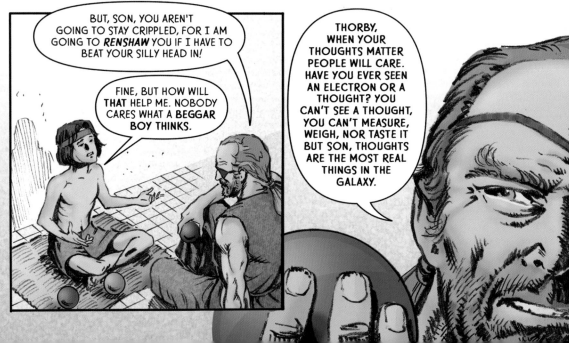

BUT, SON, YOU AREN'T GOING TO STAY CRIPPLED, FOR I AM GOING TO *RENSHAW* YOU IF I HAVE TO BEAT YOUR SILLY HEAD IN!

FINE, BUT HOW WILL *THAT* HELP ME. NOBODY CARES WHAT A *BEGGAR* BOY THINKS.

THORBY, WHEN YOUR THOUGHTS MATTER PEOPLE WILL CARE. HAVE YOU EVER SEEN AN ELECTRON OR A THOUGHT? YOU CAN'T SEE A THOUGHT, YOU CAN'T MEASURE, WEIGH, NOR TASTE IT BUT SON, THOUGHTS ARE THE MOST REAL THINGS IN THE GALAXY.

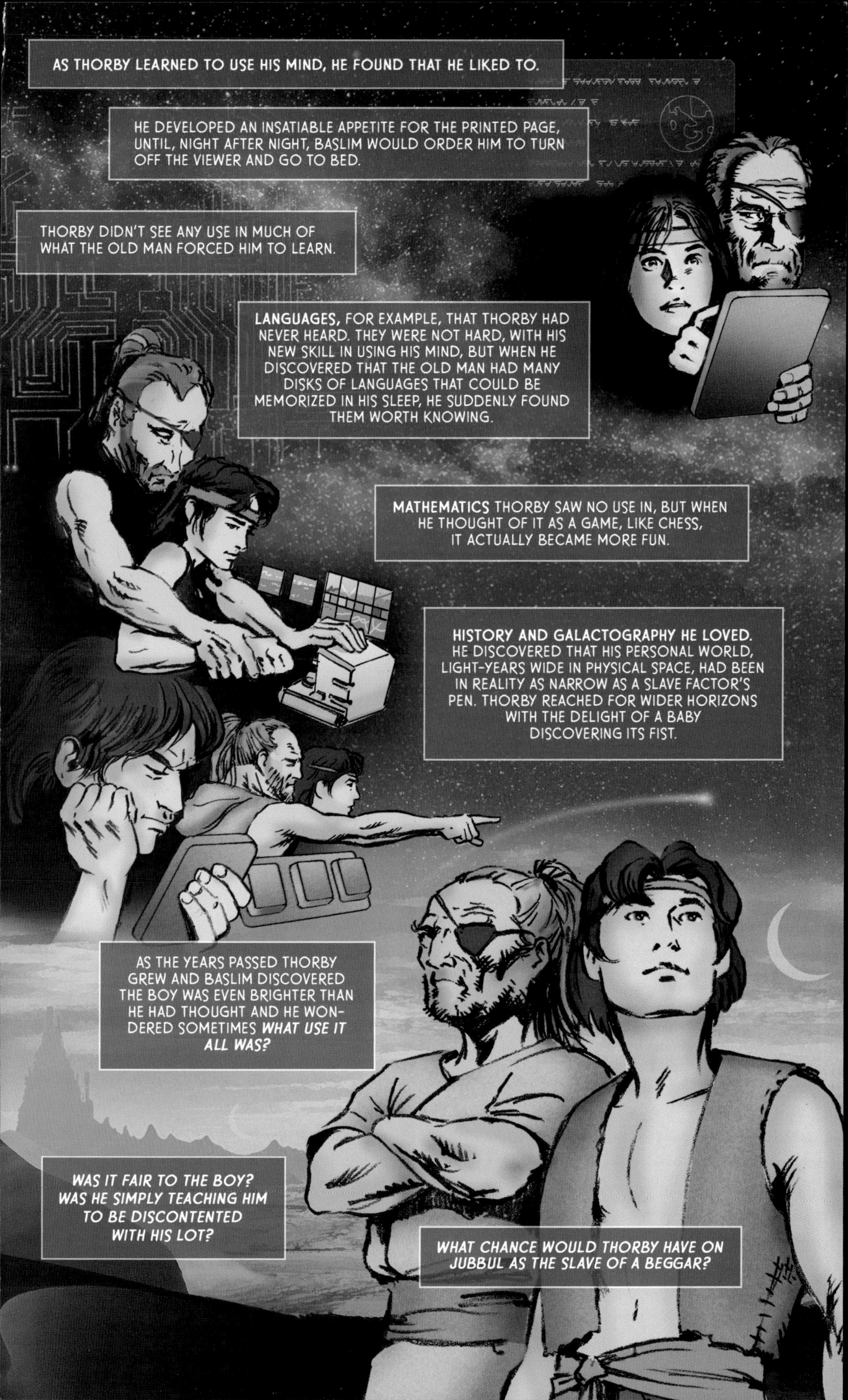
AS THORBY LEARNED TO USE HIS MIND, HE FOUND THAT HE LIKED TO.
HE DEVELOPED AN INSATIABLE APPETITE FOR THE PRINTED PAGE, UNTIL, NIGHT AFTER NIGHT, BASLIM WOULD ORDER HIM TO TURN OFF THE VIEWER AND GO TO BED.
THORBY DIDN'T SEE ANY USE IN MUCH OF WHAT THE OLD MAN FORCED HIM TO LEARN.
LANGUAGES, FOR EXAMPLE, THAT THORBY HAD NEVER HEARD. THEY WERE NOT HARD, WITH HIS NEW SKILL IN USING HIS MIND, BUT WHEN HE DISCOVERED THAT THE OLD MAN HAD MANY DISKS OF LANGUAGES THAT COULD BE MEMORIZED IN HIS SLEEP, HE SUDDENLY FOUND THEM WORTH KNOWING.
MATHEMATICS THORBY SAW NO USE IN, BUT WHEN HE THOUGHT OF IT AS A GAME, LIKE CHESS, IT ACTUALLY BECAME MORE FUN.
HISTORY AND GALACTOGRAPHY HE LOVED. HE DISCOVERED THAT HIS PERSONAL WORLD, LIGHT-YEARS WIDE IN PHYSICAL SPACE, HAD BEEN IN REALITY AS NARROW AS A SLAVE FACTOR'S PEN. THORBY REACHED FOR WIDER HORIZONS WITH THE DELIGHT OF A BABY DISCOVERING ITS FIST.
AS THE YEARS PASSED THORBY GREW AND BASLIM DISCOVERED THE BOY WAS EVEN BRIGHTER THAN HE HAD THOUGHT AND HE WON-DERED SOMETIMES WHAT USE IT ALL WAS?
WAS IT FAIR TO THE BOY? WAS HE SIMPLY TEACHING HIM TO BE DISCONTENTED WITH HIS LOT?
WHAT CHANCE WOULD THORBY HAVE ON JUBBUL AS THE SLAVE OF A BEGGAR?

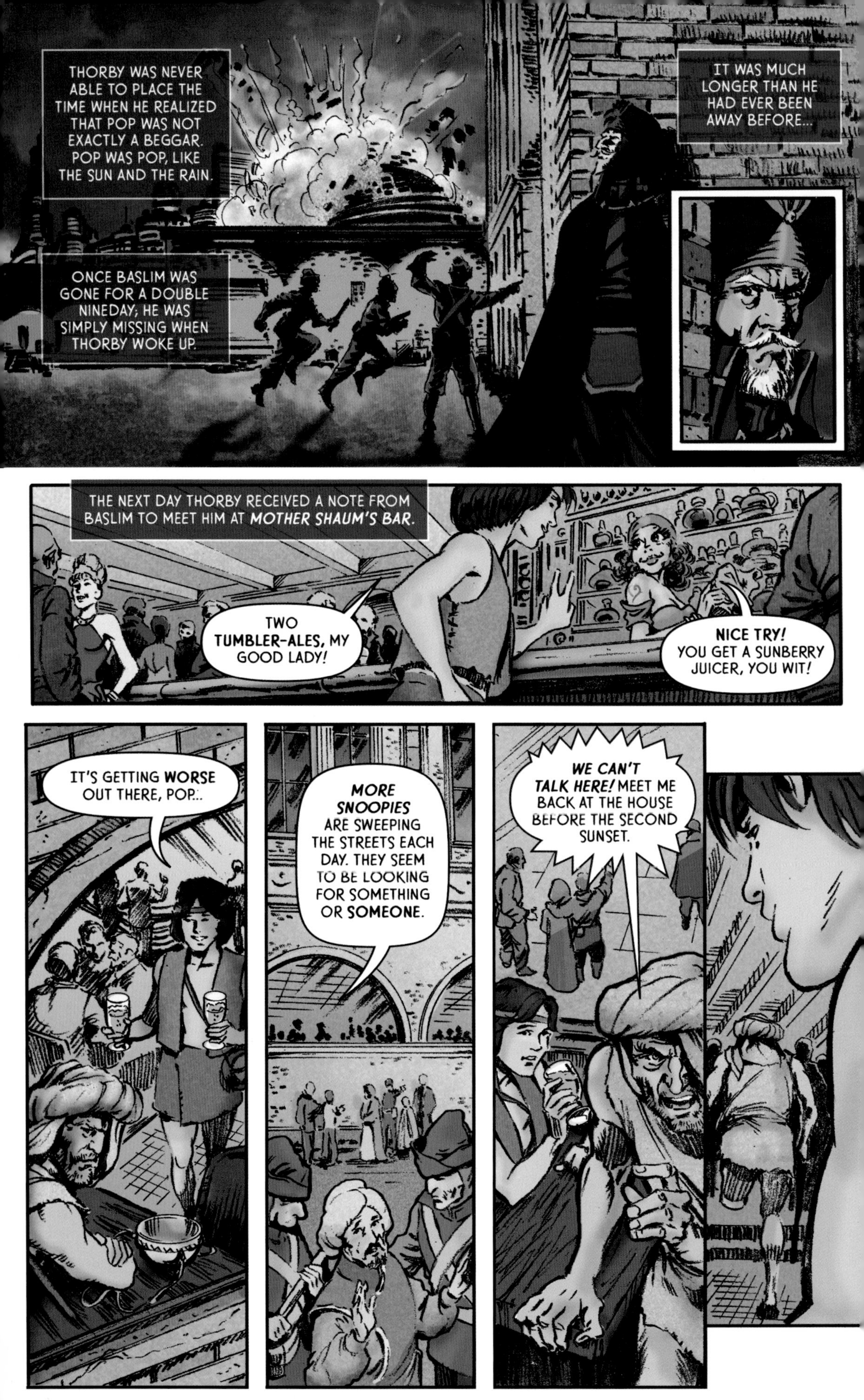
THORBY WAS NEVER ABLE TO PLACE THE TIME WHEN HE REALIZED THAT POP WAS NOT EXACTLY A BEGGAR. POP WAS POP, LIKE THE SUN AND THE RAIN.
ONCE BASLIM WAS GONE FOR A DOUBLE NINEDAY; HE WAS SIMPLY MISSING WHEN THORBY WOKE UP.
IT WAS MUCH LONGER THAN HE HAD EVER BEEN AWAY BEFORE...
THE NEXT DAY THORBY RECEIVED A NOTE FROM BASLIM TO MEET HIM AT MOTHER SHAUM'S BAR.
TWO TUMBLER-ALES, MY GOOD LADY!
NICE TRY! YOU GET A SUNBERRY JUICER, YOU WIT!
IT'S GETTING WORSE OUT THERE, POP...
MORE SNOOPIES ARE SWEEPING THE STREETS EACH DAY. THEY SEEM TO BE LOOKING FOR SOMETHING OR SOMEONE.
WE CAN'T TALK HERE! MEET ME BACK AT THE HOUSE BEFORE THE SECOND SUNSET.

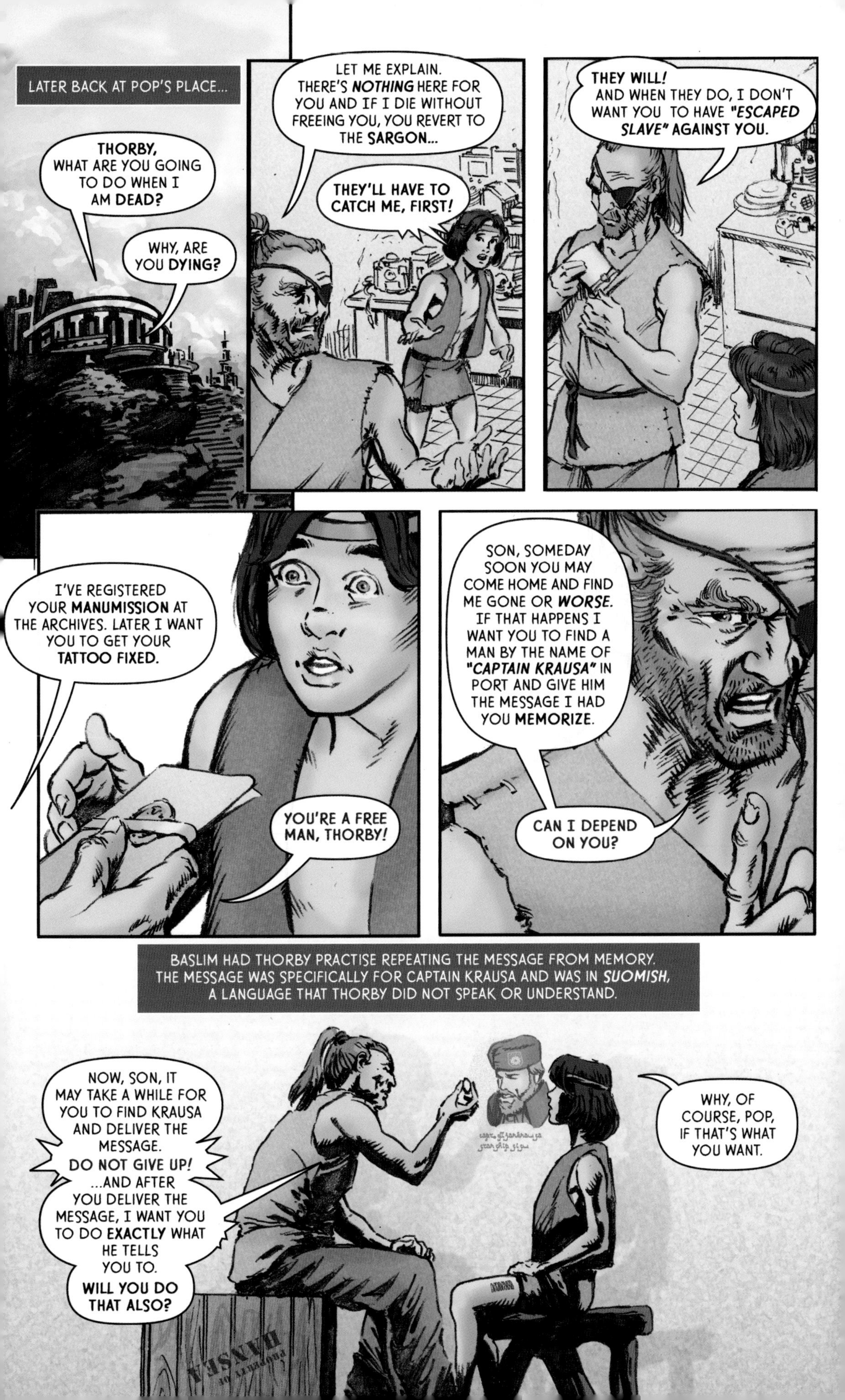
LATER BACK AT POP'S PLACE...
THORBY, WHAT ARE YOU GOING TO DO WHEN I AM DEAD?
WHY, ARE YOU DYING?
LET ME EXPLAIN. THERE'S NOTHING HERE FOR YOU AND IF I DIE WITHOUT FREEING YOU, YOU REVERT TO THE SARGON...
THEY'LL HAVE TO CATCH ME, FIRST!
THEY WILL! AND WHEN THEY DO, I DON'T WANT YOU TO HAVE "ESCAPED SLAVE" AGAINST YOU.
I'VE REGISTERED YOUR MANUMISSION AT THE ARCHIVES. LATER I WANT YOU TO GET YOUR TATTOO FIXED.
YOU'RE A FREE MAN, THORBY!
SON, SOMEDAY SOON YOU MAY COME HOME AND FIND ME GONE OR WORSE. IF THAT HAPPENS I WANT YOU TO FIND A MAN BY THE NAME OF "CAPTAIN KRAUSA" IN PORT AND GIVE HIM THE MESSAGE I HAD YOU MEMORIZE.
CAN I DEPEND ON YOU?
BASLIM HAD THORBY PRACTISE REPEATING THE MESSAGE FROM MEMORY. THE MESSAGE WAS SPECIFICALLY FOR CAPTAIN KRAUSA AND WAS IN SUOMISH, A LANGUAGE THAT THORBY DID NOT SPEAK OR UNDERSTAND.
NOW, SON, IT MAY TAKE A WHILE FOR YOU TO FIND KRAUSA AND DELIVER THE MESSAGE.
DO NOT GIVE UP!
...AND AFTER YOU DELIVER THE MESSAGE, I WANT YOU TO DO EXACTLY WHAT HE TELLS YOU TO.
WILL YOU DO THAT ALSO?
WHY, OF COURSE, POP, IF THAT'S WHAT YOU WANT.

BUT NOW THERE'S NO TIME TO WASTE... GET MOVING.

I DON'T WANT TO LEAVE HERE, POP.

THIS WILL **ALWAYS** BE YOUR HOME, THORBY.

LATER THORBY ARRIVES AT THE SARGONIAN TATTOO PARLOR.

SO WHAT'S YOUR STORY...YOUR OLD MASTER GO BANKRUPT?

NONE OF YOUR BUSINESS.

DON'T GET SMART, KID, OR THIS LASER CAN HURT EVEN MORE. NOW GIVE ME A CIVIL ANSWER. HOW **OLD** WERE YA WHEN THEY **BRANDED** YA?

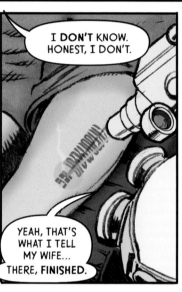

I **DON'T** KNOW. HONEST, I DON'T.

YEAH, THAT'S WHAT I TELL MY WIFE... THERE, FINISHED.

AUNTIE SINGHAM, WHAT'S BURNING?

THORBY, IT'S A RAID!

THEY'VE TAKEN YOUR MASTER, CLAIMING HE WAS **SPYING** AGAINST THE SARGON!

THERE'S A REWARD OUT FOR YOU! YOU BEST CRAWL IN A HOLE AND PULL IT IN AFTER YOU.

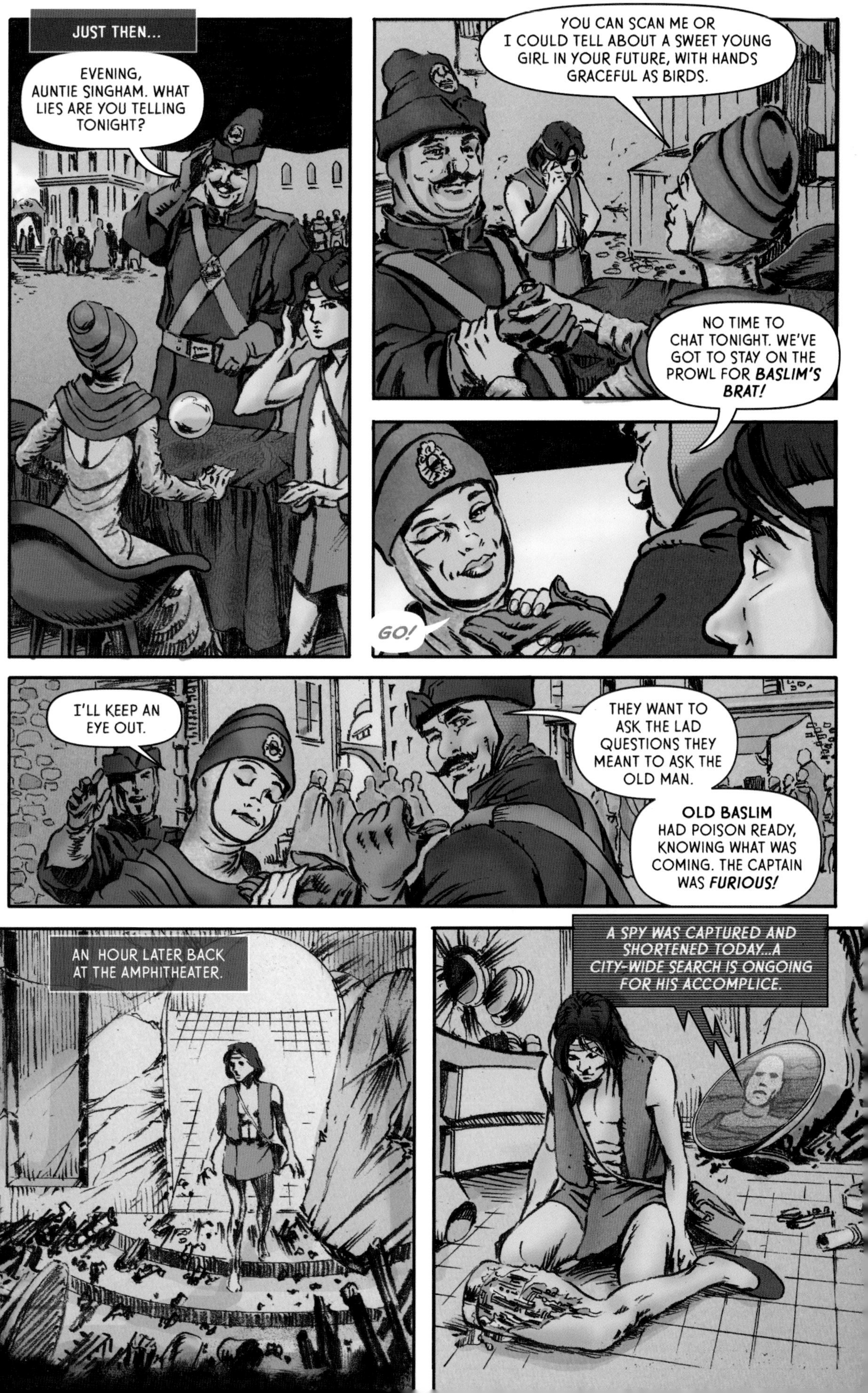
JUST THEN...
EVENING, AUNTIE SINGHAM. WHAT LIES ARE YOU TELLING TONIGHT?
YOU CAN SCAN ME OR I COULD TELL ABOUT A SWEET YOUNG GIRL IN YOUR FUTURE, WITH HANDS GRACEFUL AS BIRDS.
NO TIME TO CHAT TONIGHT. WE'VE GOT TO STAY ON THE PROWL FOR BASLIM'S BRAT!
GO!
I'LL KEEP AN EYE OUT.
THEY WANT TO ASK THE LAD QUESTIONS THEY MEANT TO ASK THE OLD MAN.
OLD BASLIM HAD POISON READY, KNOWING WHAT WAS COMING. THE CAPTAIN WAS FURIOUS!
AN HOUR LATER BACK AT THE AMPHITHEATER.
A SPY WAS CAPTURED AND SHORTENED TODAY...A CITY-WIDE SEARCH IS ONGOING FOR HIS ACCOMPLICE.

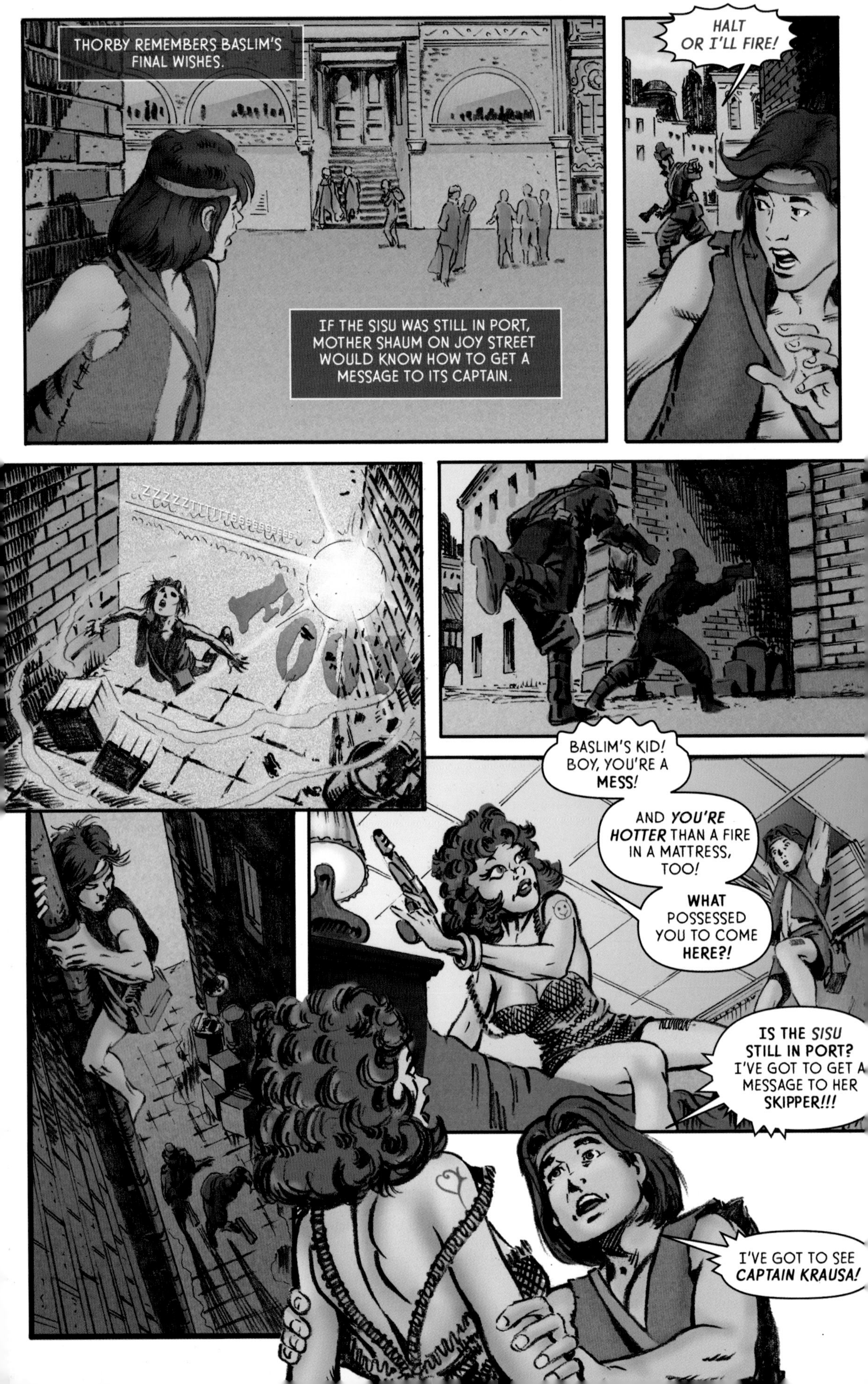
THORBY REMEMBERS BASLIM'S FINAL WISHES.
IF THE SISU WAS STILL IN PORT, MOTHER SHAUM ON JOY STREET WOULD KNOW HOW TO GET A MESSAGE TO ITS CAPTAIN.
HALT OR I'LL FIRE!
BASLIM'S KID! BOY, YOU'RE A MESS!
AND YOU'RE HOTTER THAN A FIRE IN A MATTRESS, TOO!
WHAT POSSESSED YOU TO COME HERE?!
IS THE SISU STILL IN PORT? I'VE GOT TO GET A MESSAGE TO HER SKIPPER!!!
I'VE GOT TO SEE CAPTAIN KRAUSA!

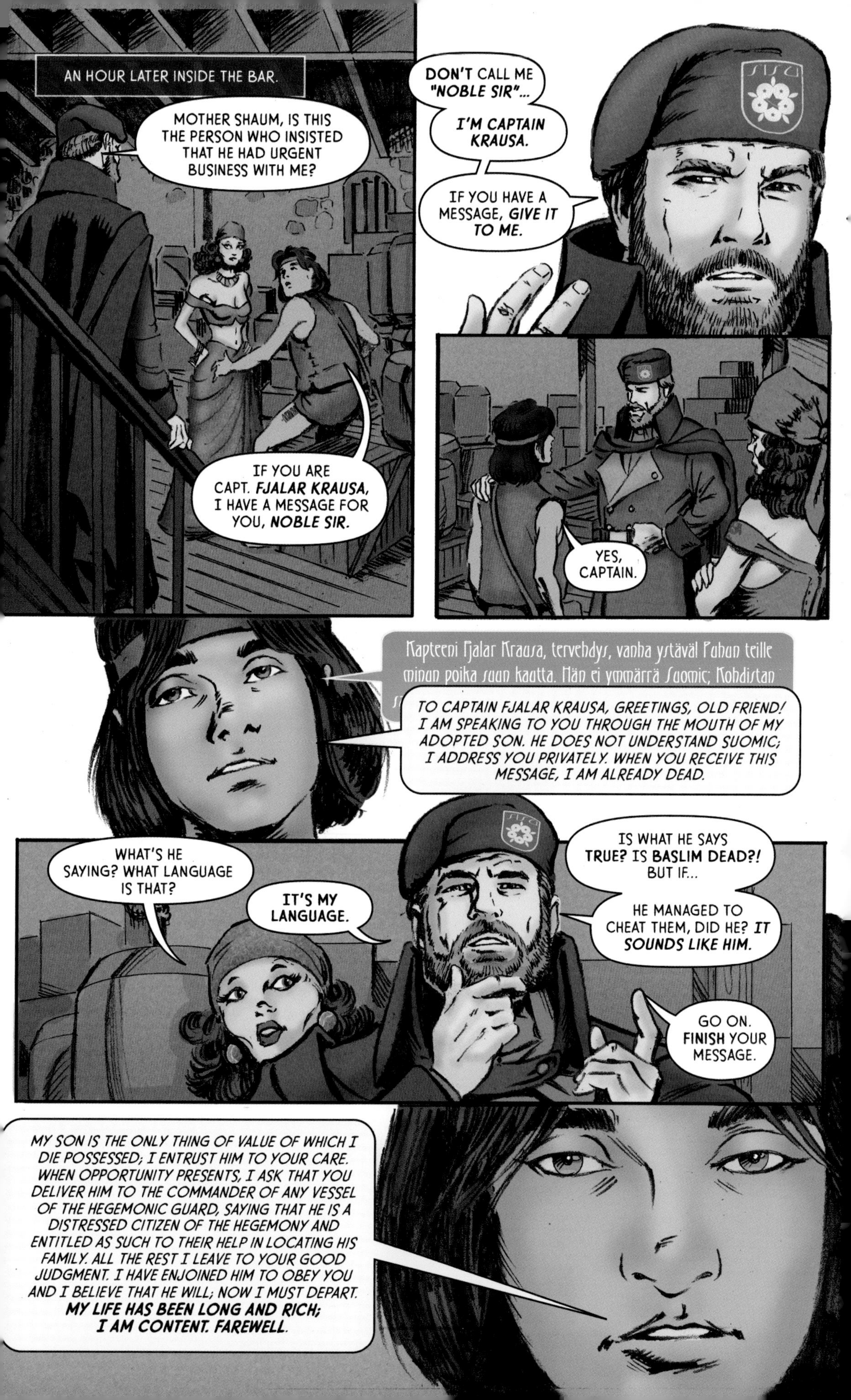
AN HOUR LATER INSIDE THE BAR.
MOTHER SHAUM, IS THIS THE PERSON WHO INSISTED THAT HE HAD URGENT BUSINESS WITH ME?
IF YOU ARE CAPT. **FJALAR KRAUSA,** I HAVE A MESSAGE FOR YOU, **NOBLE SIR.**
DON'T CALL ME ***"NOBLE SIR"...***
I'M CAPTAIN KRAUSA.
IF YOU HAVE A MESSAGE, ***GIVE IT TO ME.***
YES, CAPTAIN.
Kapteeni Fjalar Krausa, tervehdys, vanha ystävä! Puhun teille
minun poika suun kautta. Hän ei ymmärrä Suomic; Kohdistan
TO CAPTAIN FJALAR KRAUSA, GREETINGS, OLD FRIEND! I AM SPEAKING TO YOU THROUGH THE MOUTH OF MY ADOPTED SON. HE DOES NOT UNDERSTAND SUOMIC; I ADDRESS YOU PRIVATELY. WHEN YOU RECEIVE THIS MESSAGE, I AM ALREADY DEAD.
WHAT'S HE SAYING? WHAT LANGUAGE IS THAT?
IT'S MY LANGUAGE.
IS WHAT HE SAYS **TRUE?** IS **BASLIM DEAD?!** BUT IF...
HE MANAGED TO CHEAT THEM, DID HE? ***IT SOUNDS LIKE HIM.***
GO ON. **FINISH** YOUR MESSAGE.
MY SON IS THE ONLY THING OF VALUE OF WHICH I DIE POSSESSED; I ENTRUST HIM TO YOUR CARE. WHEN OPPORTUNITY PRESENTS, I ASK THAT YOU DELIVER HIM TO THE COMMANDER OF ANY VESSEL OF THE HEGEMONIC GUARD, SAYING THAT HE IS A DISTRESSED CITIZEN OF THE HEGEMONY AND ENTITLED AS SUCH TO THEIR HELP IN LOCATING HIS FAMILY. ALL THE REST I LEAVE TO YOUR GOOD JUDGMENT. I HAVE ENJOINED HIM TO OBEY YOU AND I BELIEVE THAT HE WILL; NOW I MUST DEPART. ***MY LIFE HAS BEEN LONG AND RICH; I AM CONTENT. FAREWELL.***

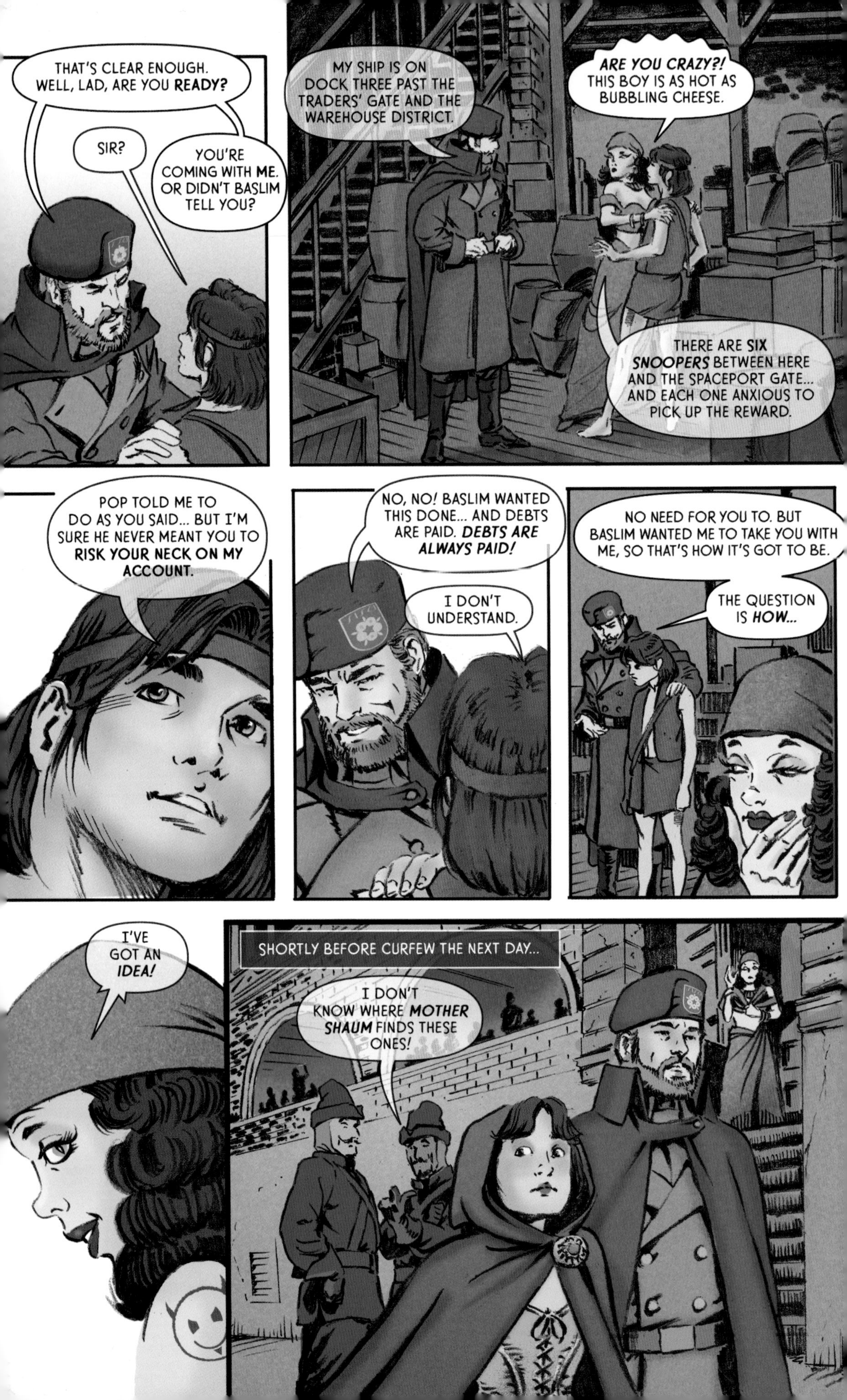
THAT'S CLEAR ENOUGH. WELL, LAD, ARE YOU **READY?**
SIR?
YOU'RE COMING WITH **ME**. OR DIDN'T BASLIM TELL YOU?
MY SHIP IS ON DOCK THREE PAST THE TRADERS' GATE AND THE WAREHOUSE DISTRICT.
ARE YOU CRAZY?! THIS BOY IS AS HOT AS BUBBLING CHEESE.
THERE ARE **SIX *SNOOPERS*** BETWEEN HERE AND THE SPACEPORT GATE... AND EACH ONE ANXIOUS TO PICK UP THE REWARD.
POP TOLD ME TO DO AS YOU SAID... BUT I'M SURE HE NEVER MEANT YOU TO **RISK YOUR NECK ON MY ACCOUNT.**
NO, NO*!* BASLIM WANTED THIS DONE... AND DEBTS ARE PAID. ***DEBTS ARE ALWAYS PAID!***
I DON'T UNDERSTAND.
NO NEED FOR YOU TO. BUT BASLIM WANTED ME TO TAKE YOU WITH ME, SO THAT'S HOW IT'S GOT TO BE.
THE QUESTION IS ***HOW...***
I'VE GOT AN ***IDEA!***
SHORTLY BEFORE CURFEW THE NEXT DAY...
I DON'T KNOW WHERE ***MOTHER SHAUM*** FINDS THESE ONES!

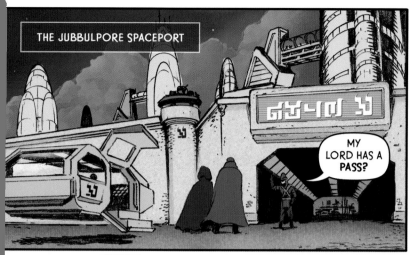

THE JUBBULPORE SPACEPORT

MY LORD HAS A PASS?

STILL LOOKING FOR THE BEGGAR'S BOY?

AS A MATTER OF FACT, YES. BUT WE'LL FIND HIM.

WHAT THE...

THOOM!

FOR THE PEOPLE!

WE WERE ON LOCKDOWN. *WHO BOARDED THAT VESSEL?!!*

RELAX, IT WAS JUST A MERCHANT AND HIS SLAVE.

THORBY AND KRAUSA CASUALLY EXIT WITH A LITTLE DIVERSIONARY HELP FROM MOTHER SHAULM AND COMPANY.

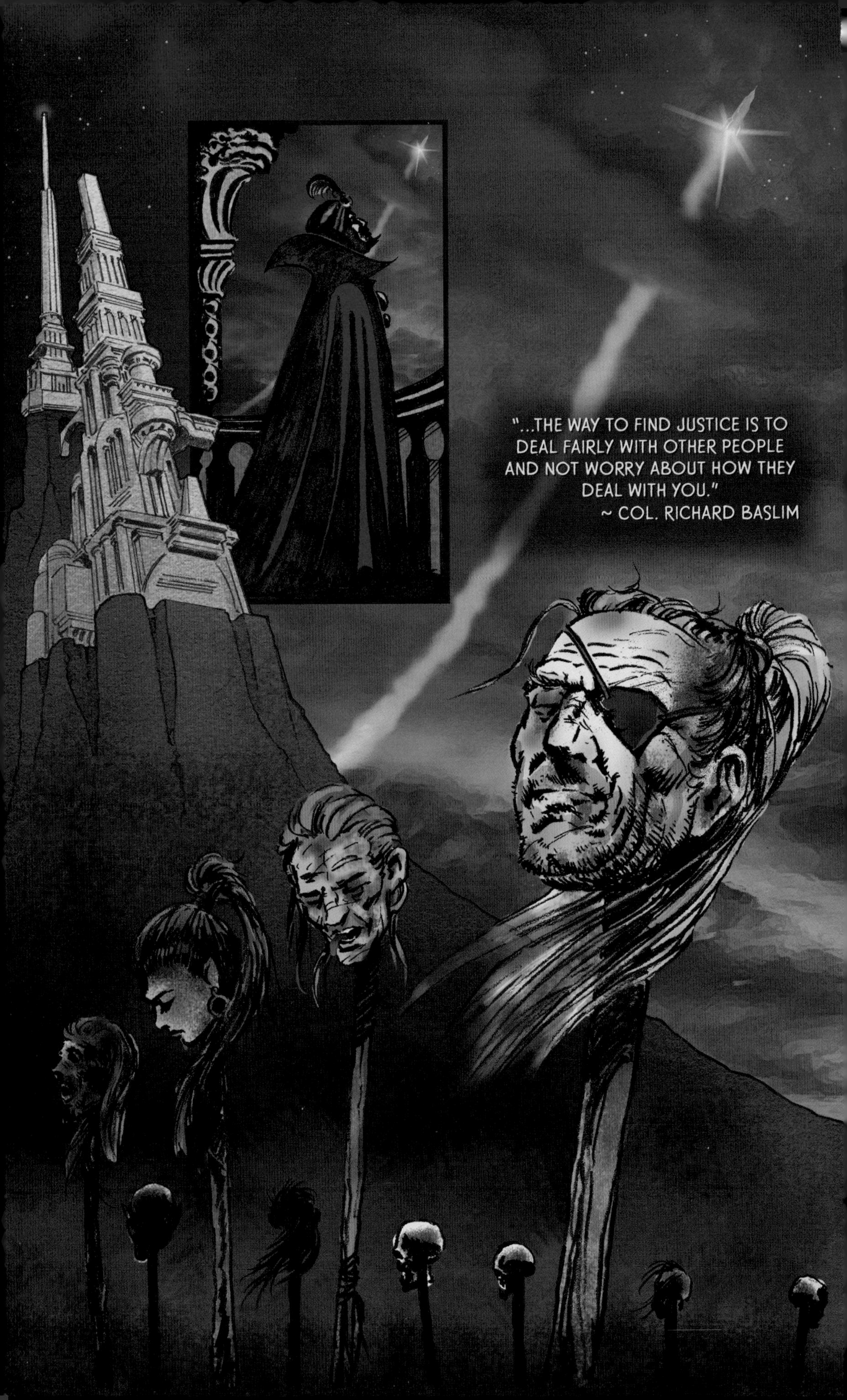
"...THE WAY TO FIND JUSTICE IS TO DEAL FAIRLY WITH OTHER PEOPLE AND NOT WORRY ABOUT HOW THEY DEAL WITH YOU."
~ COL. RICHARD BASLIM

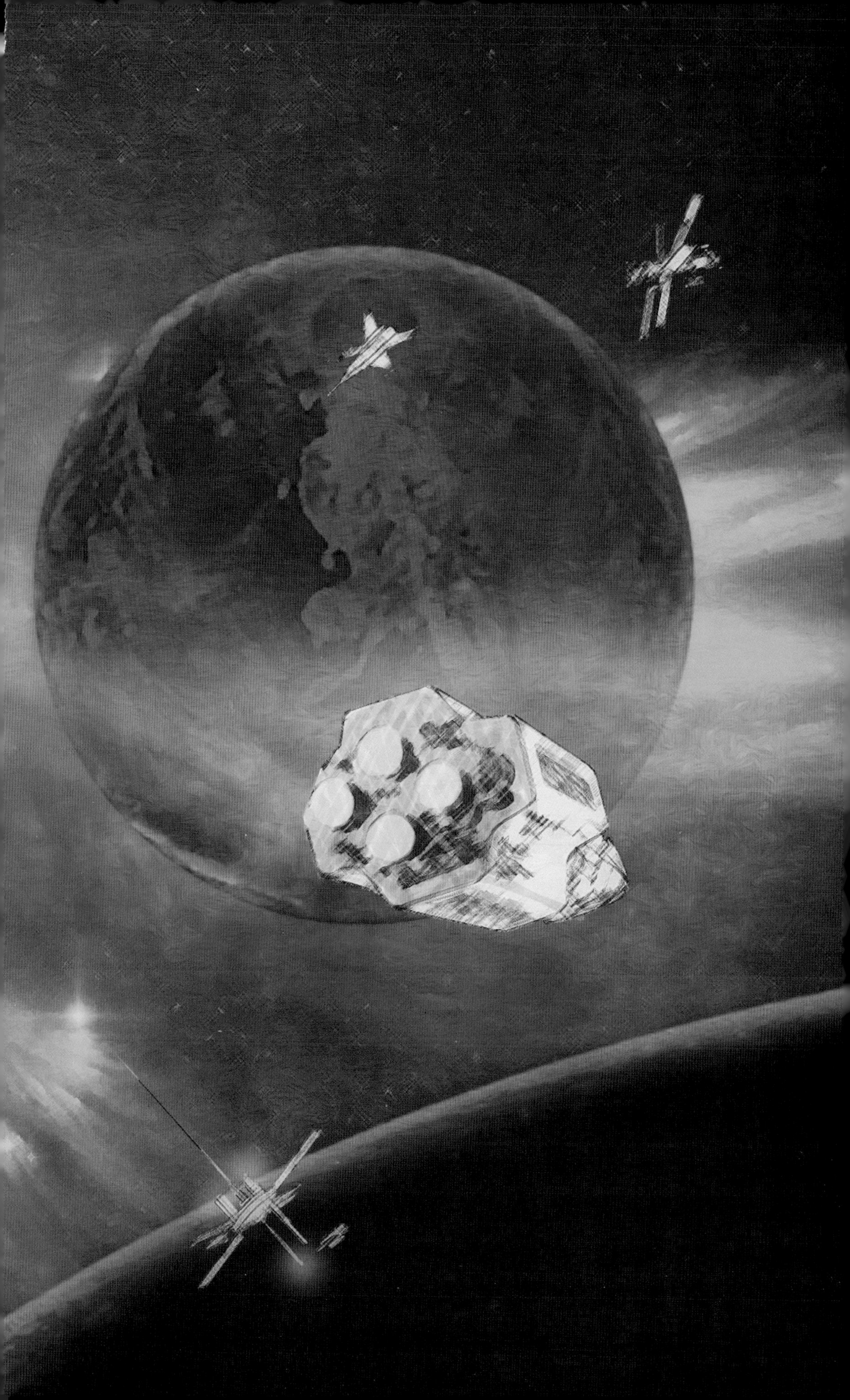

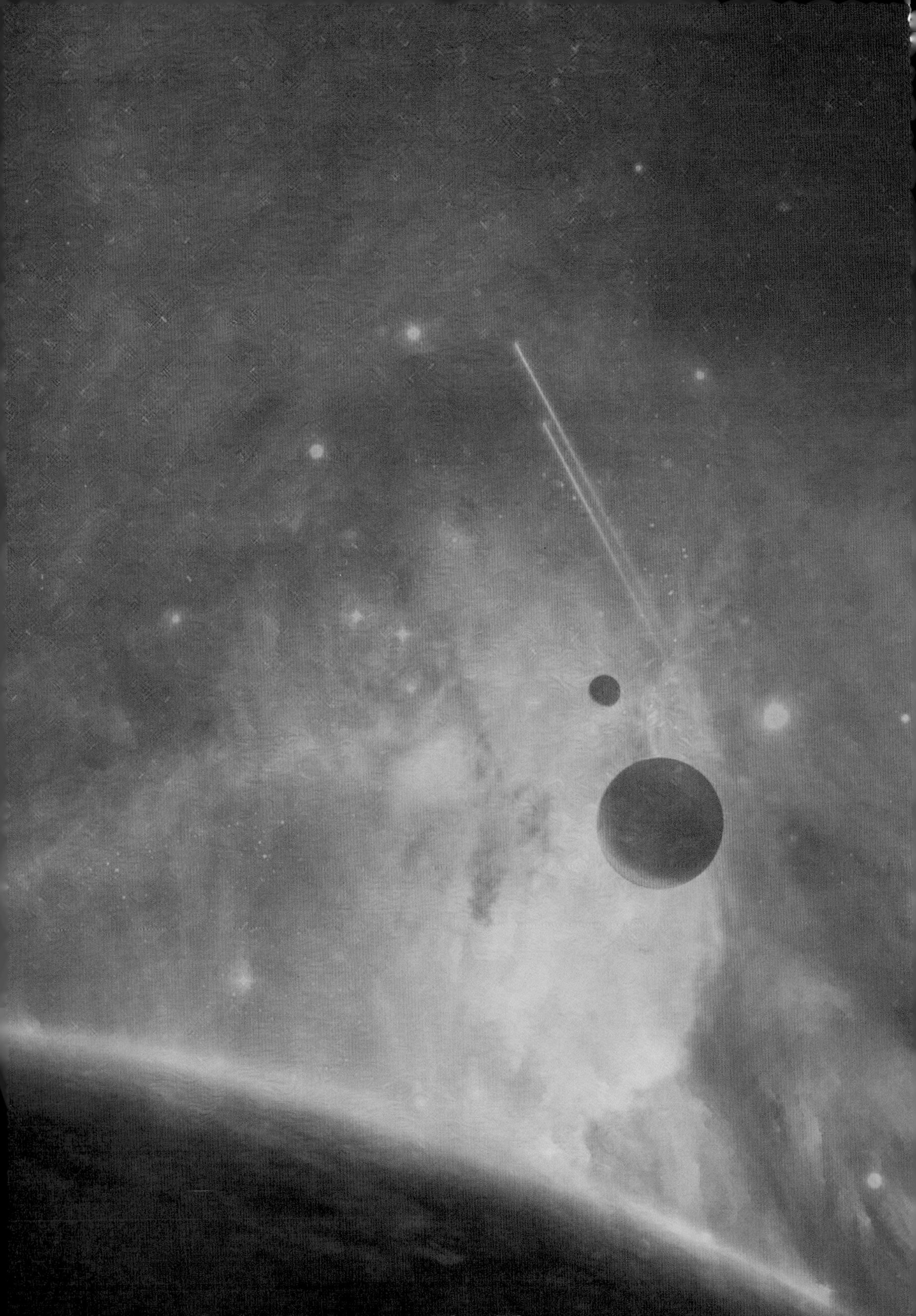

ACT II

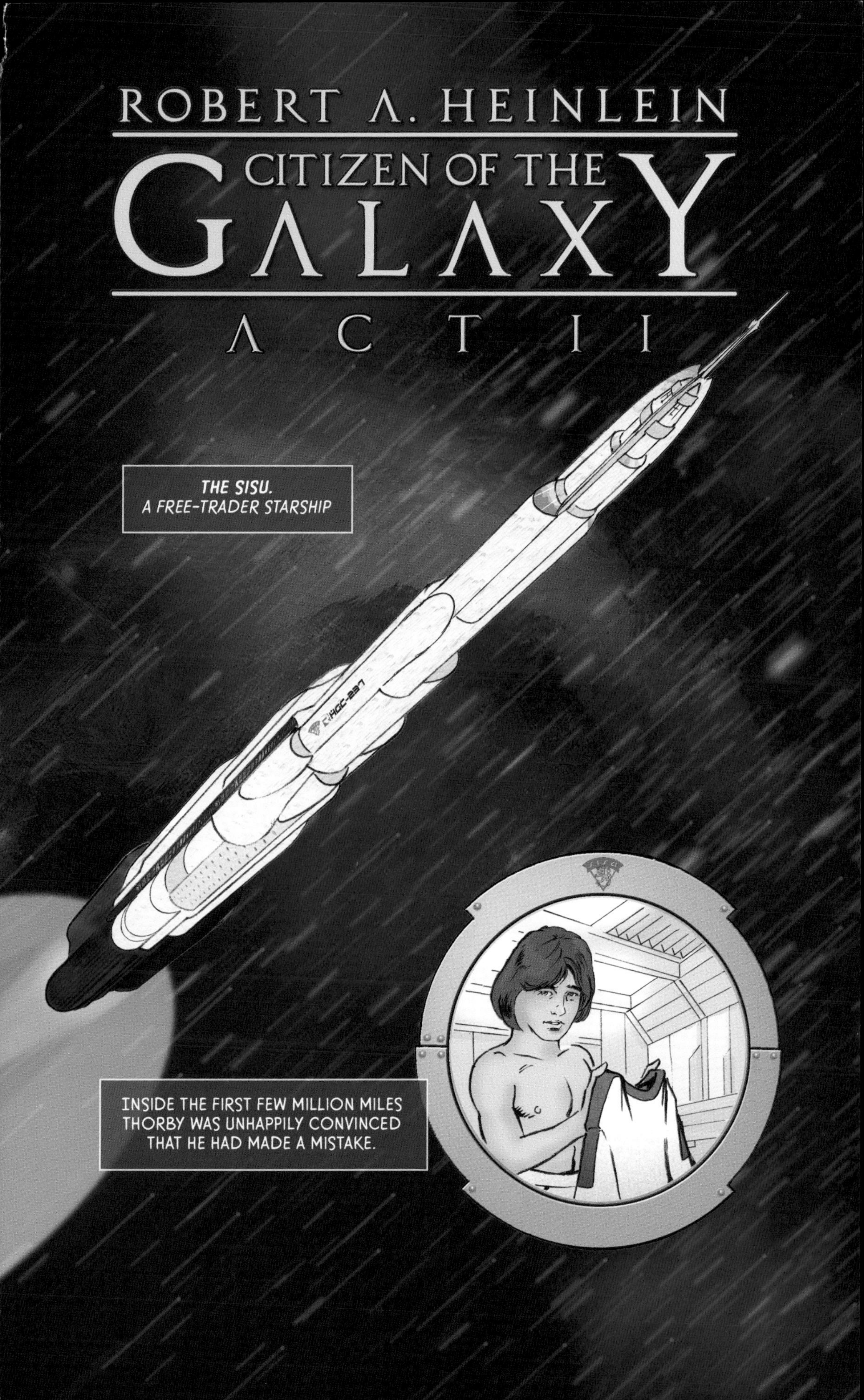
ROBERT A. HEINLEIN
CITIZEN OF THE GALAXY
ACT II
THE SISU.
A FREE-TRADER STARSHIP
INSIDE THE FIRST FEW MILLION MILES THORBY WAS UNHAPPILY CONVINCED THAT HE HAD MADE A MISTAKE.

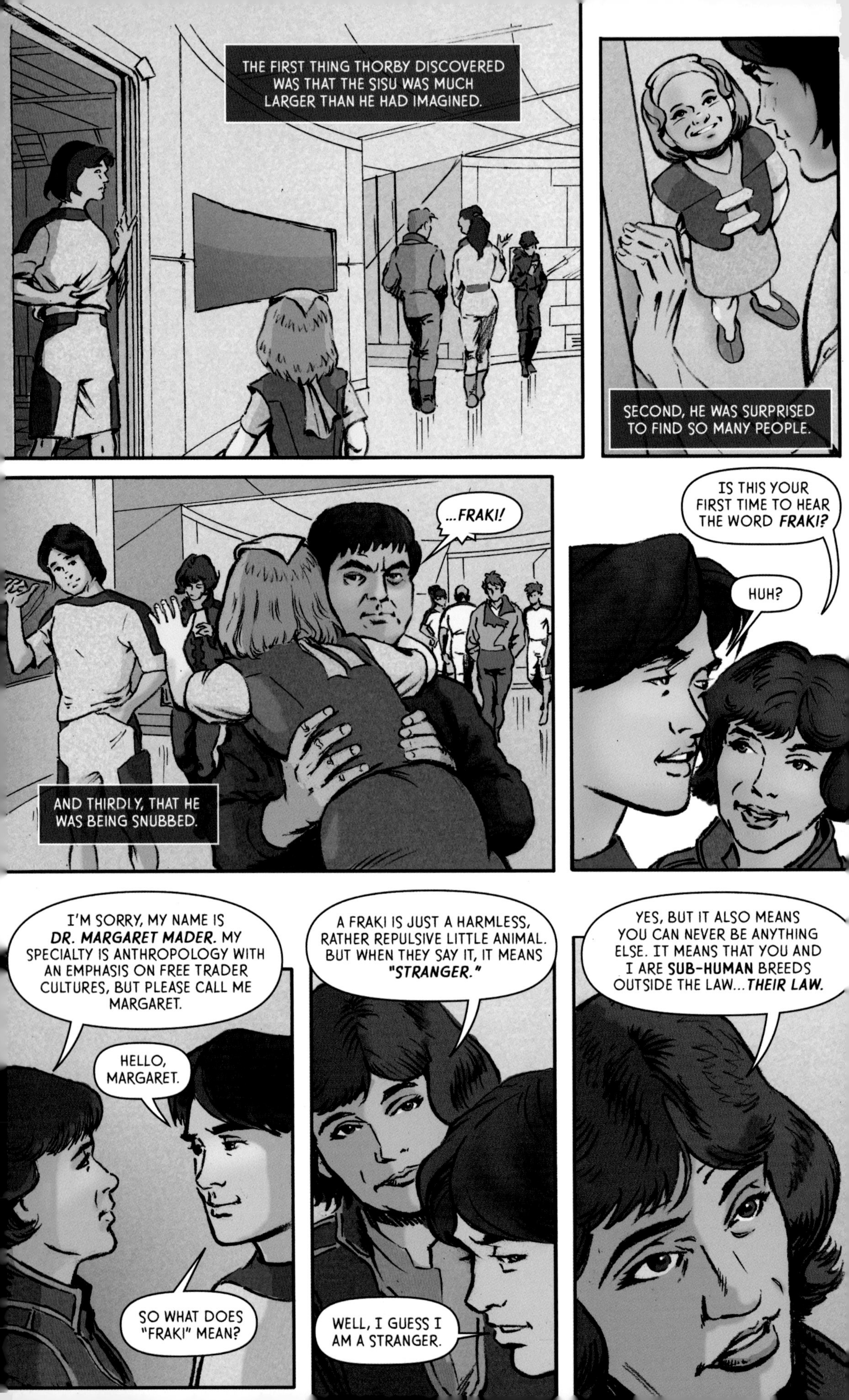
THE FIRST THING THORBY DISCOVERED WAS THAT THE SISU WAS MUCH LARGER THAN HE HAD IMAGINED.
SECOND, HE WAS SURPRISED TO FIND SO MANY PEOPLE.
...FRAKI!
AND THIRDLY, THAT HE WAS BEING SNUBBED.
IS THIS YOUR FIRST TIME TO HEAR THE WORD FRAKI?
HUH?
I'M SORRY, MY NAME IS DR. MARGARET MADER. MY SPECIALTY IS ANTHROPOLOGY WITH AN EMPHASIS ON FREE TRADER CULTURES, BUT PLEASE CALL ME MARGARET.
HELLO, MARGARET.
SO WHAT DOES "FRAKI" MEAN?
A FRAKI IS JUST A HARMLESS, RATHER REPULSIVE LITTLE ANIMAL. BUT WHEN THEY SAY IT, IT MEANS "STRANGER."
WELL, I GUESS I AM A STRANGER.
YES, BUT IT ALSO MEANS YOU CAN NEVER BE ANYTHING ELSE. IT MEANS THAT YOU AND I ARE SUB-HUMAN BREEDS OUTSIDE THE LAW...THEIR LAW.

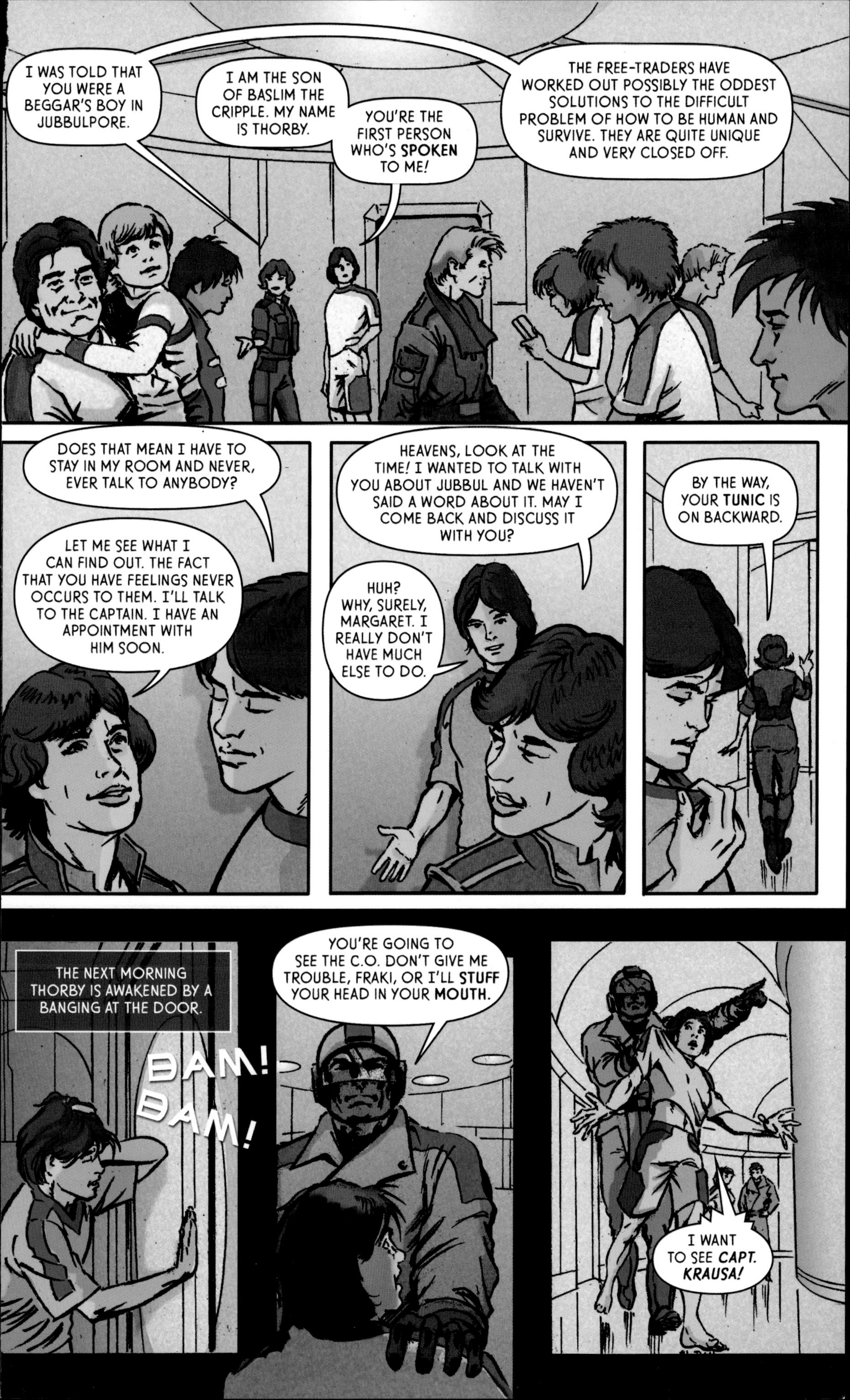

I WAS TOLD THAT YOU WERE A BEGGAR'S BOY IN JUBBULPORE.
I AM THE SON OF BASLIM THE CRIPPLE. MY NAME IS THORBY.
YOU'RE THE FIRST PERSON WHO'S SPOKEN TO ME!
THE FREE-TRADERS HAVE WORKED OUT POSSIBLY THE ODDEST SOLUTIONS TO THE DIFFICULT PROBLEM OF HOW TO BE HUMAN AND SURVIVE. THEY ARE QUITE UNIQUE AND VERY CLOSED OFF.
DOES THAT MEAN I HAVE TO STAY IN MY ROOM AND NEVER, EVER TALK TO ANYBODY?
LET ME SEE WHAT I CAN FIND OUT. THE FACT THAT YOU HAVE FEELINGS NEVER OCCURS TO THEM. I'LL TALK TO THE CAPTAIN. I HAVE AN APPOINTMENT WITH HIM SOON.
HEAVENS, LOOK AT THE TIME! I WANTED TO TALK WITH YOU ABOUT JUBBUL AND WE HAVEN'T SAID A WORD ABOUT IT. MAY I COME BACK AND DISCUSS IT WITH YOU?
HUH? WHY, SURELY, MARGARET. I REALLY DON'T HAVE MUCH ELSE TO DO.
BY THE WAY, YOUR TUNIC IS ON BACKWARD.
THE NEXT MORNING THORBY IS AWAKENED BY A BANGING AT THE DOOR.
BAM! BAM!
YOU'RE GOING TO SEE THE C.O. DON'T GIVE ME TROUBLE, FRAKI, OR I'LL STUFF YOUR HEAD IN YOUR MOUTH.
I WANT TO SEE CAPT. KRAUSA!

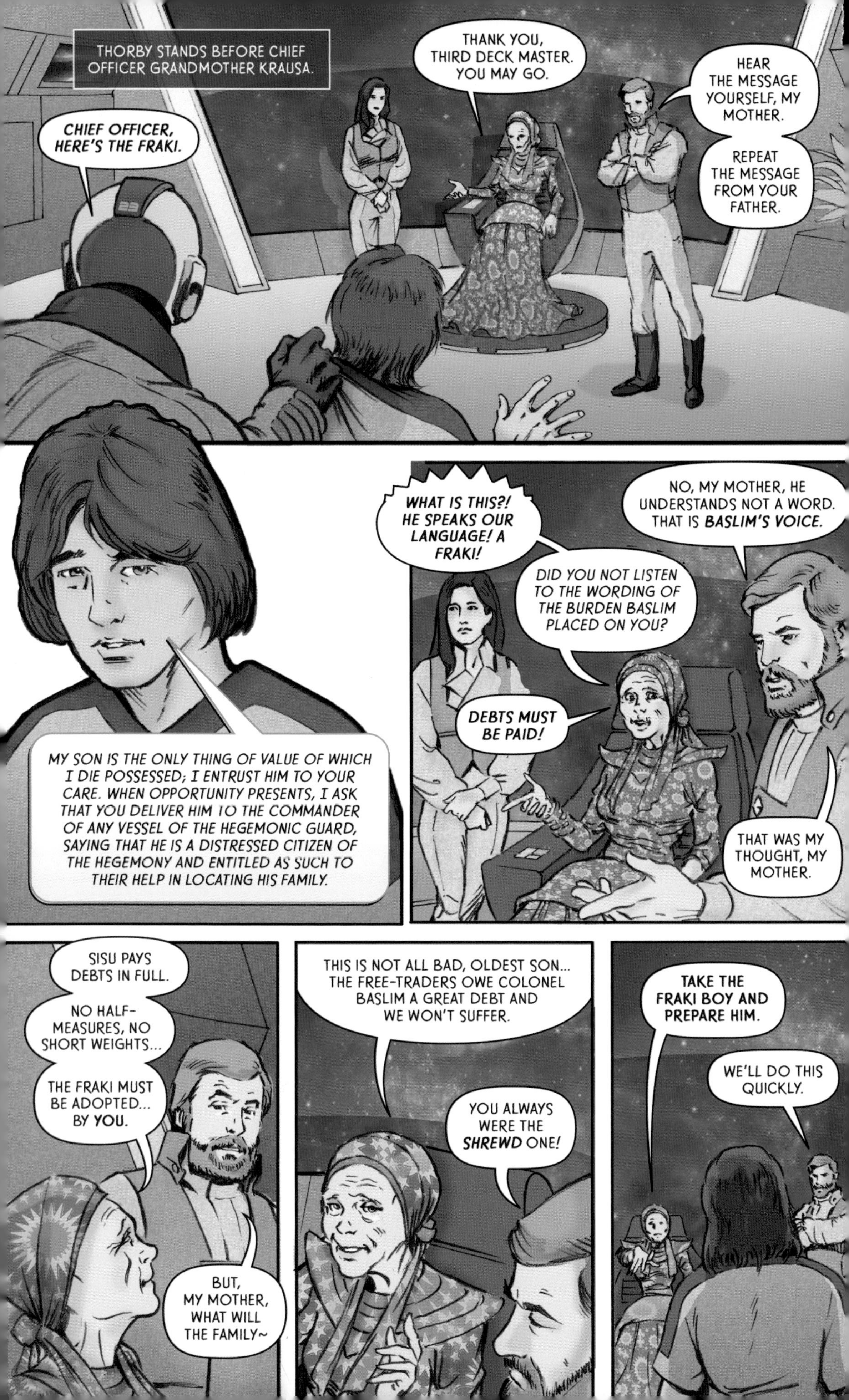

THORBY STANDS BEFORE CHIEF OFFICER GRANDMOTHER KRAUSA.
CHIEF OFFICER, HERE'S THE FRAKI.
THANK YOU, THIRD DECK MASTER. YOU MAY GO.
HEAR THE MESSAGE YOURSELF, MY MOTHER.
REPEAT THE MESSAGE FROM YOUR FATHER.
MY SON IS THE ONLY THING OF VALUE OF WHICH I DIE POSSESSED; I ENTRUST HIM TO YOUR CARE. WHEN OPPORTUNITY PRESENTS, I ASK THAT YOU DELIVER HIM TO THE COMMANDER OF ANY VESSEL OF THE HEGEMONIC GUARD, SAYING THAT HE IS A DISTRESSED CITIZEN OF THE HEGEMONY AND ENTITLED AS SUCH TO THEIR HELP IN LOCATING HIS FAMILY.
WHAT IS THIS?! HE SPEAKS OUR LANGUAGE! A FRAKI!
NO, MY MOTHER, HE UNDERSTANDS NOT A WORD. THAT IS BASLIM'S VOICE.
DID YOU NOT LISTEN TO THE WORDING OF THE BURDEN BASLIM PLACED ON YOU?
DEBTS MUST BE PAID!
THAT WAS MY THOUGHT, MY MOTHER.
SISU PAYS DEBTS IN FULL.
NO HALF-MEASURES, NO SHORT WEIGHTS...
THE FRAKI MUST BE ADOPTED... BY YOU.
BUT, MY MOTHER, WHAT WILL THE FAMILY~
THIS IS NOT ALL BAD, OLDEST SON... THE FREE-TRADERS OWE COLONEL BASLIM A GREAT DEBT AND WE WON'T SUFFER.
YOU ALWAYS WERE THE SHREWD ONE!
TAKE THE FRAKI BOY AND PREPARE HIM.
WE'LL DO THIS QUICKLY.

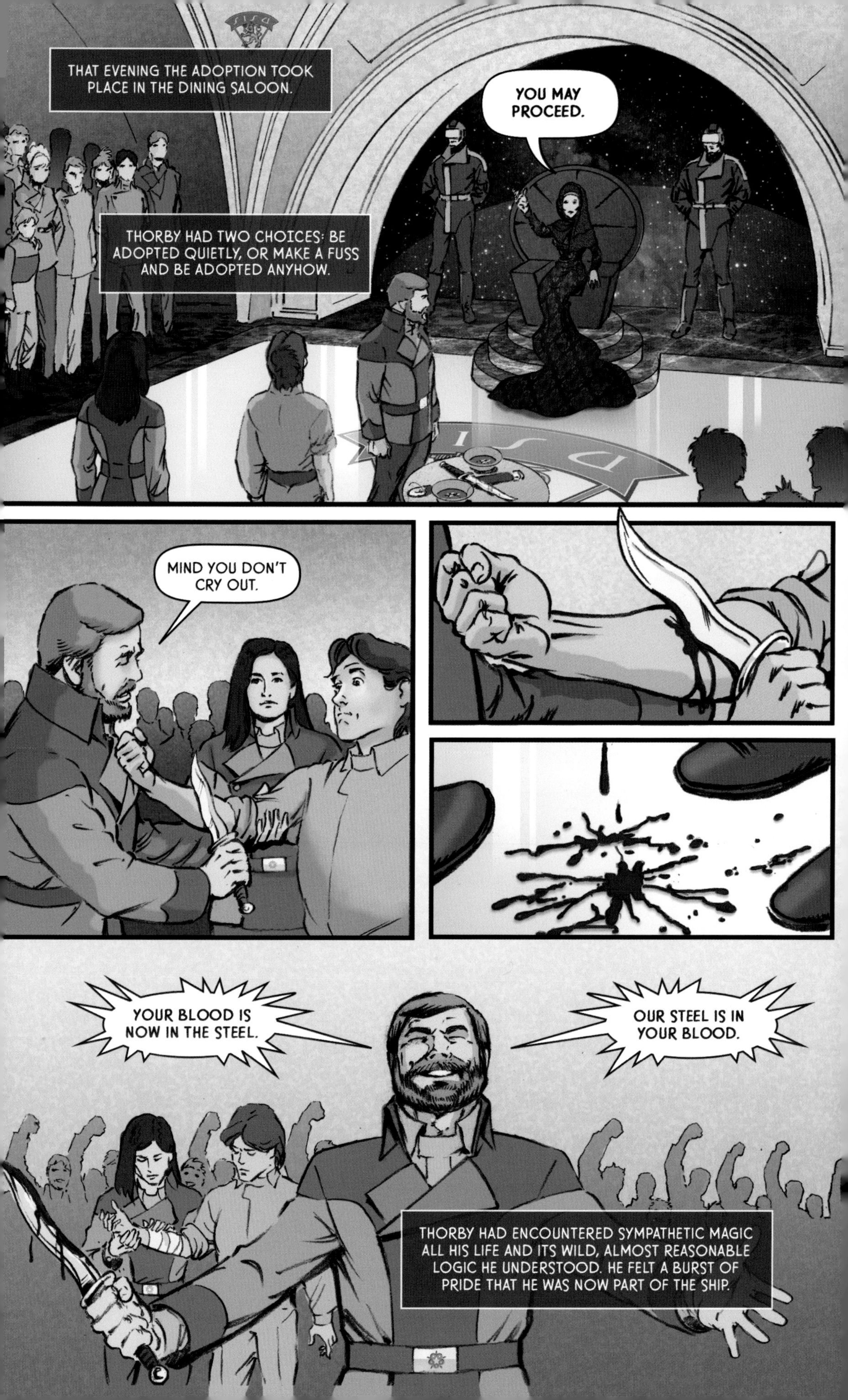
THAT EVENING THE ADOPTION TOOK PLACE IN THE DINING SALOON.
YOU MAY PROCEED.
THORBY HAD TWO CHOICES: BE ADOPTED QUIETLY, OR MAKE A FUSS AND BE ADOPTED ANYHOW.
MIND YOU DON'T CRY OUT.
YOUR BLOOD IS NOW IN THE STEEL.
OUR STEEL IS IN YOUR BLOOD.
THORBY HAD ENCOUNTERED SYMPATHETIC MAGIC ALL HIS LIFE AND ITS WILD, ALMOST REASONABLE LOGIC HE UNDERSTOOD. HE FELT A BURST OF PRIDE THAT HE WAS NOW PART OF THE SHIP.

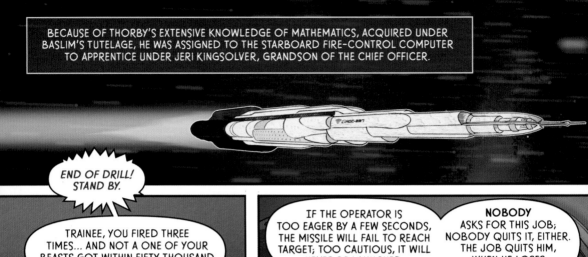

BECAUSE OF THORBY'S EXTENSIVE KNOWLEDGE OF MATHEMATICS, ACQUIRED UNDER BASLIM'S TUTELAGE, HE WAS ASSIGNED TO THE STARBOARD FIRE-CONTROL COMPUTER TO APPRENTICE UNDER JERI KINGSOLVER, GRANDSON OF THE CHIEF OFFICER.

END OF DRILL! STAND BY.

TRAINEE, YOU FIRED THREE TIMES... AND NOT A ONE OF YOUR BEASTS GOT WITHIN FIFTY THOUSAND KILOMETERS OF THE ENEMY.

I DID MY BEST!

NOT GOOD ENOUGH.

IF THE OPERATOR IS TOO EAGER BY A FEW SECONDS, THE MISSILE WILL FAIL TO REACH TARGET; TOO CAUTIOUS, IT WILL NEVER BE LAUNCHED.

NOBODY ASKS FOR THIS JOB; NOBODY QUITS IT, EITHER. THE JOB QUITS HIM, WHEN HE LOSES HIS TOUCH.

SIMULATION ENDED

MATA FINISHED WITH A NEAR PERFECT RUN.

VERY NICE, SIS! YOU'RE WITHIN A SECOND OF POST-ANALYZED OPTIMUM.

MATA AGAIN "SAVED THE SHIP" WHILE THORBY HAD FAILED.

YOU'LL GET THE HANG OF IT.

I CAN RUN EXTRA PRACTICE DRILLS WITH YOU IF YOU WANT?

FORGET IT.

LATER, THORBY PONDERS THE LESSON ON HIS WAY BACK TO HIS BUNK.

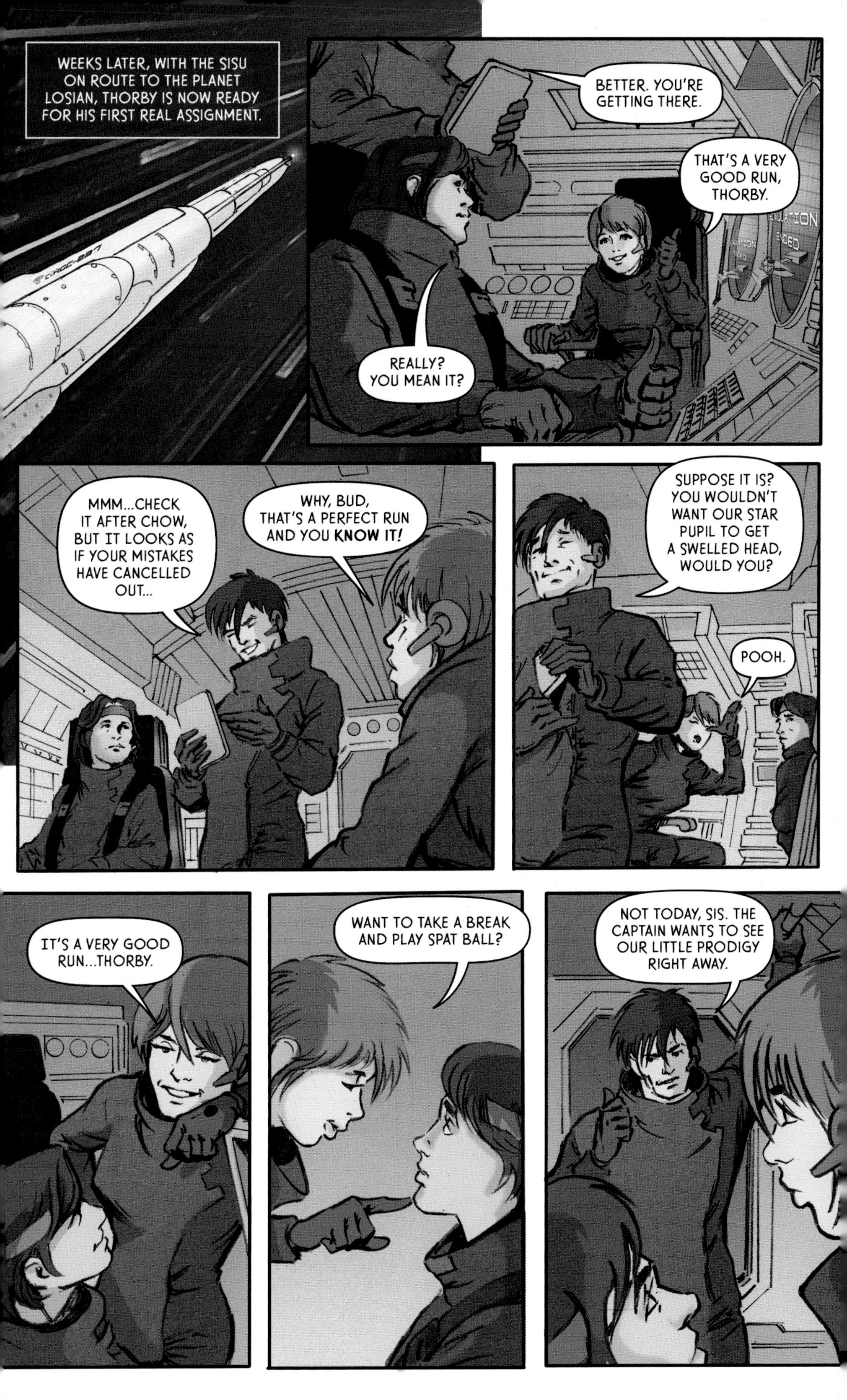
WEEKS LATER, WITH THE SISU ON ROUTE TO THE PLANET LOSIAN, THORBY IS NOW READY FOR HIS FIRST REAL ASSIGNMENT.
BETTER. YOU'RE GETTING THERE.
THAT'S A VERY GOOD RUN, THORBY.
REALLY? YOU MEAN IT?
MMM...CHECK IT AFTER CHOW, BUT IT LOOKS AS IF YOUR MISTAKES HAVE CANCELLED OUT...
WHY, BUD, THAT'S A PERFECT RUN AND YOU **KNOW IT!**
SUPPOSE IT IS? YOU WOULDN'T WANT OUR STAR PUPIL TO GET A SWELLED HEAD, WOULD YOU?
POOH.
IT'S A VERY GOOD RUN...THORBY.
WANT TO TAKE A BREAK AND PLAY SPAT BALL?
NOT TODAY, SIS. THE CAPTAIN WANTS TO SEE OUR LITTLE PRODIGY RIGHT AWAY.

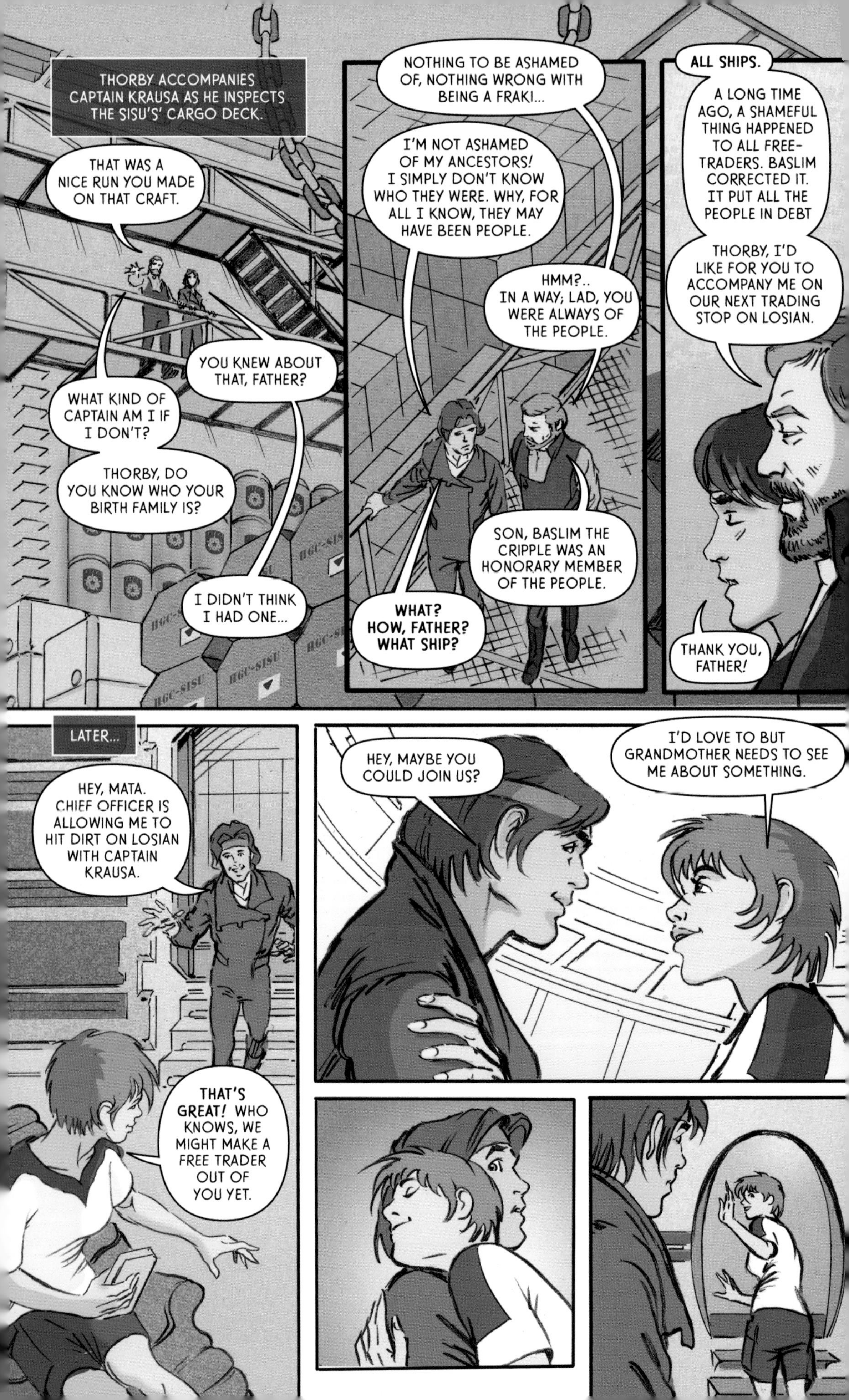
THORBY ACCOMPANIES CAPTAIN KRAUSA AS HE INSPECTS THE SISU'S' CARGO DECK.
THAT WAS A NICE RUN YOU MADE ON THAT CRAFT.
YOU KNEW ABOUT THAT, FATHER?
WHAT KIND OF CAPTAIN AM I IF I DON'T?
THORBY, DO YOU KNOW WHO YOUR BIRTH FAMILY IS?
I DIDN'T THINK I HAD ONE...
HGC-SISU
NOTHING TO BE ASHAMED OF, NOTHING WRONG WITH BEING A FRAKI...
I'M NOT ASHAMED OF MY ANCESTORS! I SIMPLY DON'T KNOW WHO THEY WERE. WHY, FOR ALL I KNOW, THEY MAY HAVE BEEN PEOPLE.
HMM?.. IN A WAY; LAD, YOU WERE ALWAYS OF THE PEOPLE.
SON, BASLIM THE CRIPPLE WAS AN HONORARY MEMBER OF THE PEOPLE.
WHAT? HOW, FATHER? WHAT SHIP?
ALL SHIPS.
A LONG TIME AGO, A SHAMEFUL THING HAPPENED TO ALL FREE-TRADERS. BASLIM CORRECTED IT. IT PUT ALL THE PEOPLE IN DEBT
THORBY, I'D LIKE FOR YOU TO ACCOMPANY ME ON OUR NEXT TRADING STOP ON LOSIAN.
THANK YOU, FATHER!
LATER...
HEY, MATA. CHIEF OFFICER IS ALLOWING ME TO HIT DIRT ON LOSIAN WITH CAPTAIN KRAUSA.
THAT'S GREAT! WHO KNOWS, WE MIGHT MAKE A FREE TRADER OUT OF YOU YET.
HEY, MAYBE YOU COULD JOIN US?
I'D LOVE TO BUT GRANDMOTHER NEEDS TO SEE ME ABOUT SOMETHING.

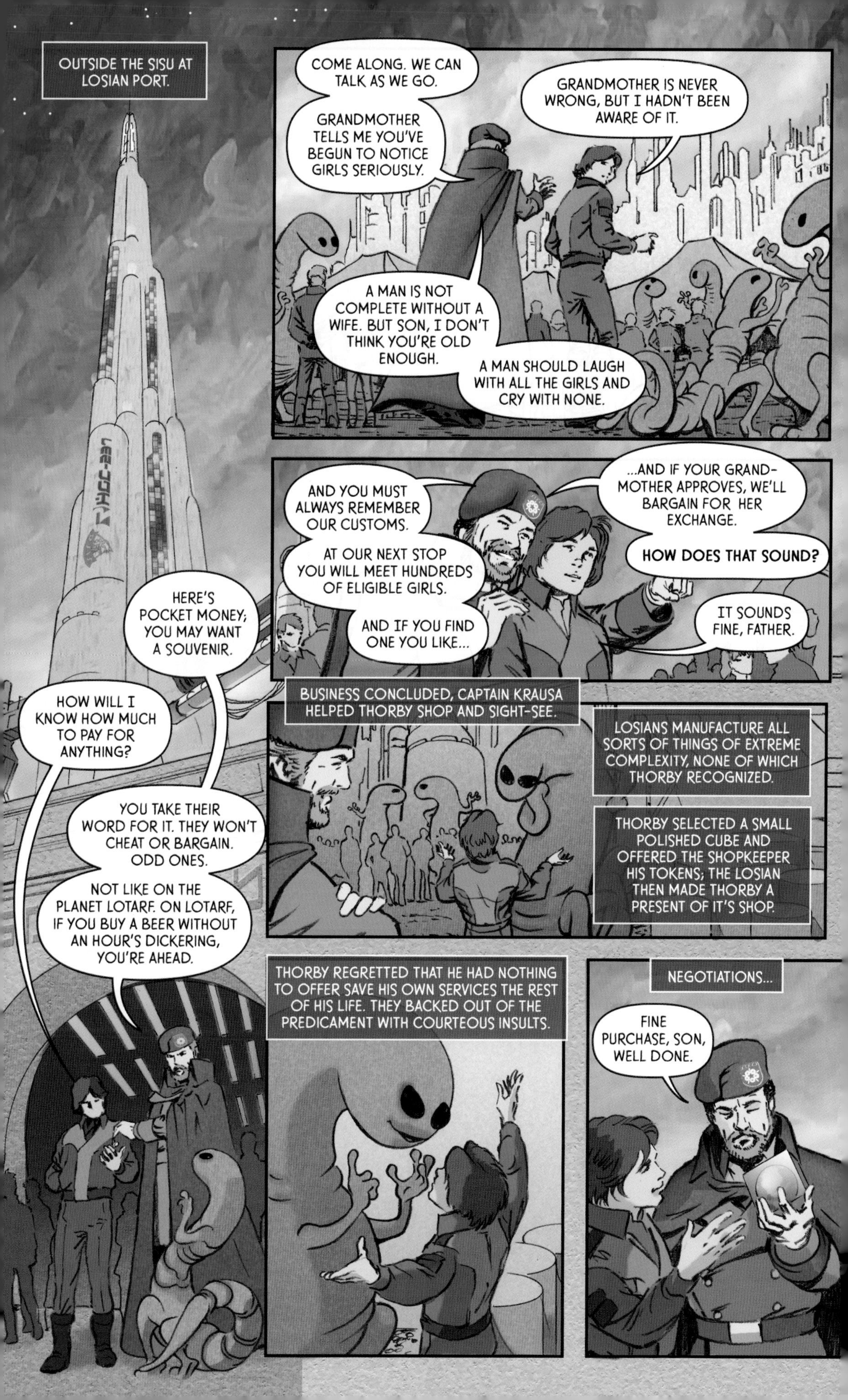
OUTSIDE THE SISU AT LOSIAN PORT.
COME ALONG. WE CAN TALK AS WE GO.
GRANDMOTHER TELLS ME YOU'VE BEGUN TO NOTICE GIRLS SERIOUSLY.
GRANDMOTHER IS NEVER WRONG, BUT I HADN'T BEEN AWARE OF IT.
A MAN IS NOT COMPLETE WITHOUT A WIFE. BUT SON, I DON'T THINK YOU'RE OLD ENOUGH.
A MAN SHOULD LAUGH WITH ALL THE GIRLS AND CRY WITH NONE.
AND YOU MUST ALWAYS REMEMBER OUR CUSTOMS.
AT OUR NEXT STOP YOU WILL MEET HUNDREDS OF ELIGIBLE GIRLS.
AND IF YOU FIND ONE YOU LIKE...
...AND IF YOUR GRAND-MOTHER APPROVES, WE'LL BARGAIN FOR HER EXCHANGE.
HOW DOES THAT SOUND?
IT SOUNDS FINE, FATHER.
HERE'S POCKET MONEY; YOU MAY WANT A SOUVENIR.
HOW WILL I KNOW HOW MUCH TO PAY FOR ANYTHING?
YOU TAKE THEIR WORD FOR IT. THEY WON'T CHEAT OR BARGAIN. ODD ONES.
NOT LIKE ON THE PLANET LOTARF. ON LOTARF, IF YOU BUY A BEER WITHOUT AN HOUR'S DICKERING, YOU'RE AHEAD.
BUSINESS CONCLUDED, CAPTAIN KRAUSA HELPED THORBY SHOP AND SIGHT-SEE.
LOSIANS MANUFACTURE ALL SORTS OF THINGS OF EXTREME COMPLEXITY, NONE OF WHICH THORBY RECOGNIZED.
THORBY SELECTED A SMALL POLISHED CUBE AND OFFERED THE SHOPKEEPER HIS TOKENS; THE LOSIAN THEN MADE THORBY A PRESENT OF IT'S SHOP.
THORBY REGRETTED THAT HE HAD NOTHING TO OFFER SAVE HIS OWN SERVICES THE REST OF HIS LIFE. THEY BACKED OUT OF THE PREDICAMENT WITH COURTEOUS INSULTS.
NEGOTIATIONS...
FINE PURCHASE, SON, WELL DONE.

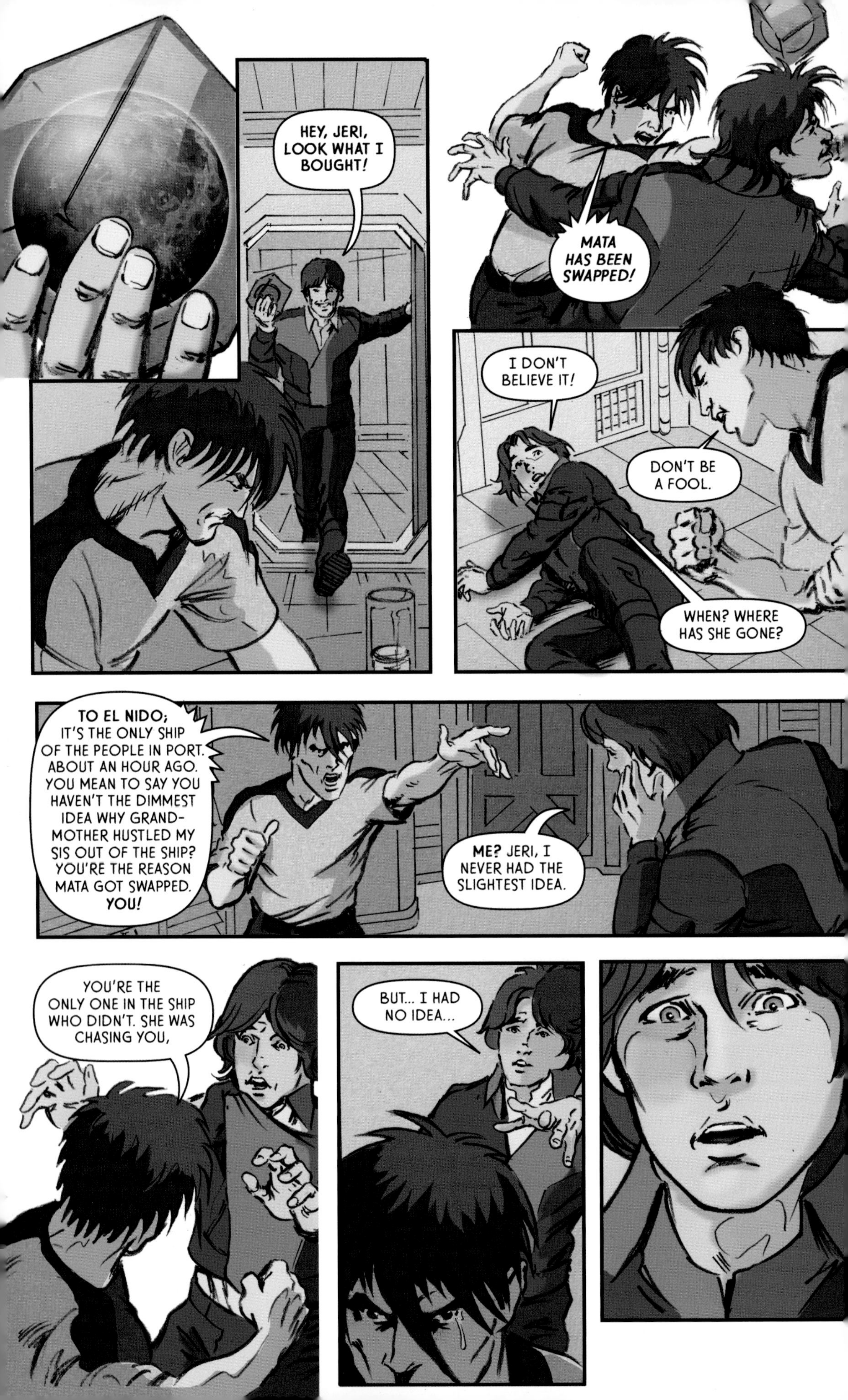

HEY, JERI, LOOK WHAT I BOUGHT!
MATA HAS BEEN SWAPPED!
I DON'T BELIEVE IT!
DON'T BE A FOOL.
WHEN? WHERE HAS SHE GONE?
TO EL NIDO; IT'S THE ONLY SHIP OF THE PEOPLE IN PORT. ABOUT AN HOUR AGO. YOU MEAN TO SAY YOU HAVEN'T THE DIMMEST IDEA WHY GRAND-MOTHER HUSTLED MY SIS OUT OF THE SHIP? YOU'RE THE REASON MATA GOT SWAPPED. YOU!
ME? JERI, I NEVER HAD THE SLIGHTEST IDEA.
YOU'RE THE ONLY ONE IN THE SHIP WHO DIDN'T. SHE WAS CHASING YOU,
BUT... I HAD NO IDEA...

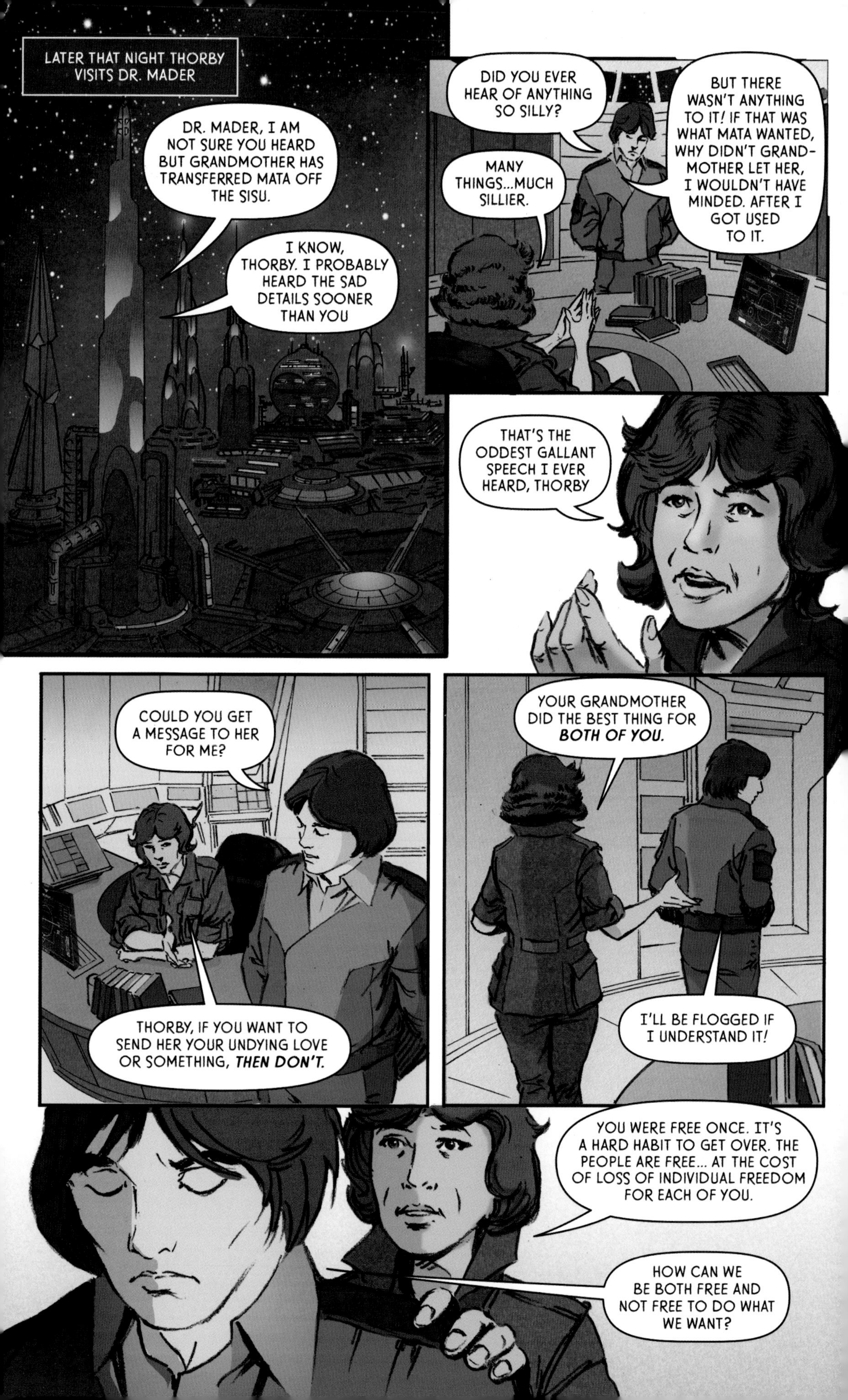
LATER THAT NIGHT THORBY VISITS DR. MADER
DR. MADER, I AM NOT SURE YOU HEARD BUT GRANDMOTHER HAS TRANSFERRED MATA OFF THE SISU.
I KNOW, THORBY. I PROBABLY HEARD THE SAD DETAILS SOONER THAN YOU
DID YOU EVER HEAR OF ANYTHING SO SILLY?
MANY THINGS...MUCH SILLIER.
BUT THERE WASN'T ANYTHING TO IT! IF THAT WAS WHAT MATA WANTED, WHY DIDN'T GRAND-MOTHER LET HER, I WOULDN'T HAVE MINDED. AFTER I GOT USED TO IT.
THAT'S THE ODDEST GALLANT SPEECH I EVER HEARD, THORBY
COULD YOU GET A MESSAGE TO HER FOR ME?
THORBY, IF YOU WANT TO SEND HER YOUR UNDYING LOVE OR SOMETHING, ***THEN DON'T.***
YOUR GRANDMOTHER DID THE BEST THING FOR ***BOTH OF YOU.***
I'LL BE FLOGGED IF I UNDERSTAND IT!
YOU WERE FREE ONCE. IT'S A HARD HABIT TO GET OVER. THE PEOPLE ARE FREE... AT THE COST OF LOSS OF INDIVIDUAL FREEDOM FOR EACH OF YOU.
HOW CAN WE BE BOTH FREE AND NOT FREE TO DO WHAT WE WANT?

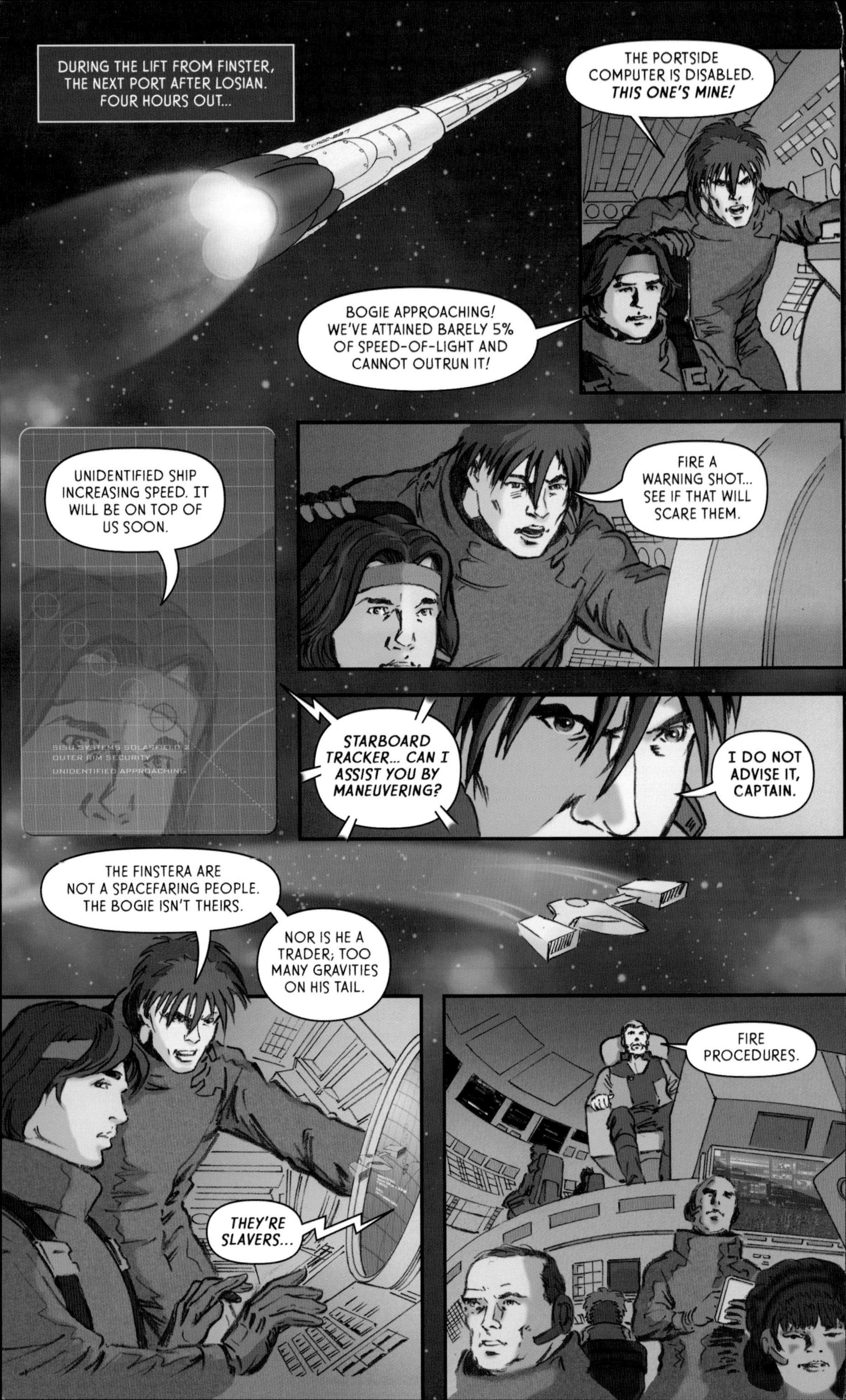
DURING THE LIFT FROM FINSTER, THE NEXT PORT AFTER LOSIAN. FOUR HOURS OUT...
THE PORTSIDE COMPUTER IS DISABLED. *THIS ONE'S MINE!*
BOGIE APPROACHING! WE'VE ATTAINED BARELY 5% OF SPEED-OF-LIGHT AND CANNOT OUTRUN IT!
UNIDENTIFIED SHIP INCREASING SPEED. IT WILL BE ON TOP OF US SOON.
SISU SYSTEMS SOLARFIELD 2
OUTER RIM SECURITY
UNIDENTIFIED APPROACHING
FIRE A WARNING SHOT... SEE IF THAT WILL SCARE THEM.
STARBOARD TRACKER... CAN I ASSIST YOU BY MANEUVERING?
I DO NOT ADVISE IT, CAPTAIN.
THE FINSTERA ARE NOT A SPACEFARING PEOPLE. THE BOGIE ISN'T THEIRS.
NOR IS HE A TRADER; TOO MANY GRAVITIES ON HIS TAIL.
THEY'RE SLAVERS...
FIRE PROCEDURES.

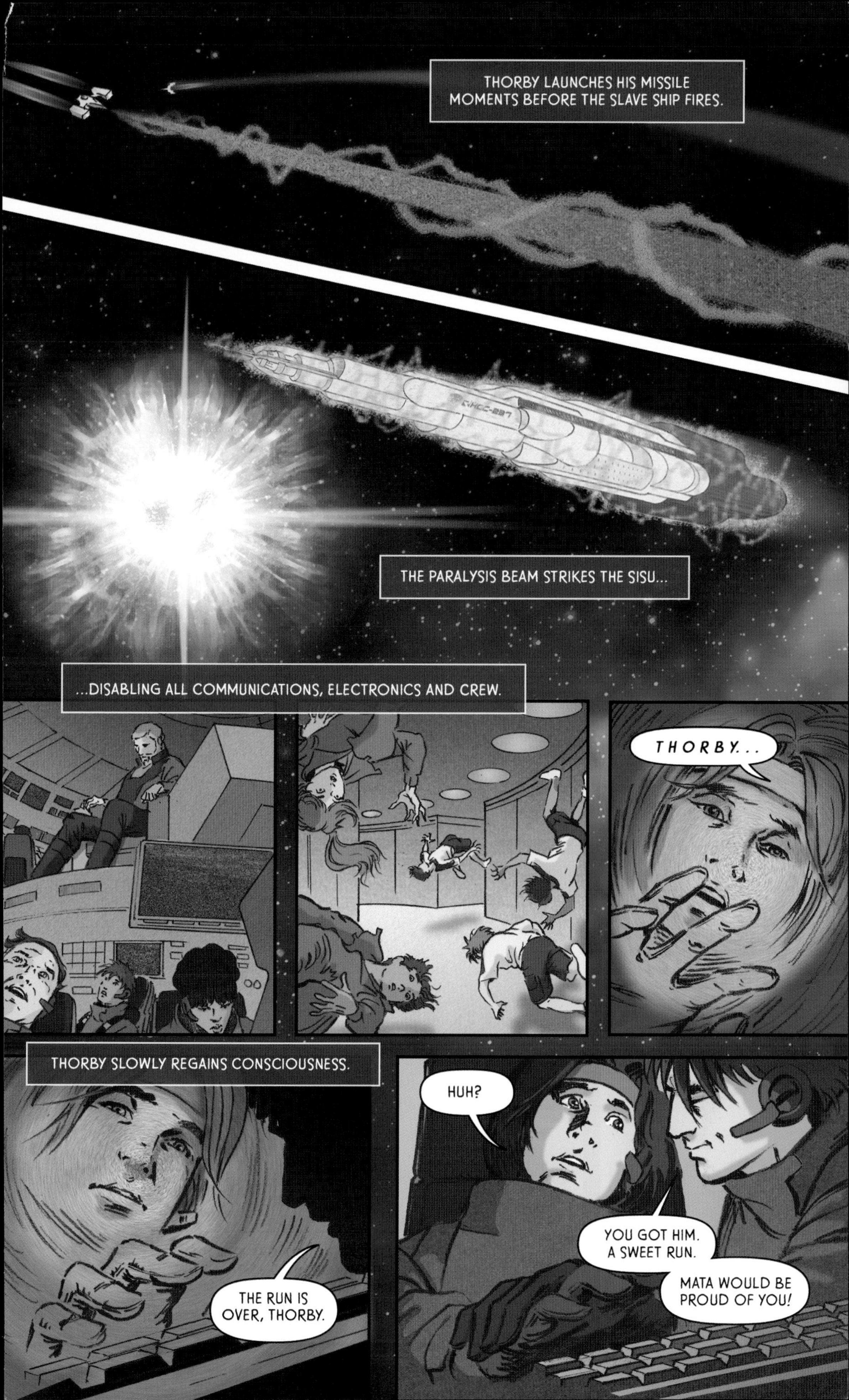

THORBY LAUNCHES HIS MISSILE MOMENTS BEFORE THE SLAVE SHIP FIRES.
THE PARALYSIS BEAM STRIKES THE SISU...
...DISABLING ALL COMMUNICATIONS, ELECTRONICS AND CREW.
THORBY...
THORBY SLOWLY REGAINS CONSCIOUSNESS.
THE RUN IS OVER, THORBY.
HUH?
YOU GOT HIM. A SWEET RUN.
MATA WOULD BE PROUD OF YOU!

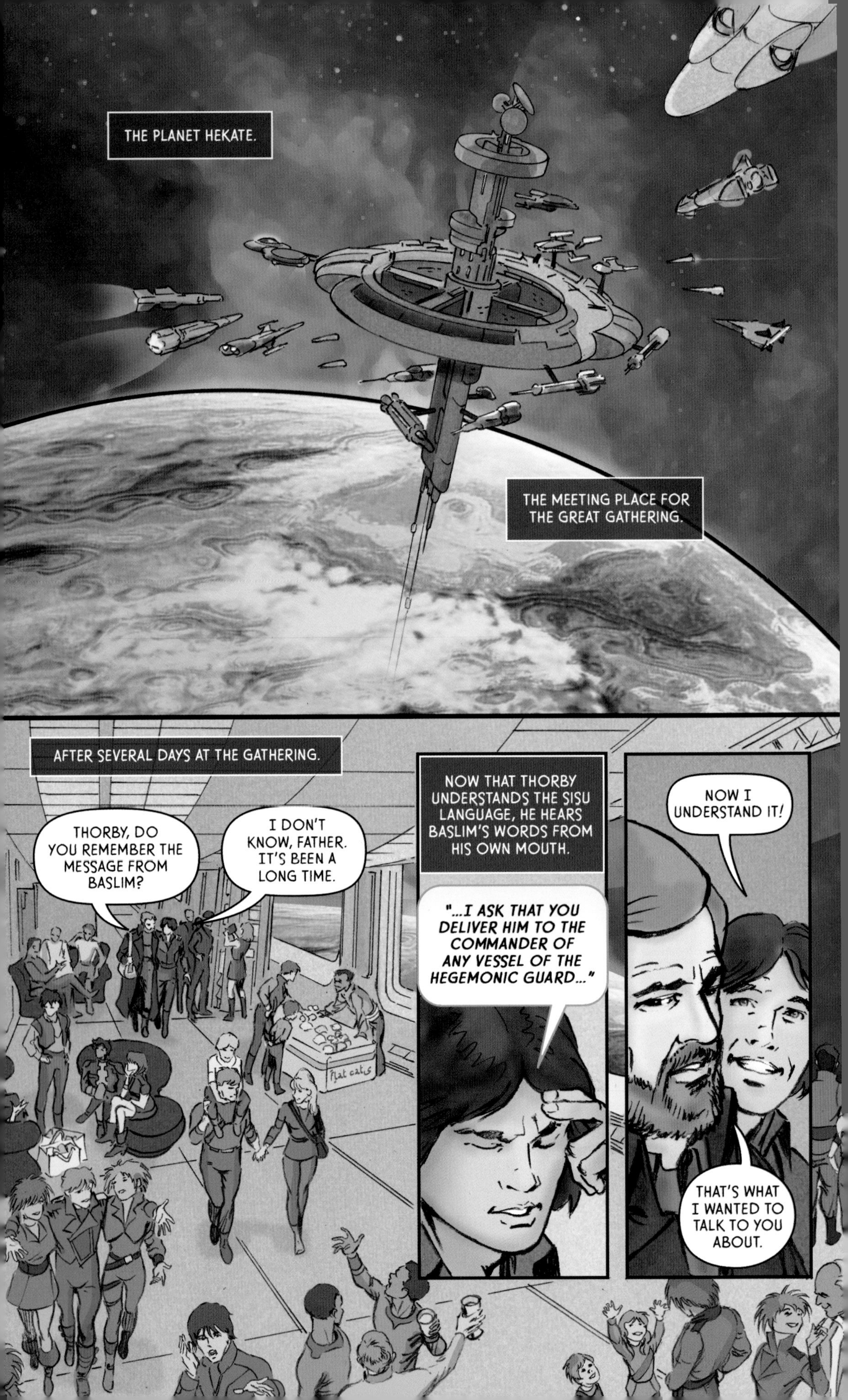
THE PLANET HEKATE.
THE MEETING PLACE FOR THE GREAT GATHERING.
AFTER SEVERAL DAYS AT THE GATHERING.
THORBY, DO YOU REMEMBER THE MESSAGE FROM BASLIM?
I DON'T KNOW, FATHER. IT'S BEEN A LONG TIME.
Flat cats
NOW THAT THORBY UNDERSTANDS THE SISU LANGUAGE, HE HEARS BASLIM'S WORDS FROM HIS OWN MOUTH.
"...I ASK THAT YOU DELIVER HIM TO THE COMMANDER OF ANY VESSEL OF THE HEGEMONIC GUARD..."
NOW I UNDERSTAND IT!
THAT'S WHAT I WANTED TO TALK TO YOU ABOUT.

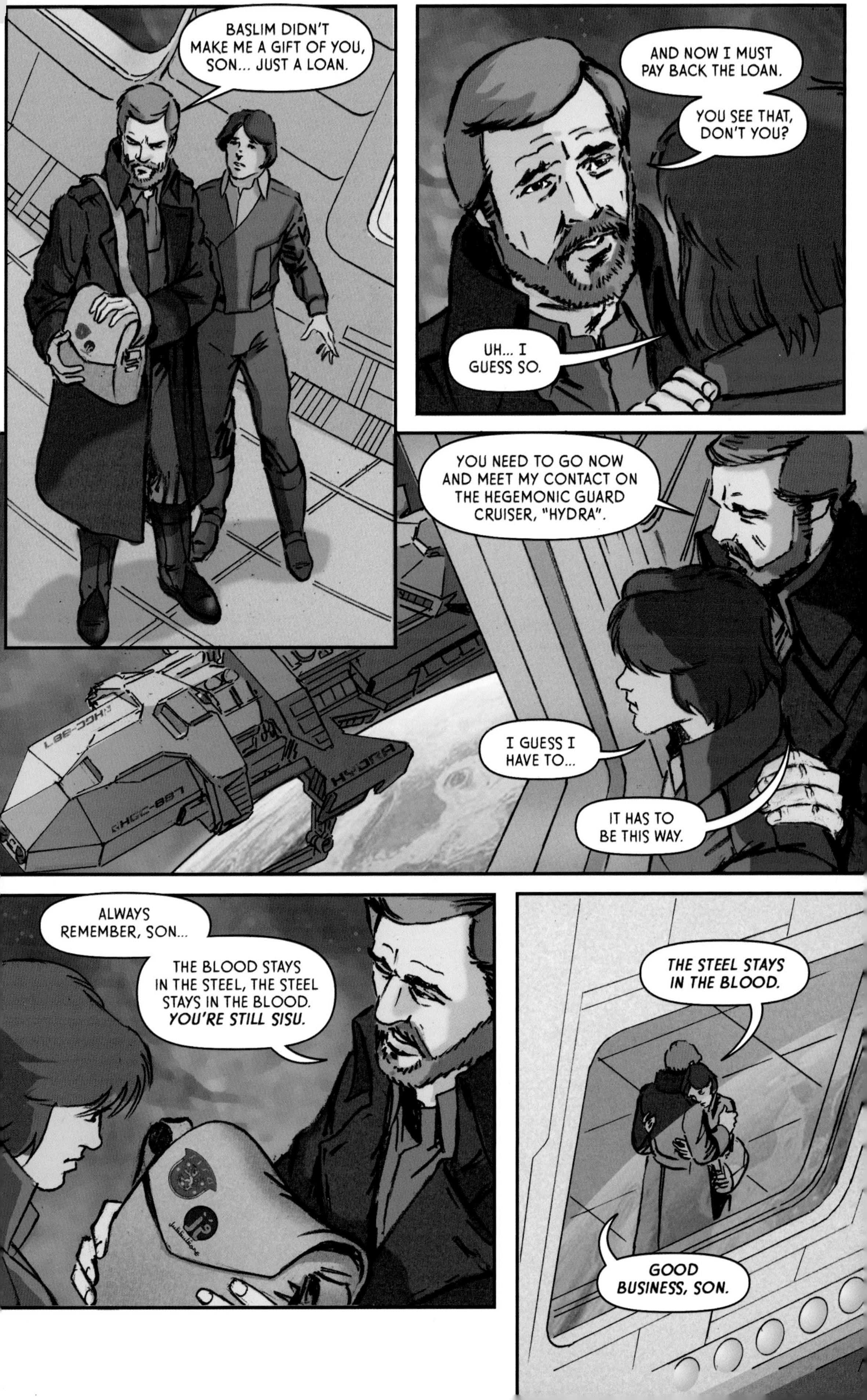
BASLIM DIDN'T MAKE ME A GIFT OF YOU, SON... JUST A LOAN.
AND NOW I MUST PAY BACK THE LOAN.
YOU SEE THAT, DON'T YOU?
UH... I GUESS SO.
YOU NEED TO GO NOW AND MEET MY CONTACT ON THE HEGEMONIC GUARD CRUISER, "HYDRA".
I GUESS I HAVE TO...
IT HAS TO BE THIS WAY.
HYDRA
HGC-887
ALWAYS REMEMBER, SON...
THE BLOOD STAYS IN THE STEEL, THE STEEL STAYS IN THE BLOOD. *YOU'RE STILL SISU.*
THE STEEL STAYS IN THE BLOOD.
GOOD BUSINESS, SON.

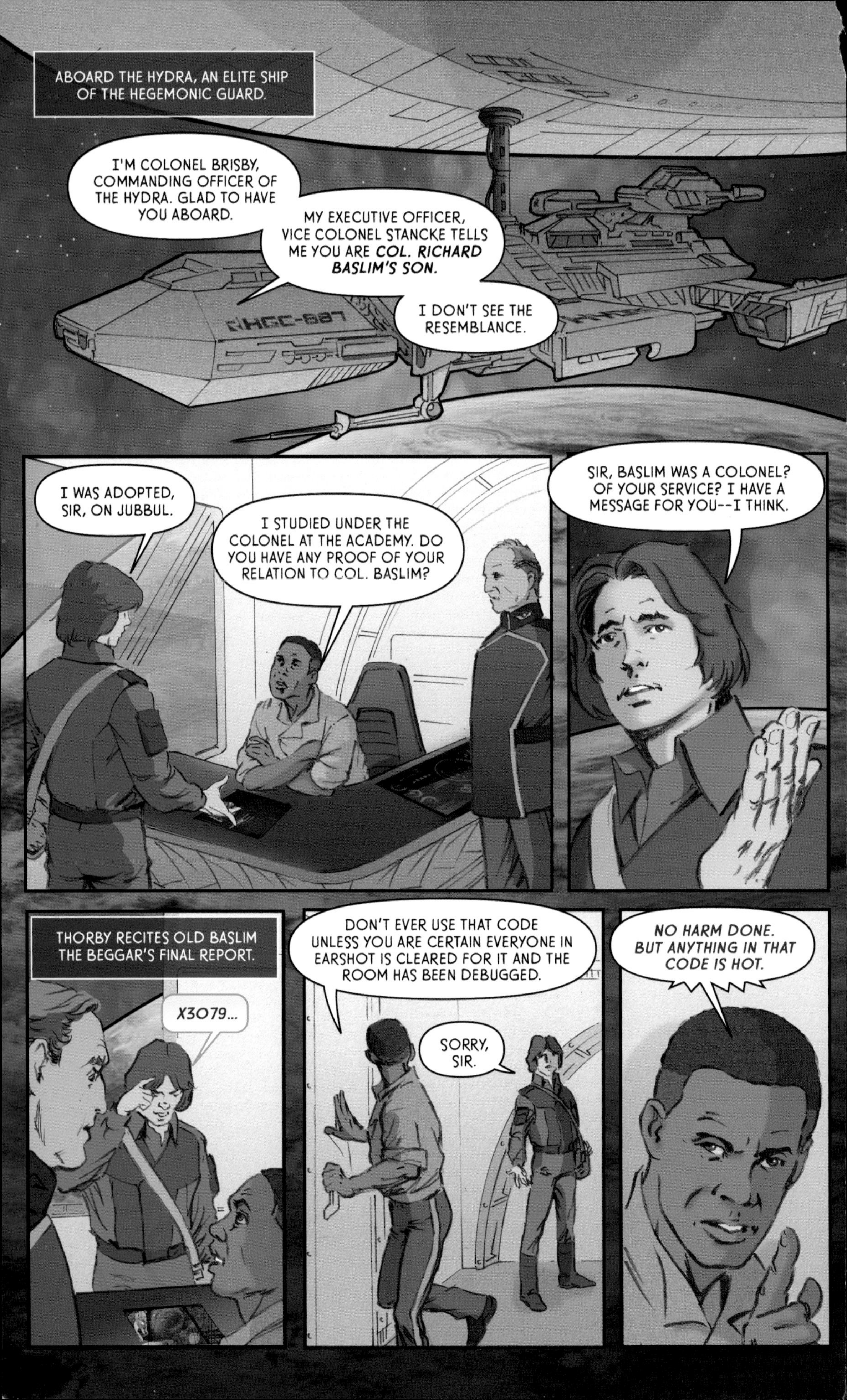
ABOARD THE HYDRA, AN ELITE SHIP OF THE HEGEMONIC GUARD.
I'M COLONEL BRISBY, COMMANDING OFFICER OF THE HYDRA. GLAD TO HAVE YOU ABOARD.
MY EXECUTIVE OFFICER, VICE COLONEL STANCKE TELLS ME YOU ARE COL. RICHARD BASLIM'S SON.
I DON'T SEE THE RESEMBLANCE.
HGC-887
I WAS ADOPTED, SIR, ON JUBBUL.
I STUDIED UNDER THE COLONEL AT THE ACADEMY. DO YOU HAVE ANY PROOF OF YOUR RELATION TO COL. BASLIM?
SIR, BASLIM WAS A COLONEL? OF YOUR SERVICE? I HAVE A MESSAGE FOR YOU--I THINK.
THORBY RECITES OLD BASLIM THE BEGGAR'S FINAL REPORT.
X3079...
DON'T EVER USE THAT CODE UNLESS YOU ARE CERTAIN EVERYONE IN EARSHOT IS CLEARED FOR IT AND THE ROOM HAS BEEN DEBUGGED.
SORRY, SIR.
NO HARM DONE. BUT ANYTHING IN THAT CODE IS HOT.

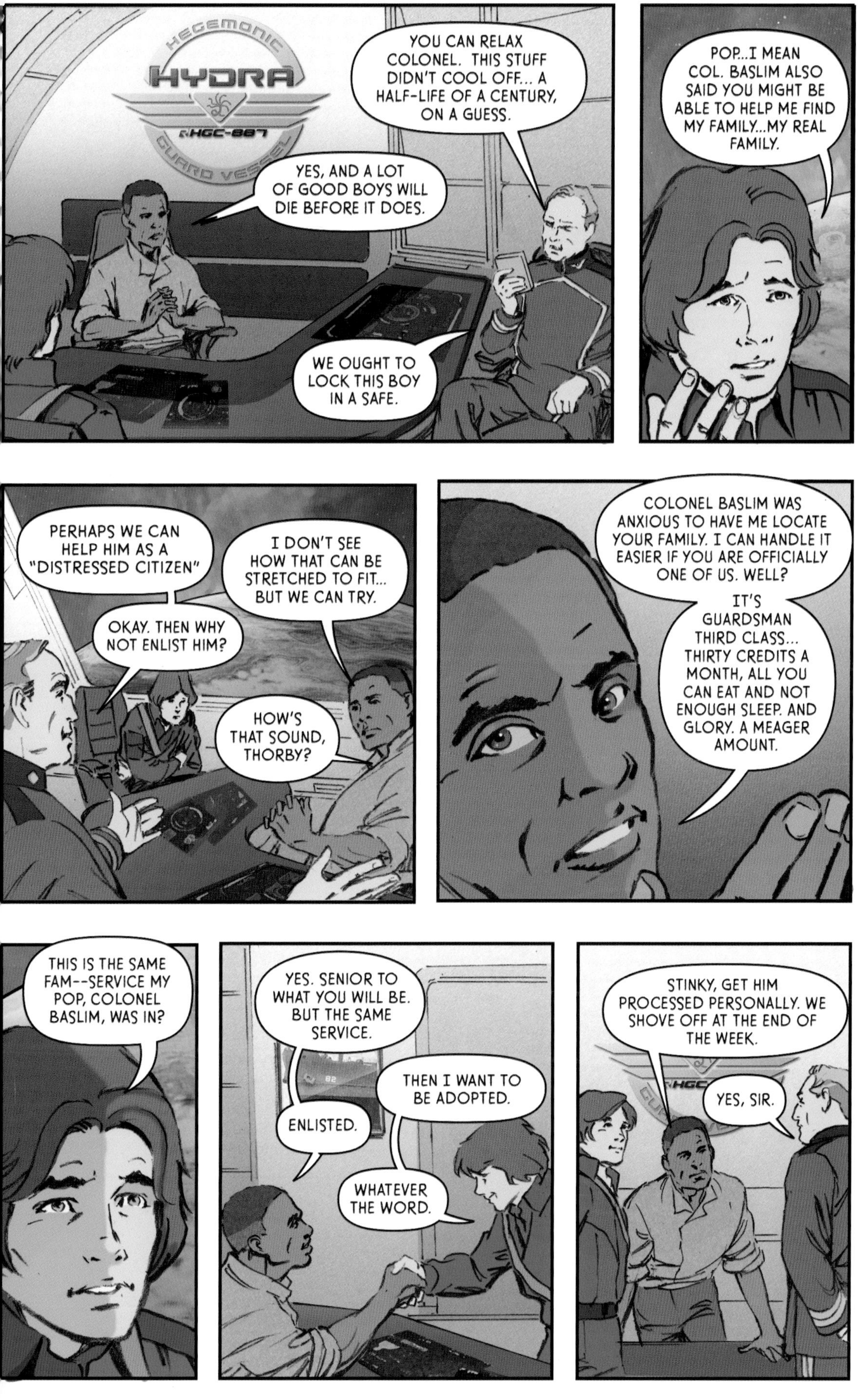
HEGEMONIC
HYDRA
HGC-887
GUARD VESSEL
YOU CAN RELAX COLONEL. THIS STUFF DIDN'T COOL OFF... A HALF-LIFE OF A CENTURY, ON A GUESS.
YES, AND A LOT OF GOOD BOYS WILL DIE BEFORE IT DOES.
WE OUGHT TO LOCK THIS BOY IN A SAFE.
POP...I MEAN COL. BASLIM ALSO SAID YOU MIGHT BE ABLE TO HELP ME FIND MY FAMILY...MY REAL FAMILY.
PERHAPS WE CAN HELP HIM AS A "DISTRESSED CITIZEN"
I DON'T SEE HOW THAT CAN BE STRETCHED TO FIT... BUT WE CAN TRY.
OKAY. THEN WHY NOT ENLIST HIM?
HOW'S THAT SOUND, THORBY?
COLONEL BASLIM WAS ANXIOUS TO HAVE ME LOCATE YOUR FAMILY. I CAN HANDLE IT EASIER IF YOU ARE OFFICIALLY ONE OF US. WELL?
IT'S GUARDSMAN THIRD CLASS... THIRTY CREDITS A MONTH, ALL YOU CAN EAT AND NOT ENOUGH SLEEP. AND GLORY. A MEAGER AMOUNT.
THIS IS THE SAME FAM--SERVICE MY POP, COLONEL BASLIM, WAS IN?
YES. SENIOR TO WHAT YOU WILL BE. BUT THE SAME SERVICE.
THEN I WANT TO BE ADOPTED.
ENLISTED.
WHATEVER THE WORD.
STINKY, GET HIM PROCESSED PERSONALLY. WE SHOVE OFF AT THE END OF THE WEEK.
YES, SIR.

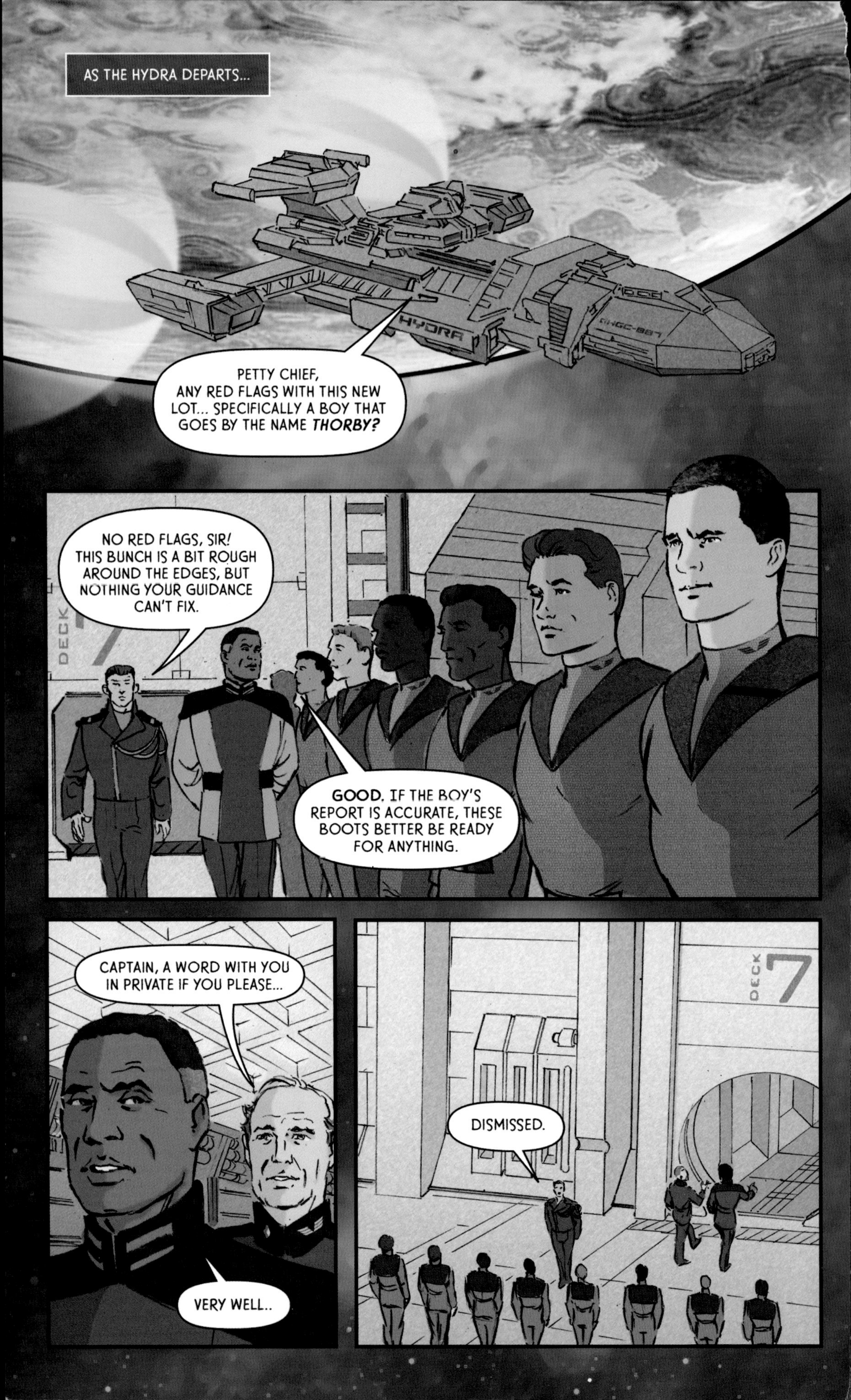
AS THE HYDRA DEPARTS...
HYDRA
HGC-887
PETTY CHIEF, ANY RED FLAGS WITH THIS NEW LOT... SPECIFICALLY A BOY THAT GOES BY THE NAME *THORBY?*
DECK 7
NO RED FLAGS, SIR! THIS BUNCH IS A BIT ROUGH AROUND THE EDGES, BUT NOTHING YOUR GUIDANCE CAN'T FIX.
GOOD. IF THE BOY'S REPORT IS ACCURATE, THESE BOOTS BETTER BE READY FOR ANYTHING.
CAPTAIN, A WORD WITH YOU IN PRIVATE IF YOU PLEASE...
VERY WELL..
DECK 7
DISMISSED.

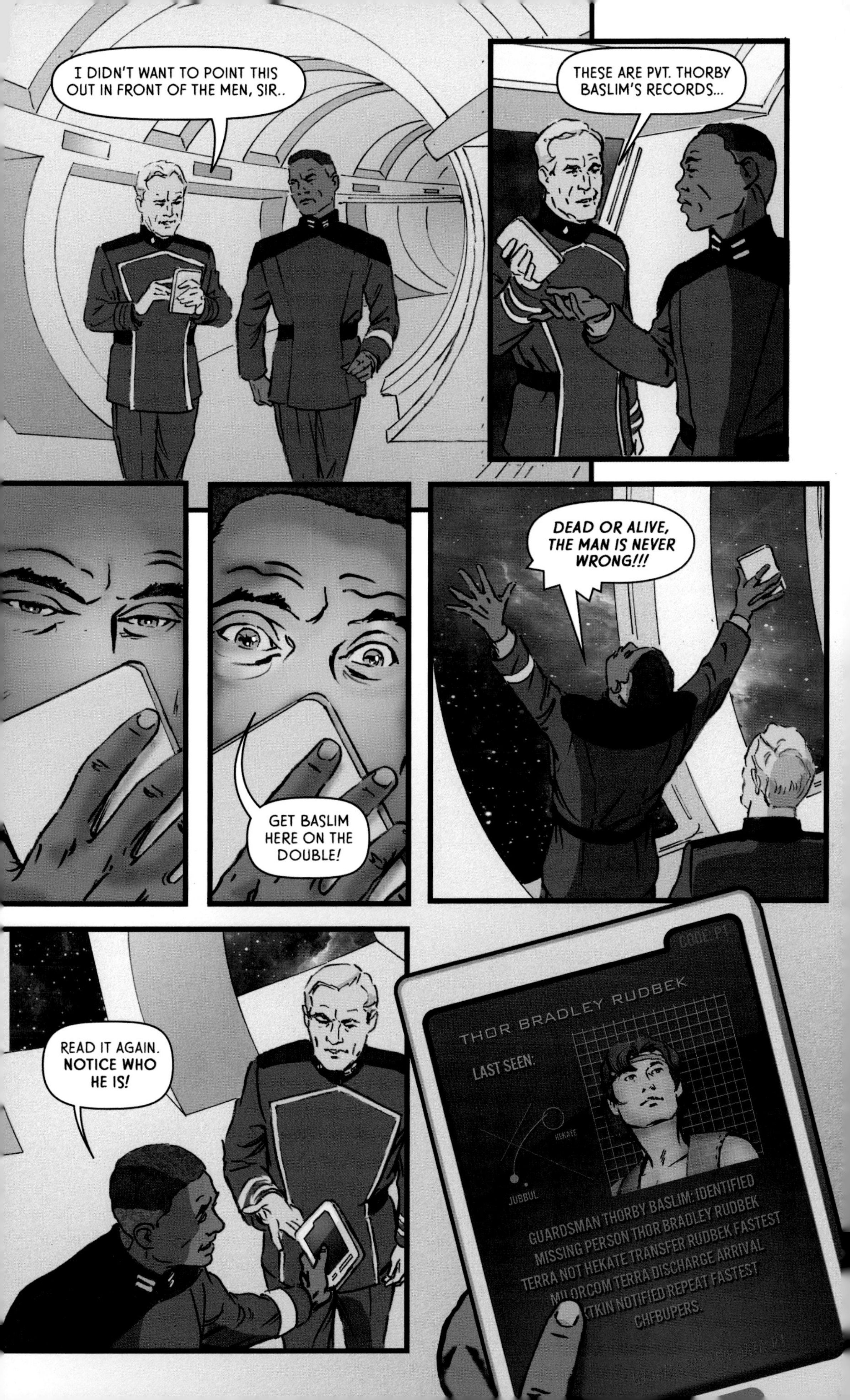
I DIDN'T WANT TO POINT THIS OUT IN FRONT OF THE MEN, SIR..
THESE ARE PVT. THORBY BASLIM'S RECORDS...
GET BASLIM HERE ON THE DOUBLE!
DEAD OR ALIVE, THE MAN IS NEVER WRONG!!!
READ IT AGAIN. **NOTICE WHO HE IS!**
CODE: P1
THOR BRADLEY RUDBEK
LAST SEEN:
HEKATE
JUBBUL
GUARDSMAN THORBY BASLIM: IDENTIFIED MISSING PERSON THOR BRADLEY RUDBEK TERRA NOT HEKATE TRANSFER RUDBEK FASTEST MILORCOM TERRA DISCHARGE ARRIVAL XTKIN NOTIFIED REPEAT FASTEST CHFBUPERS.

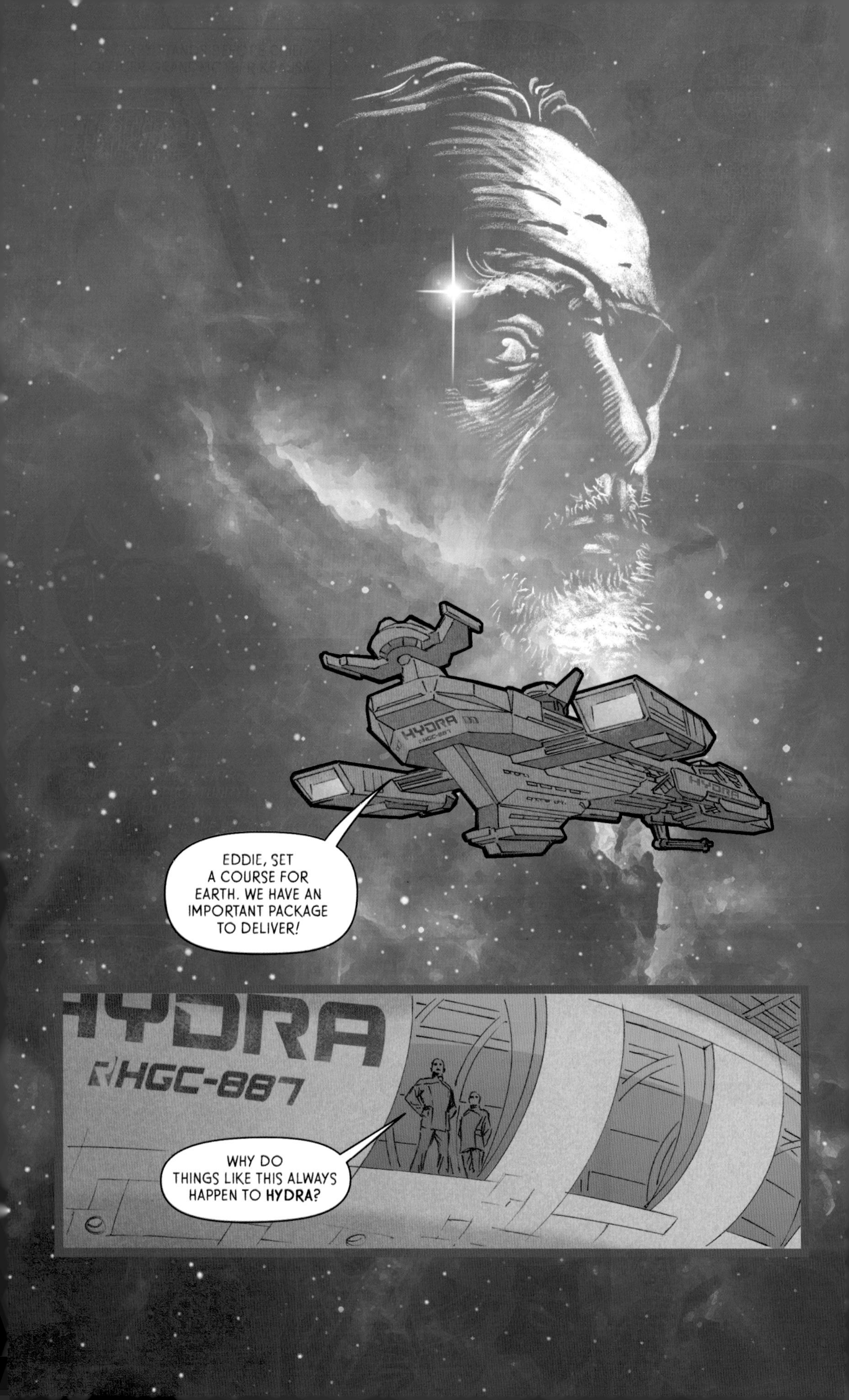
EDDIE, SET A COURSE FOR EARTH. WE HAVE AN IMPORTANT PACKAGE TO DELIVER!
HYDRA
HGC-887
WHY DO THINGS LIKE THIS ALWAYS HAPPEN TO **HYDRA**?

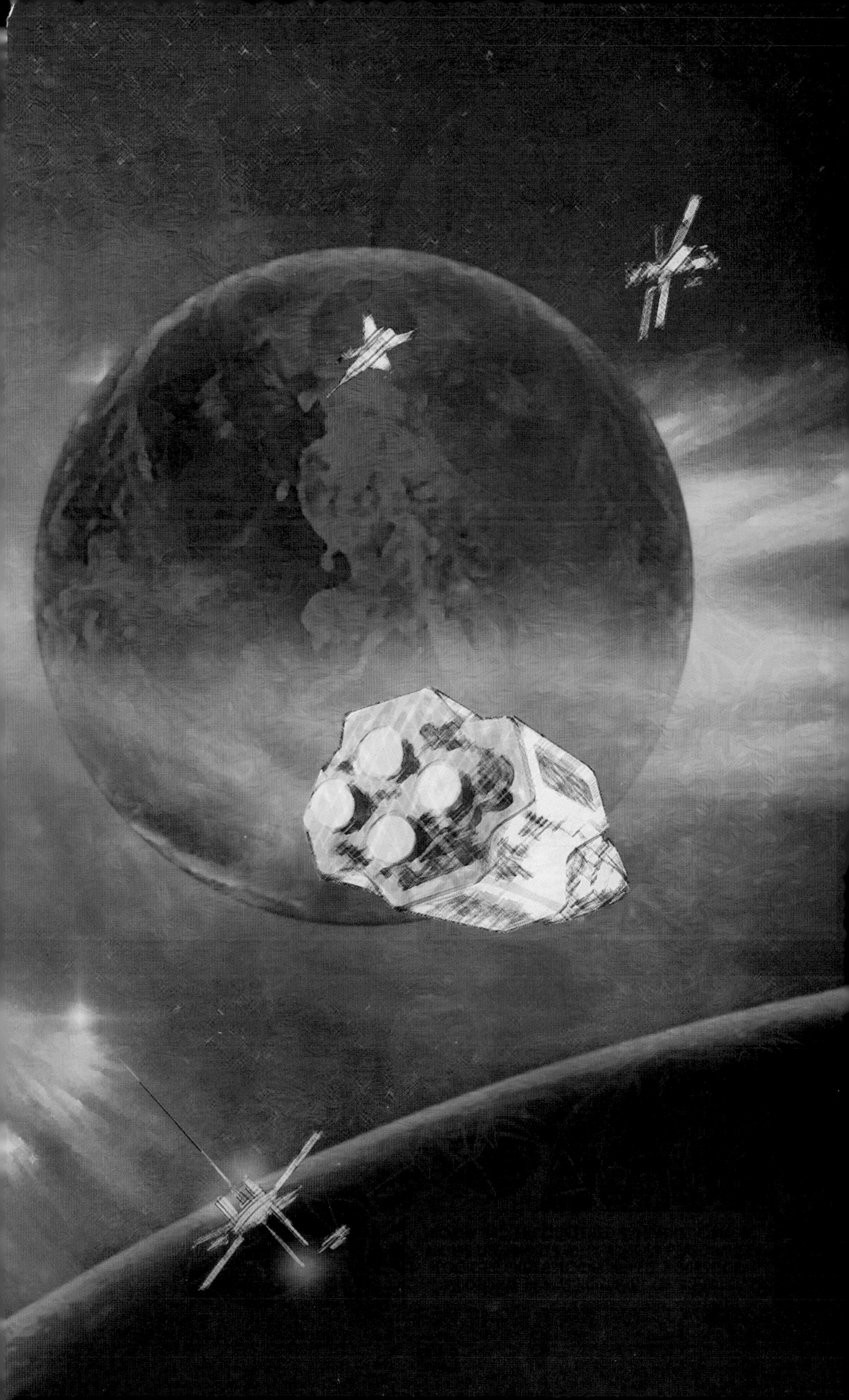

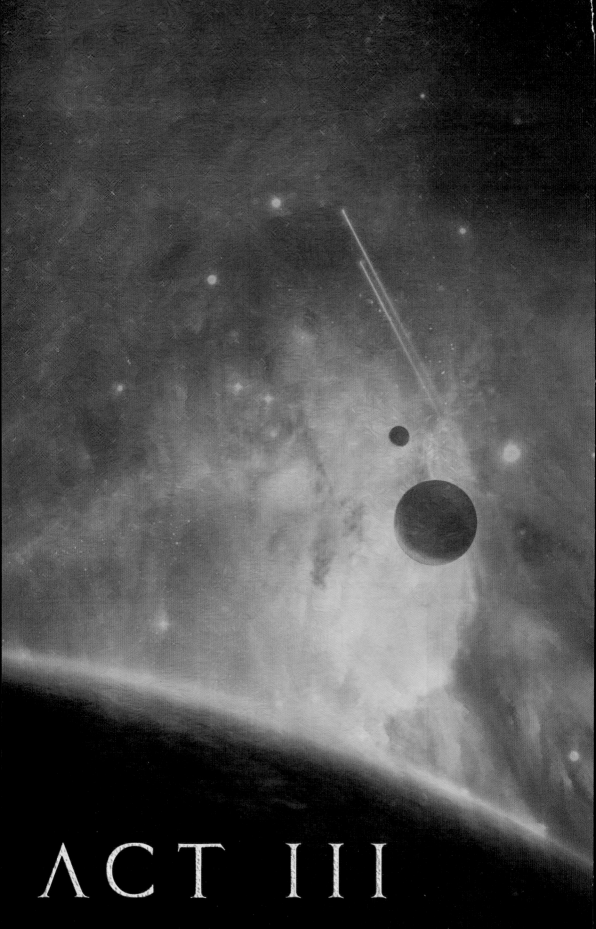

ΛCT III

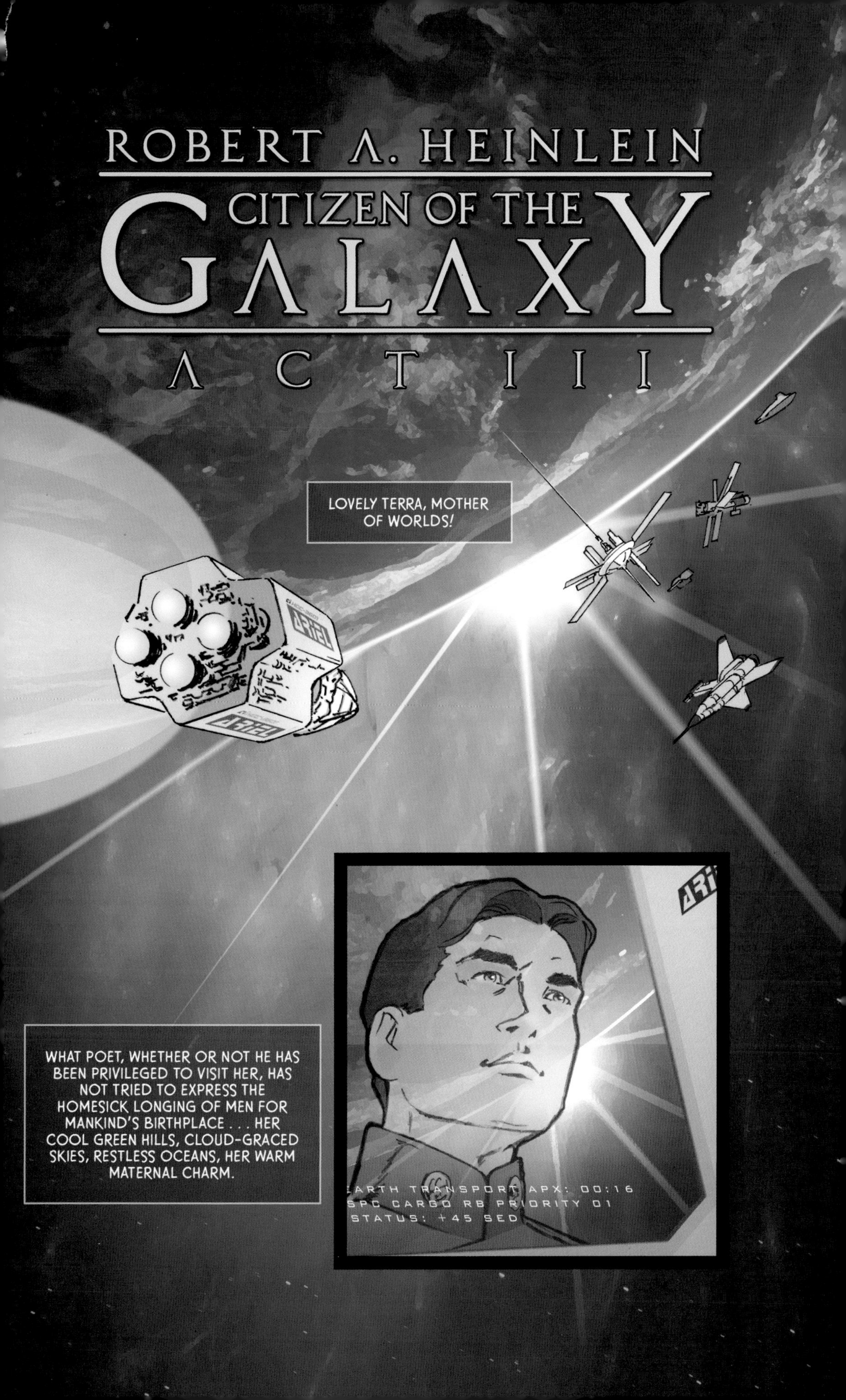
ROBERT A. HEINLEIN
CITIZEN OF THE GALAXY
ACT III
LOVELY TERRA, MOTHER OF WORLDS!
WHAT POET, WHETHER OR NOT HE HAS BEEN PRIVILEGED TO VISIT HER, HAS NOT TRIED TO EXPRESS THE HOMESICK LONGING OF MEN FOR MANKIND'S BIRTHPLACE . . . HER COOL GREEN HILLS, CLOUD-GRACED SKIES, RESTLESS OCEANS, HER WARM MATERNAL CHARM.
ARTH TRANSPORT APX: 00:16
SPC CARGO RB PRIORITY 01
STATUS: +45 SED

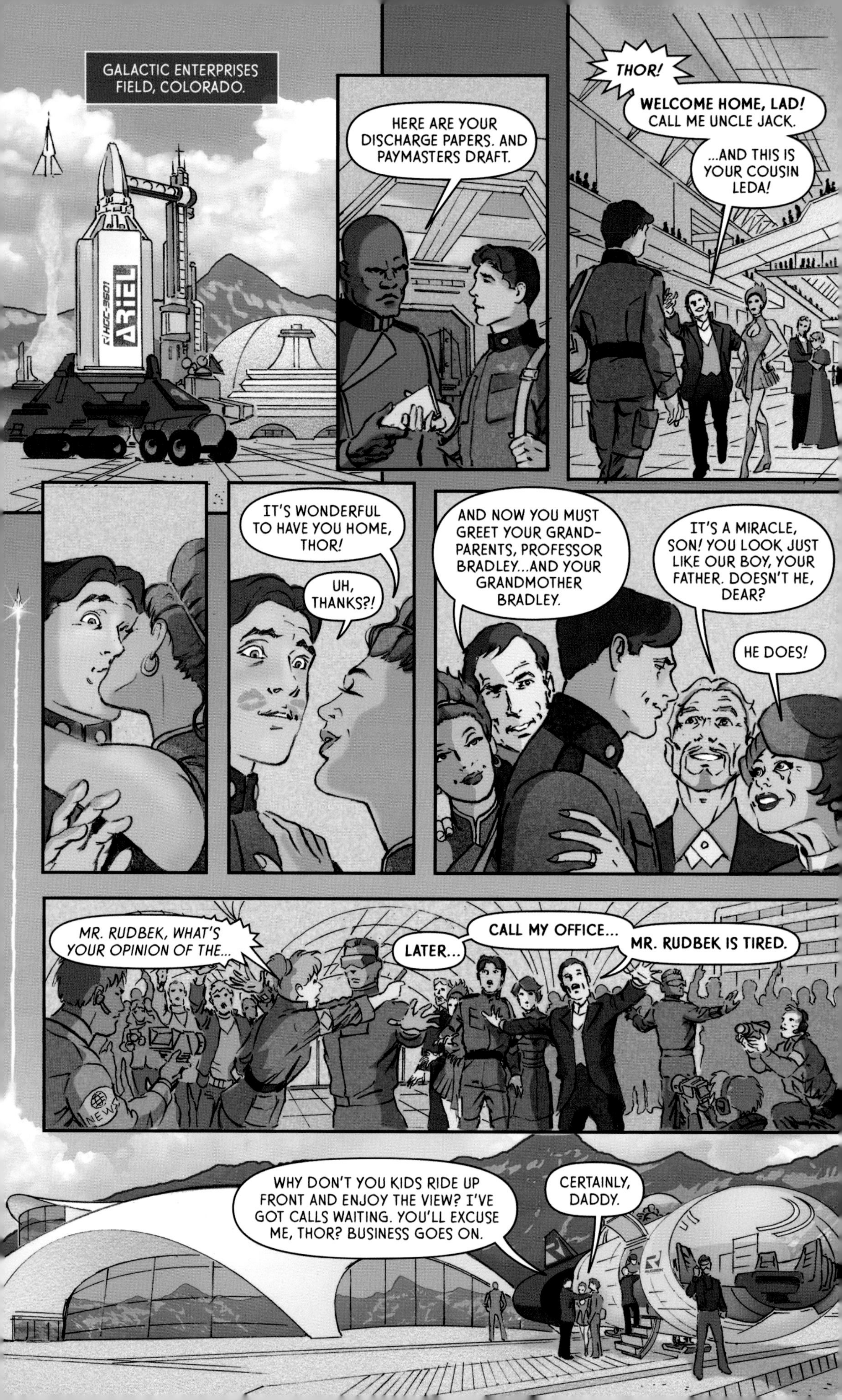
GALACTIC ENTERPRISES FIELD, COLORADO.
ARIEL
HERE ARE YOUR DISCHARGE PAPERS. AND PAYMASTERS DRAFT.
THOR!
WELCOME HOME, LAD! CALL ME UNCLE JACK.
...AND THIS IS YOUR COUSIN LEDA!
IT'S WONDERFUL TO HAVE YOU HOME, THOR!
UH, THANKS?!
AND NOW YOU MUST GREET YOUR GRAND-PARENTS, PROFESSOR BRADLEY...AND YOUR GRANDMOTHER BRADLEY.
IT'S A MIRACLE, SON! YOU LOOK JUST LIKE OUR BOY, YOUR FATHER. DOESN'T HE, DEAR?
HE DOES!
MR. RUDBEK, WHAT'S YOUR OPINION OF THE...
LATER...
CALL MY OFFICE...
MR. RUDBEK IS TIRED.
NEWS
WHY DON'T YOU KIDS RIDE UP FRONT AND ENJOY THE VIEW? I'VE GOT CALLS WAITING. YOU'LL EXCUSE ME, THOR? BUSINESS GOES ON.
CERTAINLY, DADDY.

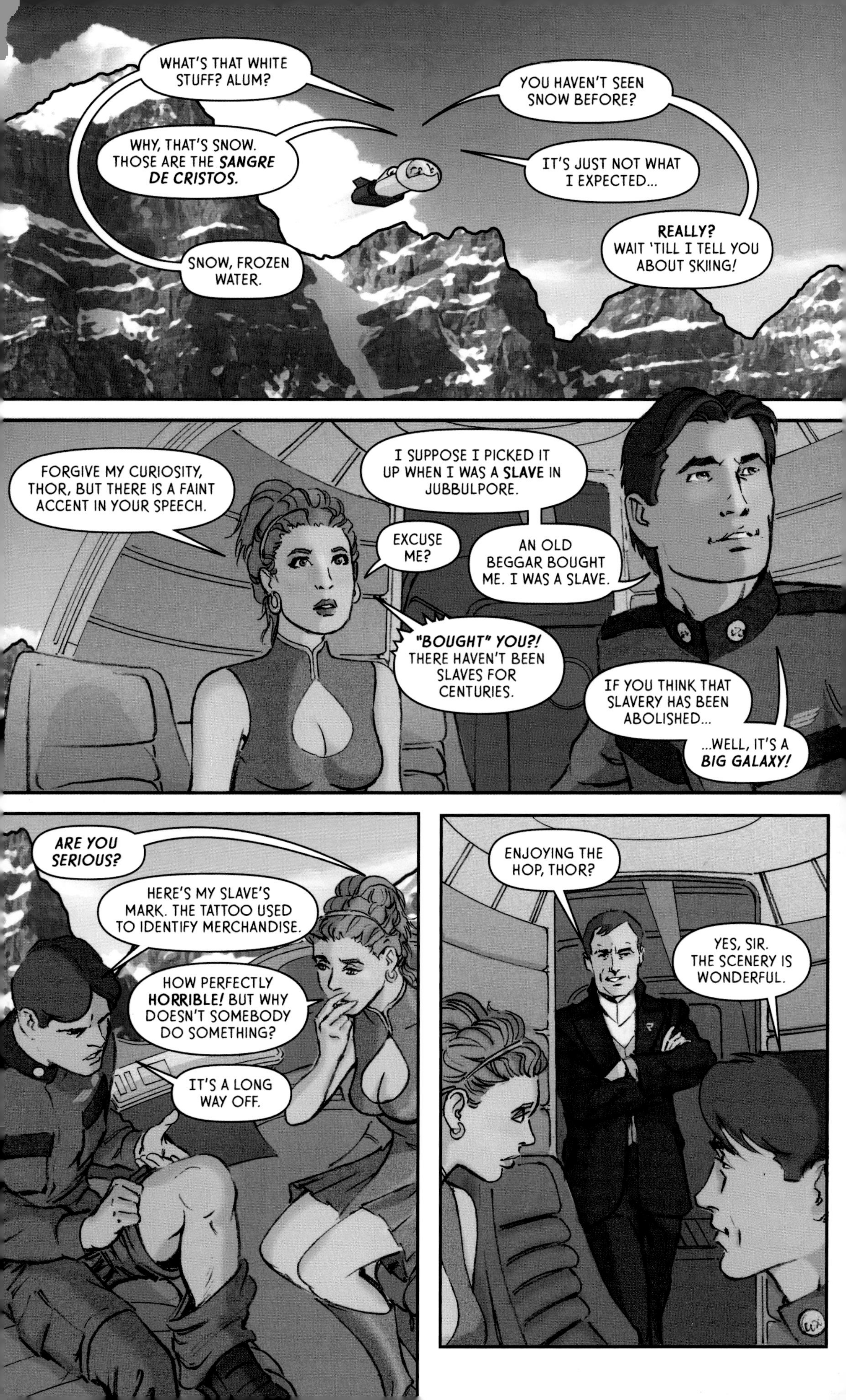
WHAT'S THAT WHITE STUFF? ALUM?
WHY, THAT'S SNOW. THOSE ARE THE **SANGRE DE CRISTOS.**
SNOW, FROZEN WATER.
YOU HAVEN'T SEEN SNOW BEFORE?
IT'S JUST NOT WHAT I EXPECTED...
REALLY? WAIT 'TILL I TELL YOU ABOUT SKIING!
FORGIVE MY CURIOSITY, THOR, BUT THERE IS A FAINT ACCENT IN YOUR SPEECH.
I SUPPOSE I PICKED IT UP WHEN I WAS A **SLAVE** IN JUBBULPORE.
EXCUSE ME?
AN OLD BEGGAR BOUGHT ME. I WAS A SLAVE.
"BOUGHT" YOU?! THERE HAVEN'T BEEN SLAVES FOR CENTURIES.
IF YOU THINK THAT SLAVERY HAS BEEN ABOLISHED...
...WELL, IT'S A ***BIG GALAXY!***
ARE YOU SERIOUS?
HERE'S MY SLAVE'S MARK. THE TATTOO USED TO IDENTIFY MERCHANDISE.
HOW PERFECTLY ***HORRIBLE!*** BUT WHY DOESN'T SOMEBODY DO SOMETHING?
IT'S A LONG WAY OFF.
ENJOYING THE HOP, THOR?
YES, SIR. THE SCENERY IS WONDERFUL.

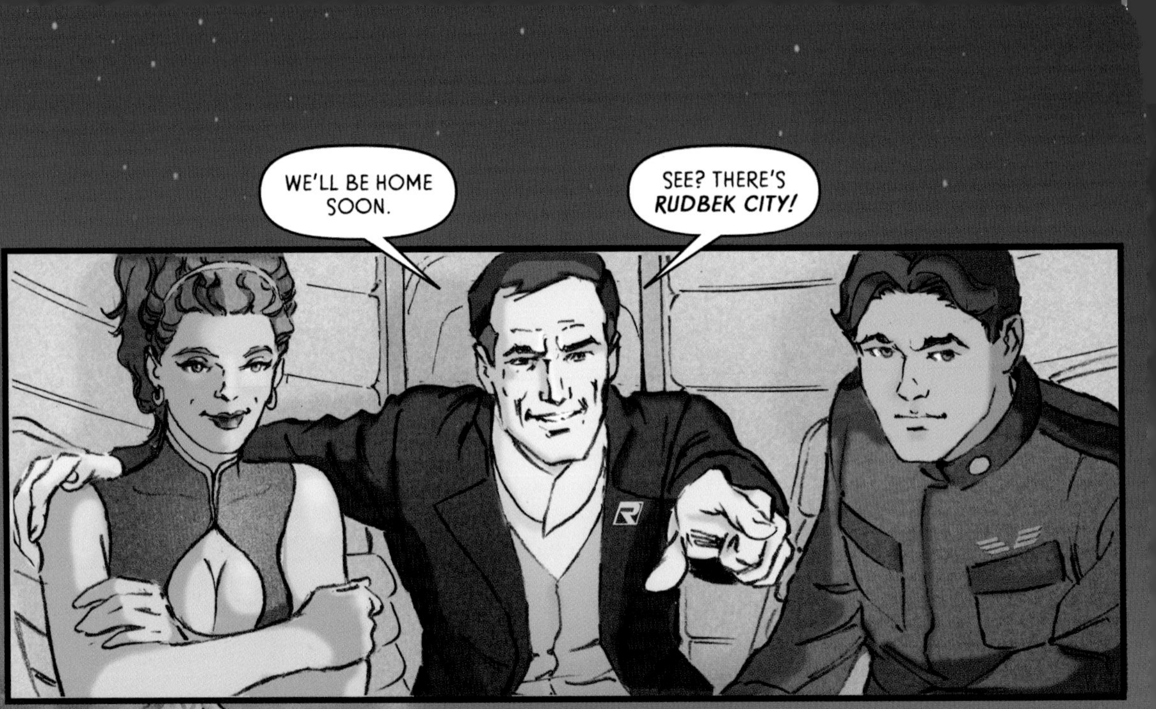
WE'LL BE HOME SOON.
SEE? THERE'S ***RUDBEK CITY!***

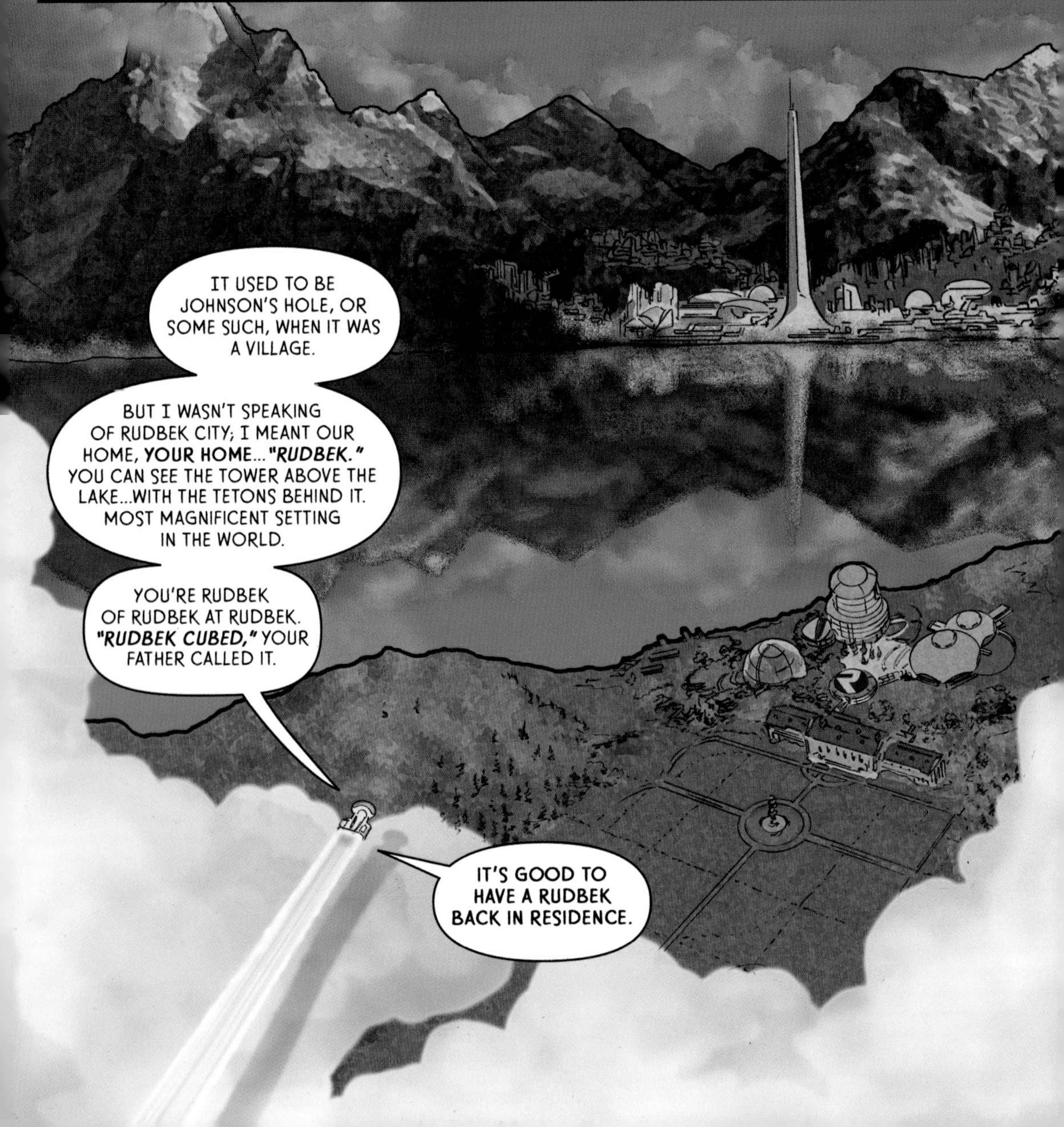
IT USED TO BE JOHNSON'S HOLE, OR SOME SUCH, WHEN IT WAS A VILLAGE.
BUT I WASN'T SPEAKING OF RUDBEK CITY; I MEANT OUR HOME, **YOUR HOME**... ***"RUDBEK."*** YOU CAN SEE THE TOWER ABOVE THE LAKE...WITH THE TETONS BEHIND IT. MOST MAGNIFICENT SETTING IN THE WORLD.
YOU'RE RUDBEK OF RUDBEK AT RUDBEK. ***"RUDBEK CUBED,"*** YOUR FATHER CALLED IT.
IT'S GOOD TO HAVE A RUDBEK BACK IN RESIDENCE.

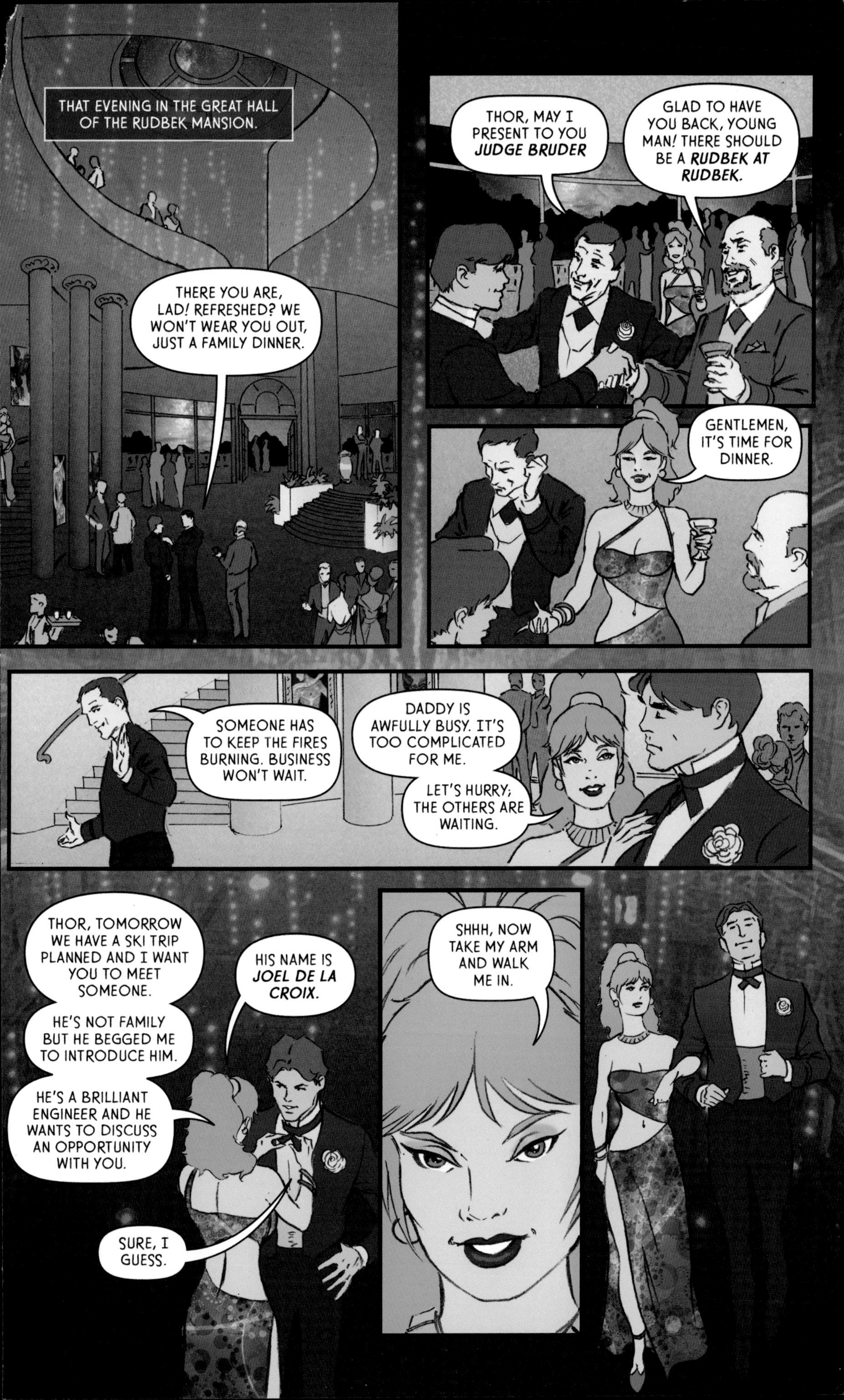
THAT EVENING IN THE GREAT HALL OF THE RUDBEK MANSION.
THERE YOU ARE, LAD! REFRESHED? WE WON'T WEAR YOU OUT, JUST A FAMILY DINNER.
THOR, MAY I PRESENT TO YOU *JUDGE BRUDER*
GLAD TO HAVE YOU BACK, YOUNG MAN! THERE SHOULD BE A *RUDBEK AT RUDBEK.*
GENTLEMEN, IT'S TIME FOR DINNER.
SOMEONE HAS TO KEEP THE FIRES BURNING. BUSINESS WON'T WAIT.
DADDY IS AWFULLY BUSY. IT'S TOO COMPLICATED FOR ME.
LET'S HURRY; THE OTHERS ARE WAITING.
THOR, TOMORROW WE HAVE A SKI TRIP PLANNED AND I WANT YOU TO MEET SOMEONE.
HE'S NOT FAMILY BUT HE BEGGED ME TO INTRODUCE HIM.
HE'S A BRILLIANT ENGINEER AND HE WANTS TO DISCUSS AN OPPORTUNITY WITH YOU.
HIS NAME IS *JOEL DE LA CROIX.*
SURE, I GUESS.
SHHH, NOW TAKE MY ARM AND WALK ME IN.

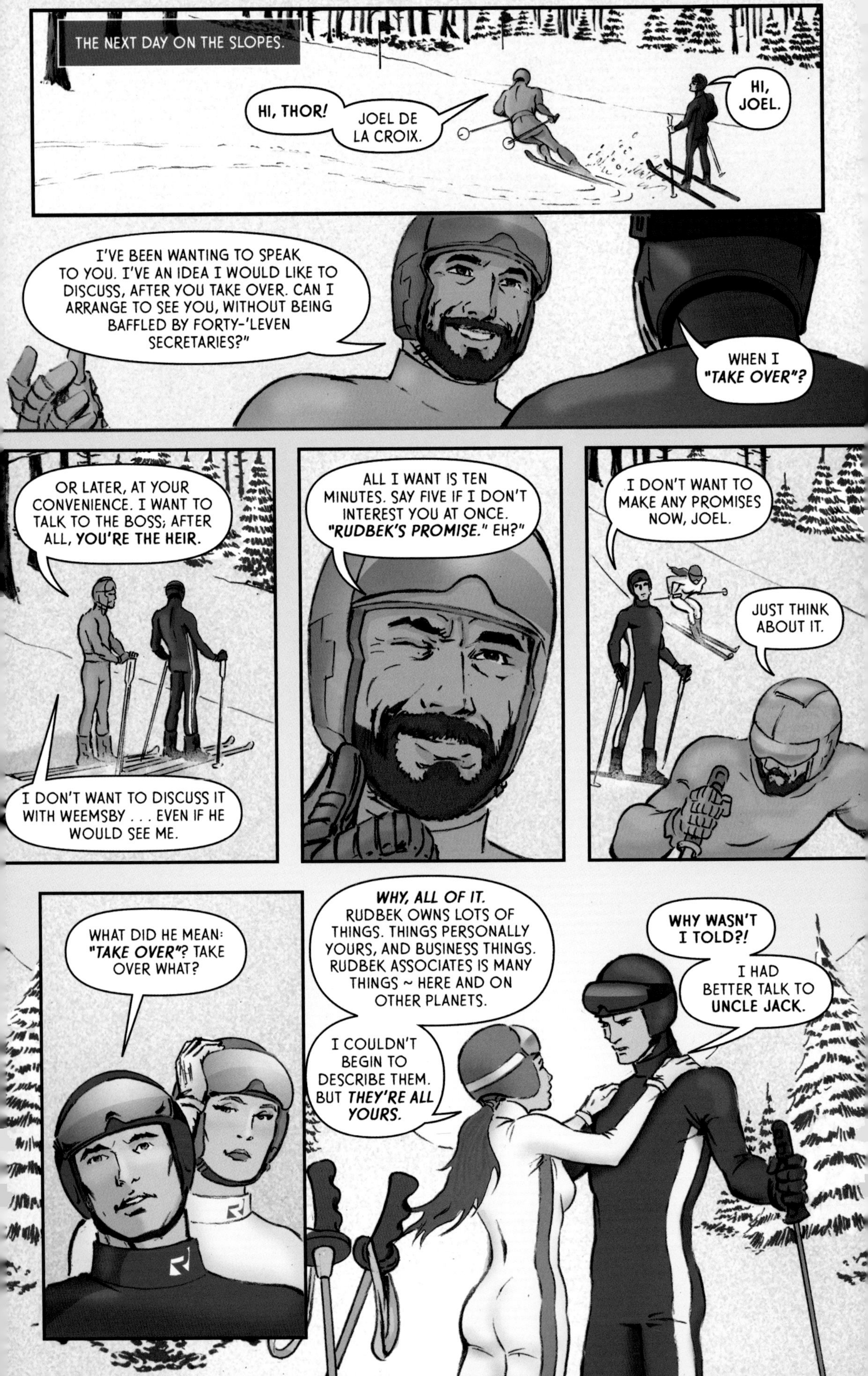
THE NEXT DAY ON THE SLOPES.
HI, THOR!
JOEL DE LA CROIX.
HI, JOEL.
I'VE BEEN WANTING TO SPEAK TO YOU. I'VE AN IDEA I WOULD LIKE TO DISCUSS, AFTER YOU TAKE OVER. CAN I ARRANGE TO SEE YOU, WITHOUT BEING BAFFLED BY FORTY-'LEVEN SECRETARIES?"
WHEN I "TAKE OVER"?
OR LATER, AT YOUR CONVENIENCE. I WANT TO TALK TO THE BOSS; AFTER ALL, YOU'RE THE HEIR.
I DON'T WANT TO DISCUSS IT WITH WEEMSBY . . . EVEN IF HE WOULD SEE ME.
ALL I WANT IS TEN MINUTES. SAY FIVE IF I DON'T INTEREST YOU AT ONCE. "RUDBEK'S PROMISE." EH?"
I DON'T WANT TO MAKE ANY PROMISES NOW, JOEL.
JUST THINK ABOUT IT.
WHAT DID HE MEAN: "TAKE OVER"? TAKE OVER WHAT?
WHY, ALL OF IT. RUDBEK OWNS LOTS OF THINGS. THINGS PERSONALLY YOURS, AND BUSINESS THINGS. RUDBEK ASSOCIATES IS MANY THINGS ~ HERE AND ON OTHER PLANETS.
I COULDN'T BEGIN TO DESCRIBE THEM. BUT THEY'RE ALL YOURS.
WHY WASN'T I TOLD?!
I HAD BETTER TALK TO UNCLE JACK.

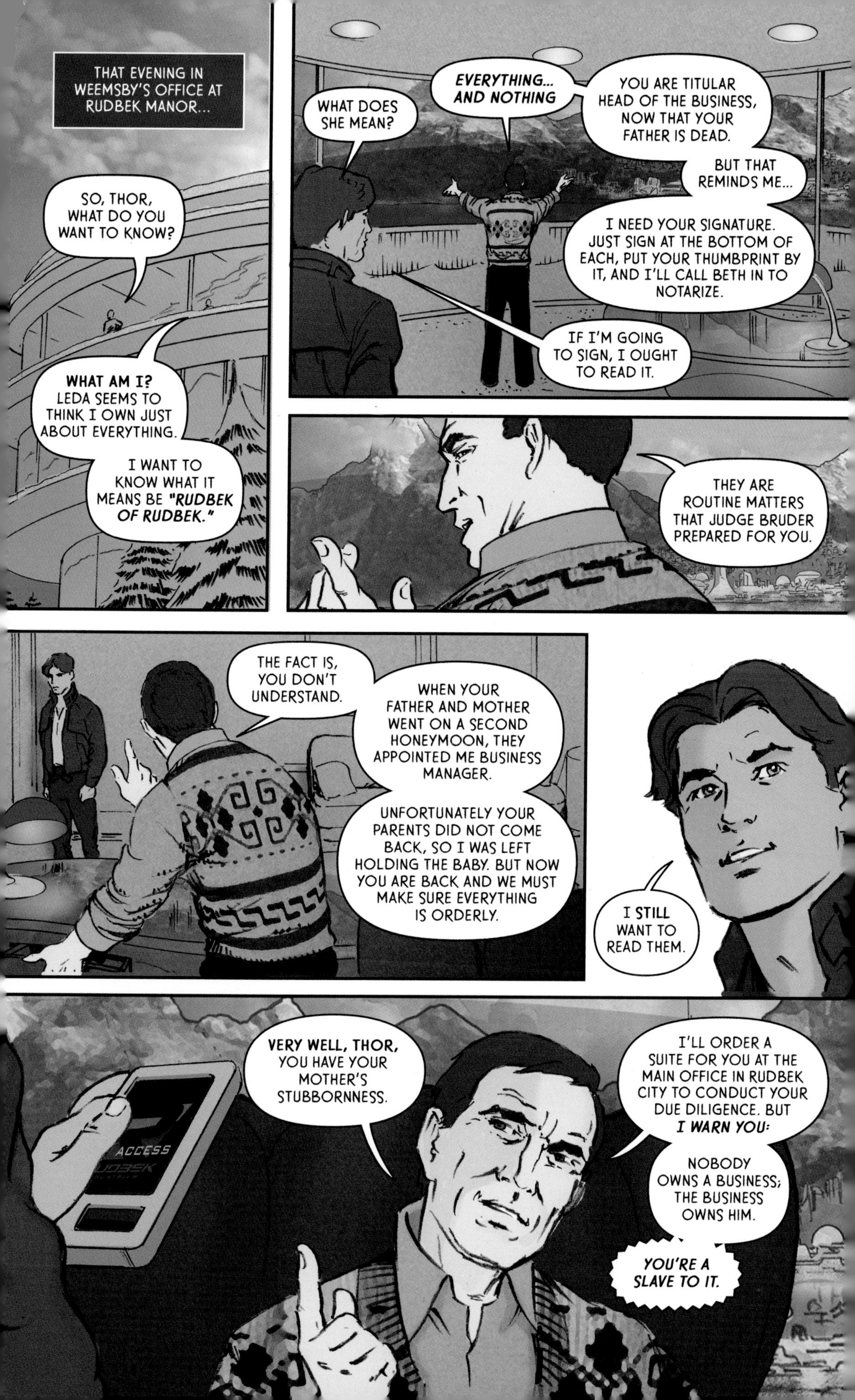
THAT EVENING IN WEEMSBY'S OFFICE AT RUDBEK MANOR...
SO, THOR, WHAT DO YOU WANT TO KNOW?
WHAT AM I? LEDA SEEMS TO THINK I OWN JUST ABOUT EVERYTHING.
I WANT TO KNOW WHAT IT MEANS BE "RUDBEK OF RUDBEK."
WHAT DOES SHE MEAN?
EVERYTHING... AND NOTHING
YOU ARE TITULAR HEAD OF THE BUSINESS, NOW THAT YOUR FATHER IS DEAD.
BUT THAT REMINDS ME...
I NEED YOUR SIGNATURE. JUST SIGN AT THE BOTTOM OF EACH, PUT YOUR THUMBPRINT BY IT, AND I'LL CALL BETH IN TO NOTARIZE.
IF I'M GOING TO SIGN, I OUGHT TO READ IT.
THEY ARE ROUTINE MATTERS THAT JUDGE BRUDER PREPARED FOR YOU.
THE FACT IS, YOU DON'T UNDERSTAND.
WHEN YOUR FATHER AND MOTHER WENT ON A SECOND HONEYMOON, THEY APPOINTED ME BUSINESS MANAGER.
UNFORTUNATELY YOUR PARENTS DID NOT COME BACK, SO I WAS LEFT HOLDING THE BABY. BUT NOW YOU ARE BACK AND WE MUST MAKE SURE EVERYTHING IS ORDERLY.
I STILL WANT TO READ THEM.
VERY WELL, THOR, YOU HAVE YOUR MOTHER'S STUBBORNNESS.
I'LL ORDER A SUITE FOR YOU AT THE MAIN OFFICE IN RUDBEK CITY TO CONDUCT YOUR DUE DILIGENCE. BUT I WARN YOU:
NOBODY OWNS A BUSINESS; THE BUSINESS OWNS HIM.
YOU'RE A SLAVE TO IT.
ACCESS

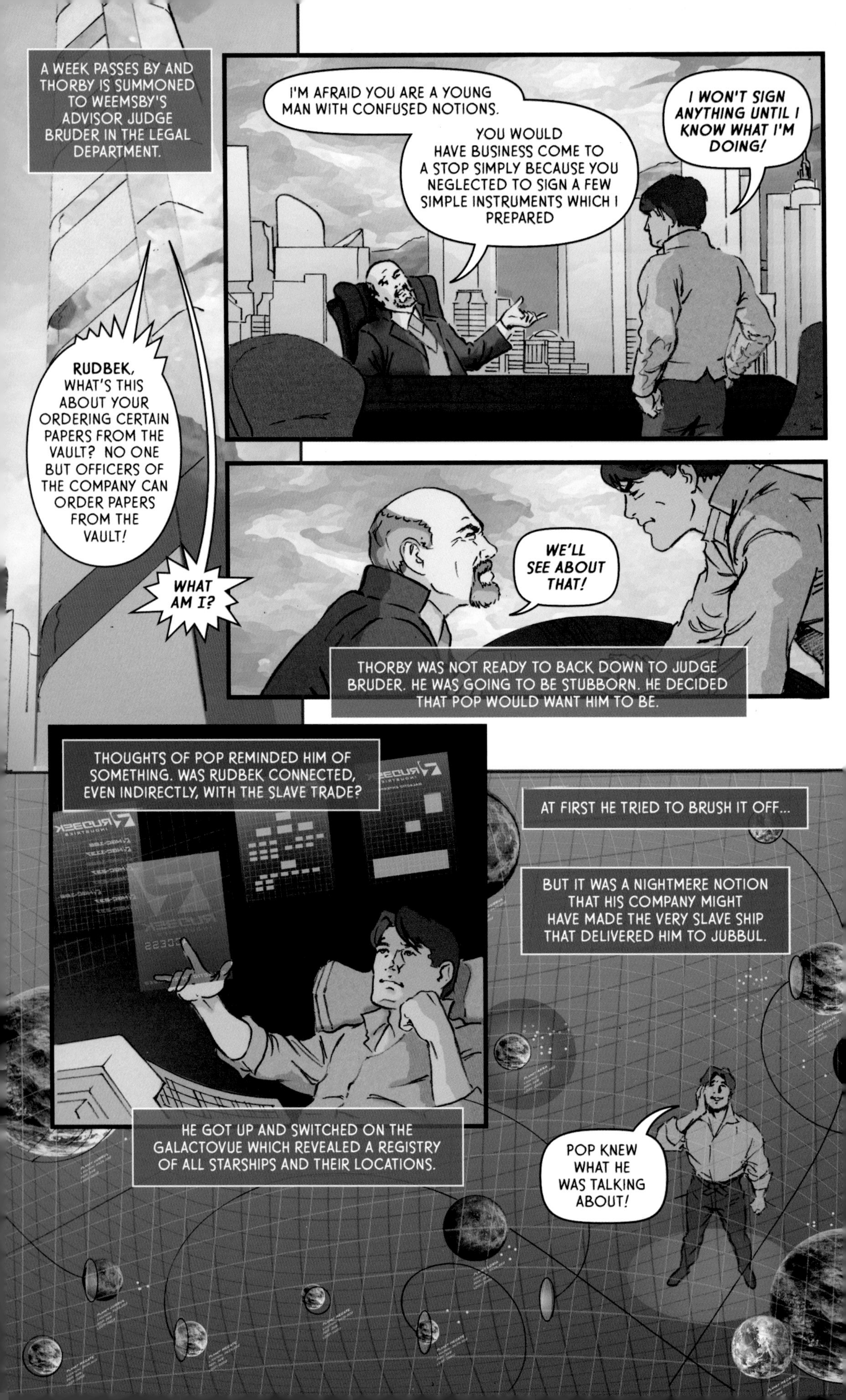
A WEEK PASSES BY AND THORBY IS SUMMONED TO WEEMSBY'S ADVISOR JUDGE BRUDER IN THE LEGAL DEPARTMENT.
I'M AFRAID YOU ARE A YOUNG MAN WITH CONFUSED NOTIONS.
YOU WOULD HAVE BUSINESS COME TO A STOP SIMPLY BECAUSE YOU NEGLECTED TO SIGN A FEW SIMPLE INSTRUMENTS WHICH I PREPARED
I WON'T SIGN ANYTHING UNTIL I KNOW WHAT I'M DOING!
RUDBEK, WHAT'S THIS ABOUT YOUR ORDERING CERTAIN PAPERS FROM THE VAULT? NO ONE BUT OFFICERS OF THE COMPANY CAN ORDER PAPERS FROM THE VAULT!
WHAT AM I?
WE'LL SEE ABOUT THAT!
THORBY WAS NOT READY TO BACK DOWN TO JUDGE BRUDER. HE WAS GOING TO BE STUBBORN. HE DECIDED THAT POP WOULD WANT HIM TO BE.
THOUGHTS OF POP REMINDED HIM OF SOMETHING. WAS RUDBEK CONNECTED, EVEN INDIRECTLY, WITH THE SLAVE TRADE?
HE GOT UP AND SWITCHED ON THE GALACTOVUE WHICH REVEALED A REGISTRY OF ALL STARSHIPS AND THEIR LOCATIONS.
AT FIRST HE TRIED TO BRUSH IT OFF...
BUT IT WAS A NIGHTMERE NOTION THAT HIS COMPANY MIGHT HAVE MADE THE VERY SLAVE SHIP THAT DELIVERED HIM TO JUBBUL.
POP KNEW WHAT HE WAS TALKING ABOUT!

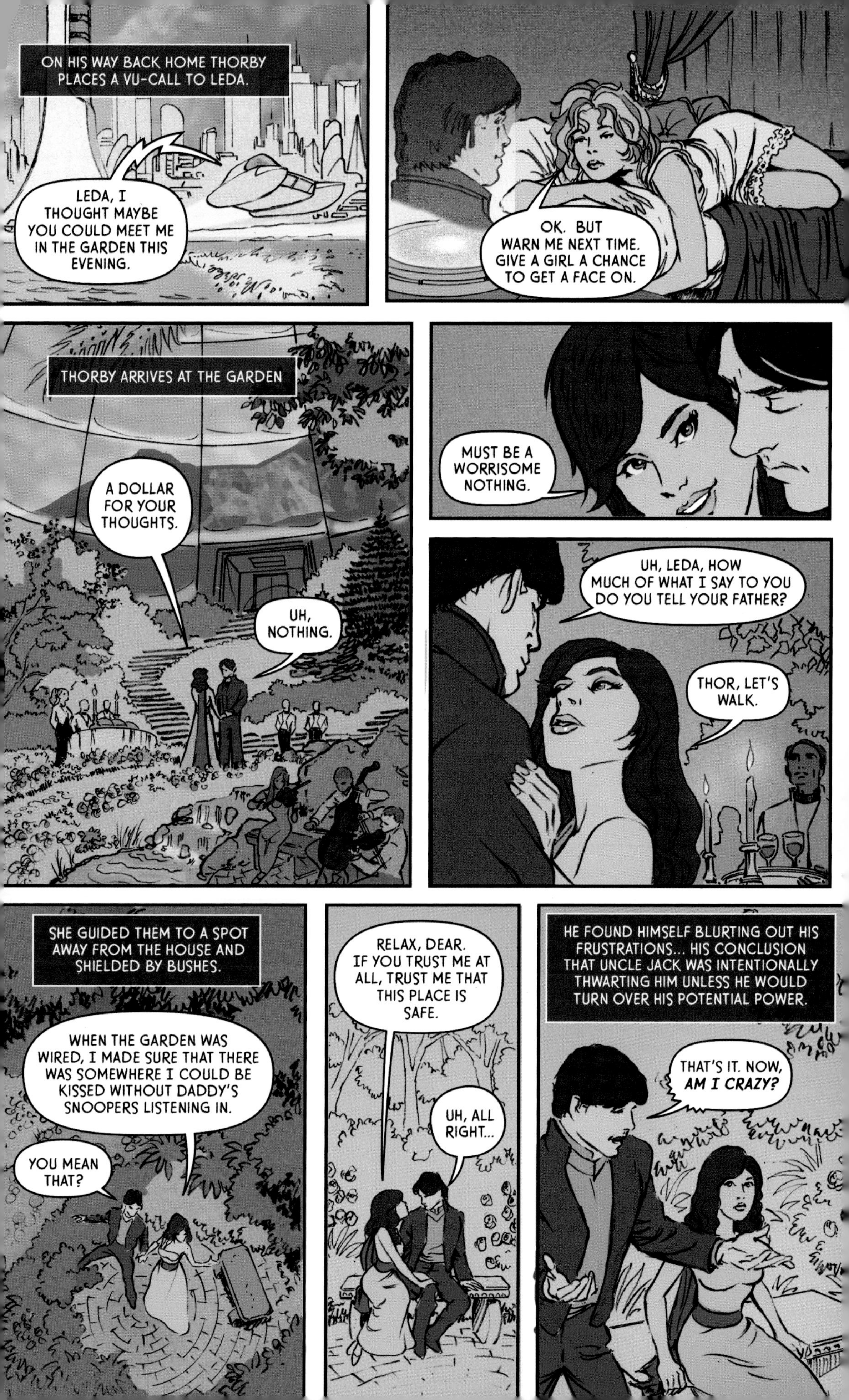
ON HIS WAY BACK HOME THORBY PLACES A VU-CALL TO LEDA.
LEDA, I THOUGHT MAYBE YOU COULD MEET ME IN THE GARDEN THIS EVENING.
OK. BUT WARN ME NEXT TIME. GIVE A GIRL A CHANCE TO GET A FACE ON.
THORBY ARRIVES AT THE GARDEN
A DOLLAR FOR YOUR THOUGHTS.
UH, NOTHING.
MUST BE A WORRISOME NOTHING.
UH, LEDA, HOW MUCH OF WHAT I SAY TO YOU DO YOU TELL YOUR FATHER?
THOR, LET'S WALK.
SHE GUIDED THEM TO A SPOT AWAY FROM THE HOUSE AND SHIELDED BY BUSHES.
WHEN THE GARDEN WAS WIRED, I MADE SURE THAT THERE WAS SOMEWHERE I COULD BE KISSED WITHOUT DADDY'S SNOOPERS LISTENING IN.
YOU MEAN THAT?
RELAX, DEAR. IF YOU TRUST ME AT ALL, TRUST ME THAT THIS PLACE IS SAFE.
UH, ALL RIGHT...
HE FOUND HIMSELF BLURTING OUT HIS FRUSTRATIONS... HIS CONCLUSION THAT UNCLE JACK WAS INTENTIONALLY THWARTING HIM UNLESS HE WOULD TURN OVER HIS POTENTIAL POWER.
THAT'S IT. NOW, *AM I CRAZY?*

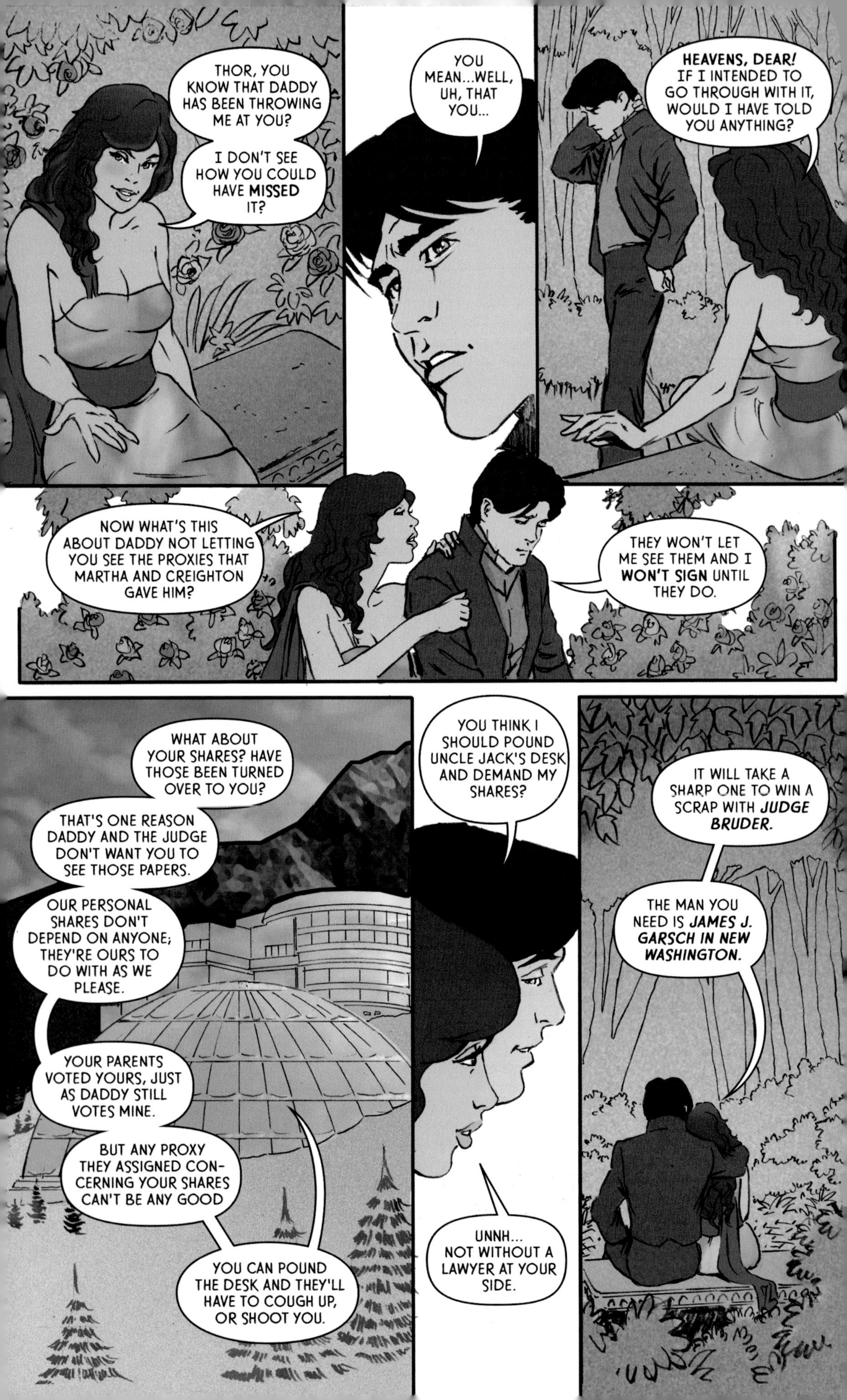
THOR, YOU KNOW THAT DADDY HAS BEEN THROWING ME AT YOU?
I DON'T SEE HOW YOU COULD HAVE **MISSED** IT?
YOU MEAN...WELL, UH, THAT YOU...
HEAVENS, DEAR! IF I INTENDED TO GO THROUGH WITH IT, WOULD I HAVE TOLD YOU ANYTHING?
NOW WHAT'S THIS ABOUT DADDY NOT LETTING YOU SEE THE PROXIES THAT MARTHA AND CREIGHTON GAVE HIM?
THEY WON'T LET ME SEE THEM AND I **WON'T SIGN** UNTIL THEY DO.
WHAT ABOUT YOUR SHARES? HAVE THOSE BEEN TURNED OVER TO YOU?
THAT'S ONE REASON DADDY AND THE JUDGE DON'T WANT YOU TO SEE THOSE PAPERS.
OUR PERSONAL SHARES DON'T DEPEND ON ANYONE; THEY'RE OURS TO DO WITH AS WE PLEASE.
YOUR PARENTS VOTED YOURS, JUST AS DADDY STILL VOTES MINE.
BUT ANY PROXY THEY ASSIGNED CON-CERNING YOUR SHARES CAN'T BE ANY GOOD
YOU CAN POUND THE DESK AND THEY'LL HAVE TO COUGH UP, OR SHOOT YOU.
YOU THINK I SHOULD POUND UNCLE JACK'S DESK AND DEMAND MY SHARES?
UNNH... NOT WITHOUT A LAWYER AT YOUR SIDE.
IT WILL TAKE A SHARP ONE TO WIN A SCRAP WITH ***JUDGE BRUDER.***
THE MAN YOU NEED IS ***JAMES J. GARSCH IN NEW WASHINGTON.***

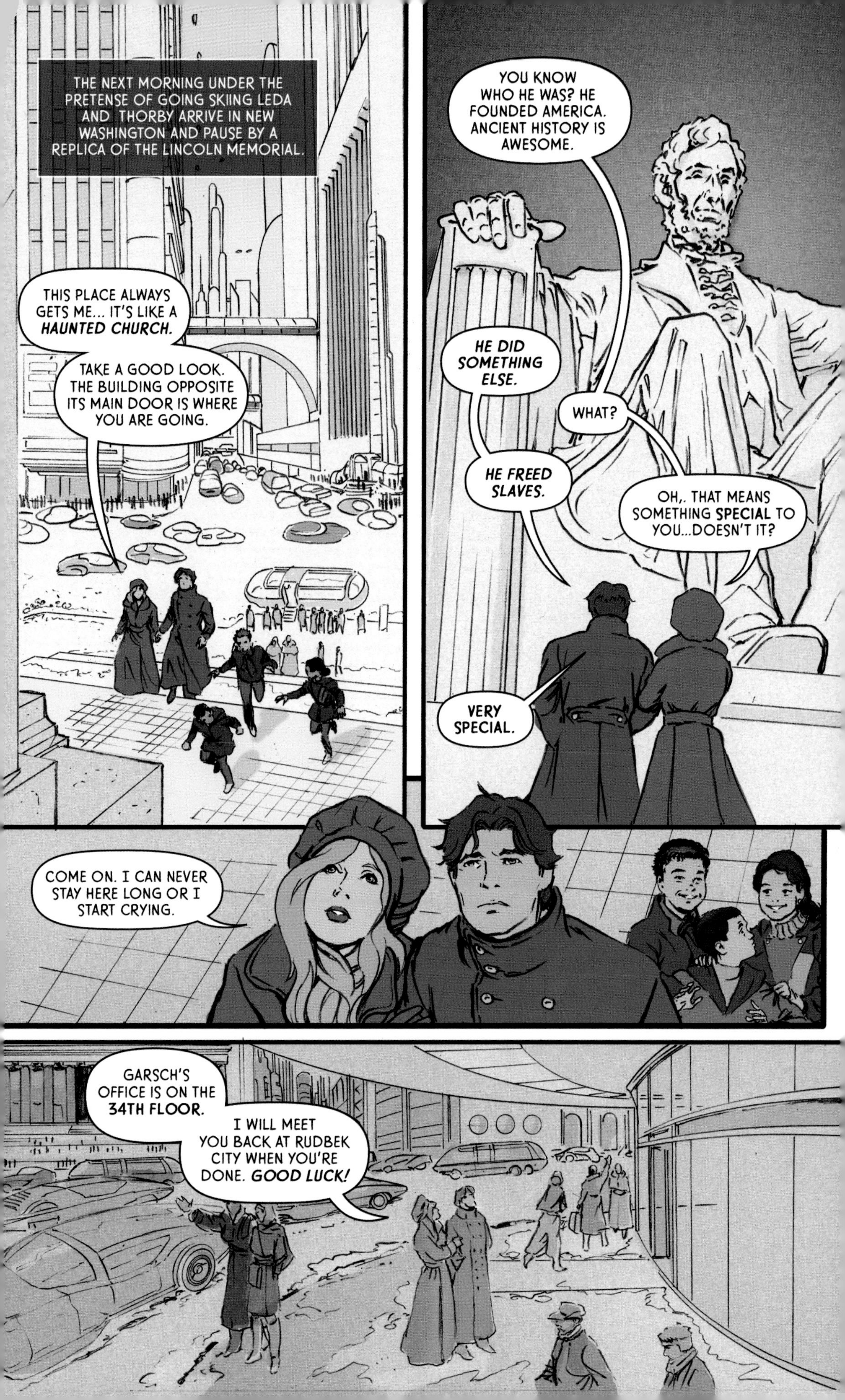
THE NEXT MORNING UNDER THE PRETENSE OF GOING SKIING LEDA AND THORBY ARRIVE IN NEW WASHINGTON AND PAUSE BY A REPLICA OF THE LINCOLN MEMORIAL.
THIS PLACE ALWAYS GETS ME... IT'S LIKE A *HAUNTED CHURCH.*
TAKE A GOOD LOOK. THE BUILDING OPPOSITE ITS MAIN DOOR IS WHERE YOU ARE GOING.
YOU KNOW WHO HE WAS? HE FOUNDED AMERICA. ANCIENT HISTORY IS AWESOME.
HE DID SOMETHING ELSE.
WHAT?
HE FREED SLAVES.
OH,. THAT MEANS SOMETHING **SPECIAL** TO YOU...DOESN'T IT?
VERY SPECIAL.
COME ON. I CAN NEVER STAY HERE LONG OR I START CRYING.
GARSCH'S OFFICE IS ON THE **34TH FLOOR.**
I WILL MEET YOU BACK AT RUDBEK CITY WHEN YOU'RE DONE. ***GOOD LUCK!***

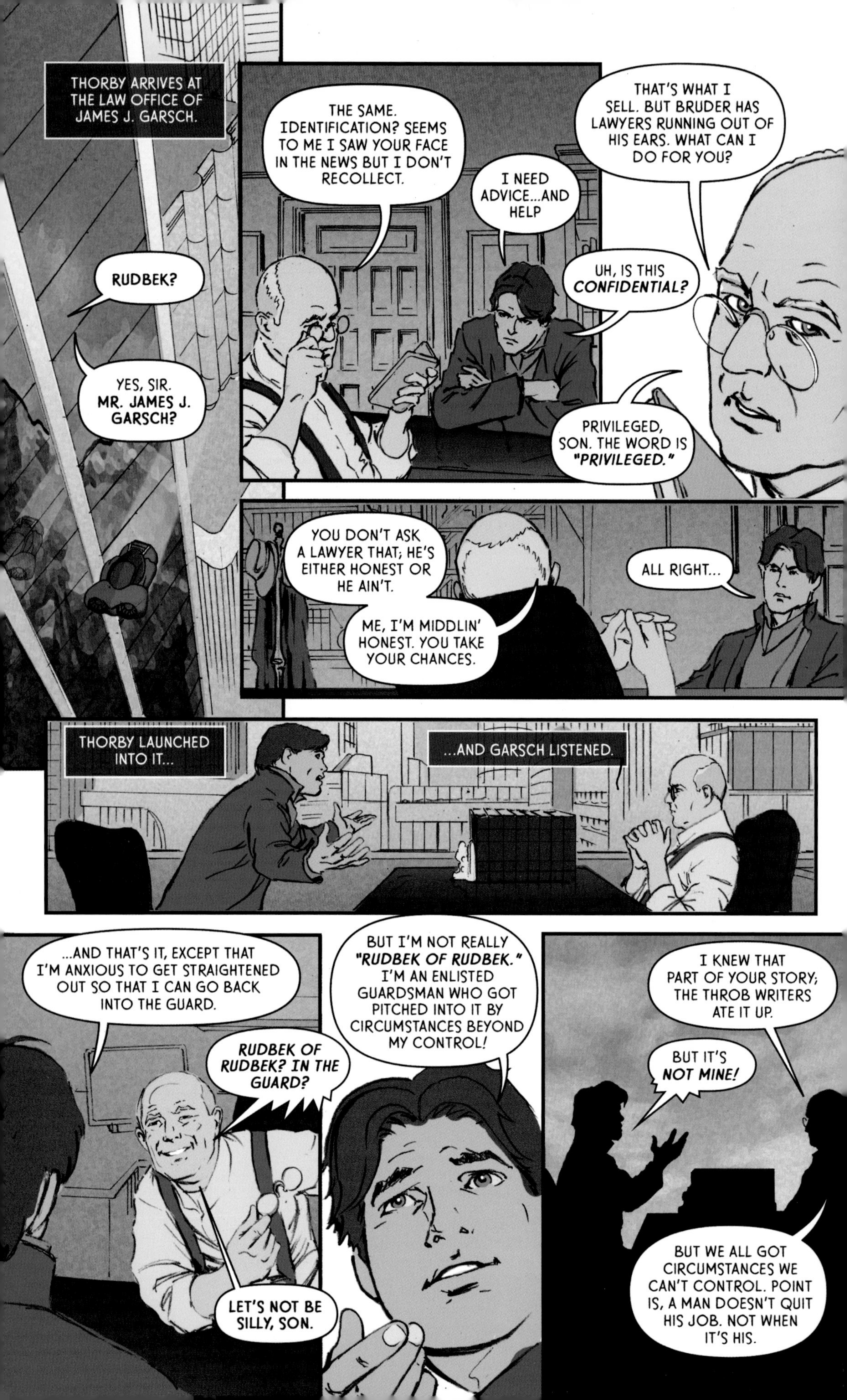
THORBY ARRIVES AT THE LAW OFFICE OF JAMES J. GARSCH.
RUDBEK?
YES, SIR. MR. JAMES J. GARSCH?
THE SAME. IDENTIFICATION? SEEMS TO ME I SAW YOUR FACE IN THE NEWS BUT I DON'T RECOLLECT.
I NEED ADVICE...AND HELP
THAT'S WHAT I SELL. BUT BRUDER HAS LAWYERS RUNNING OUT OF HIS EARS. WHAT CAN I DO FOR YOU?
UH, IS THIS CONFIDENTIAL?
PRIVILEGED, SON. THE WORD IS "PRIVILEGED."
YOU DON'T ASK A LAWYER THAT; HE'S EITHER HONEST OR HE AIN'T.
ME, I'M MIDDLIN' HONEST. YOU TAKE YOUR CHANCES.
ALL RIGHT...
THORBY LAUNCHED INTO IT...
...AND GARSCH LISTENED.
...AND THAT'S IT, EXCEPT THAT I'M ANXIOUS TO GET STRAIGHTENED OUT SO THAT I CAN GO BACK INTO THE GUARD.
RUDBEK OF RUDBEK? IN THE GUARD?
LET'S NOT BE SILLY, SON.
BUT I'M NOT REALLY "RUDBEK OF RUDBEK." I'M AN ENLISTED GUARDSMAN WHO GOT PITCHED INTO IT BY CIRCUMSTANCES BEYOND MY CONTROL!
I KNEW THAT PART OF YOUR STORY; THE THROB WRITERS ATE IT UP.
BUT IT'S NOT MINE!
BUT WE ALL GOT CIRCUMSTANCES WE CAN'T CONTROL. POINT IS, A MAN DOESN'T QUIT HIS JOB. NOT WHEN IT'S HIS.

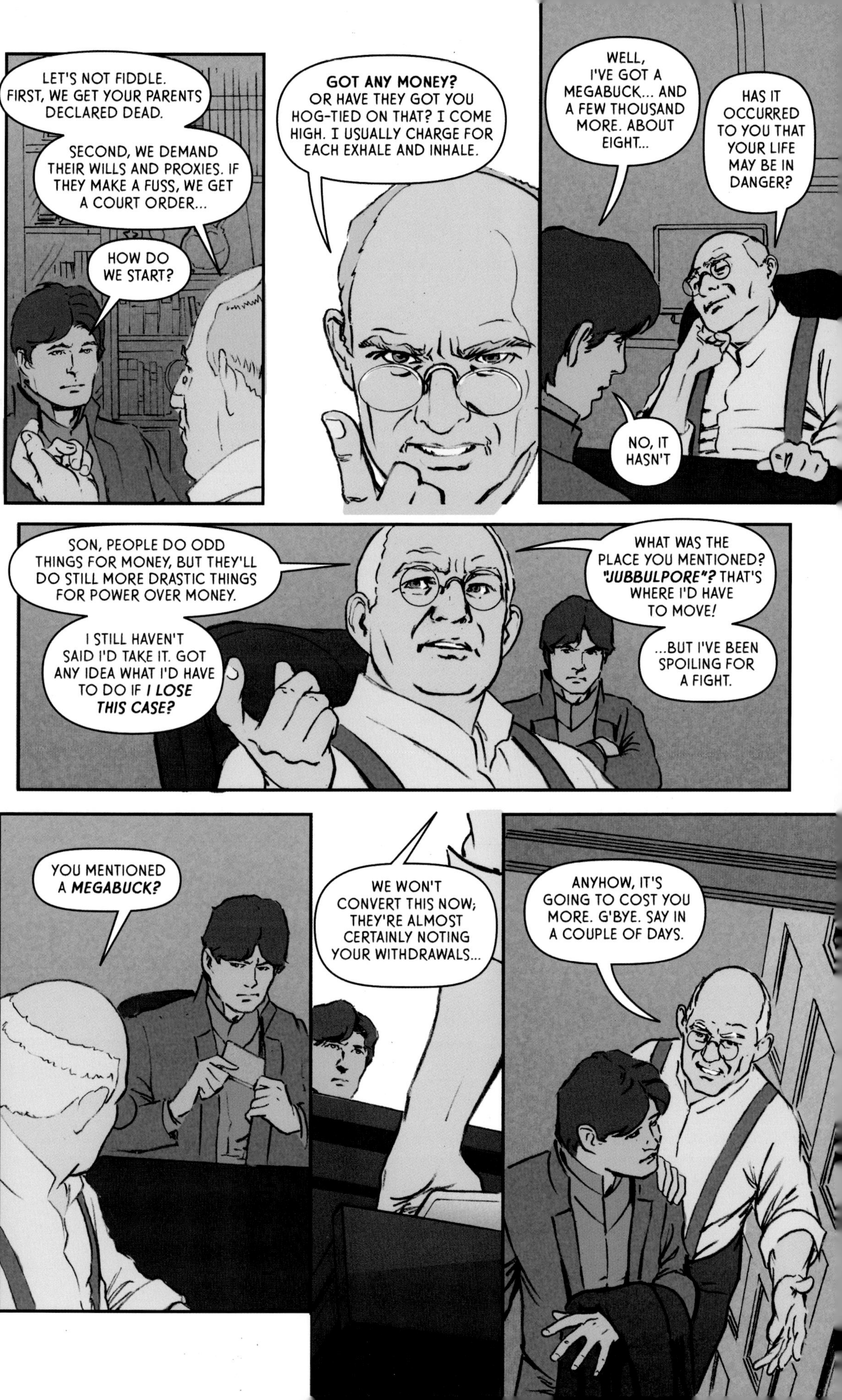

LET'S NOT FIDDLE. FIRST, WE GET YOUR PARENTS DECLARED DEAD.
SECOND, WE DEMAND THEIR WILLS AND PROXIES. IF THEY MAKE A FUSS, WE GET A COURT ORDER...
HOW DO WE START?
GOT ANY MONEY? OR HAVE THEY GOT YOU HOG-TIED ON THAT? I COME HIGH. I USUALLY CHARGE FOR EACH EXHALE AND INHALE.
WELL, I'VE GOT A MEGABUCK... AND A FEW THOUSAND MORE. ABOUT EIGHT...
HAS IT OCCURRED TO YOU THAT YOUR LIFE MAY BE IN DANGER?
NO, IT HASN'T
SON, PEOPLE DO ODD THINGS FOR MONEY, BUT THEY'LL DO STILL MORE DRASTIC THINGS FOR POWER OVER MONEY.
I STILL HAVEN'T SAID I'D TAKE IT. GOT ANY IDEA WHAT I'D HAVE TO DO IF ***I LOSE THIS CASE?***
WHAT WAS THE PLACE YOU MENTIONED? ***"JUBBULPORE"?*** THAT'S WHERE I'D HAVE TO MOVE!
...BUT I'VE BEEN SPOILING FOR A FIGHT.
YOU MENTIONED A ***MEGABUCK?***
WE WON'T CONVERT THIS NOW; THEY'RE ALMOST CERTAINLY NOTING YOUR WITHDRAWALS...
ANYHOW, IT'S GOING TO COST YOU MORE. G'BYE. SAY IN A COUPLE OF DAYS.

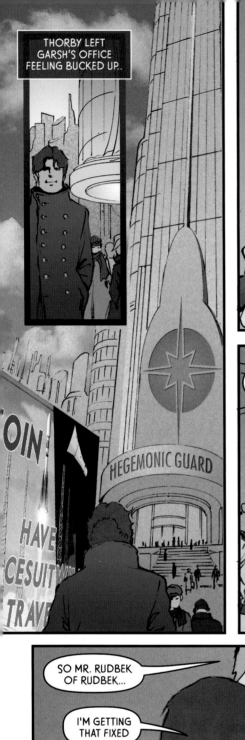

THORBY LEFT GARSH'S OFFICE FEELING BUCKED UP.

RUDBEK OF RUDBEK. I AM *WING MARSHAL SMITH*.

ACTUALLY ITS BASLIM, SIR. THORBY BASLIM.

ALL RIGHT, THORBY BASLIM... RUDBEK. WHAT CAN I DO FOR

MAYBE IT'S WHAT I CAN DO FOR YOU...

I CAME HERE FOR TWO REASONS...

THE FIRST IS, I THINK I CAN ADD SOMETHING TO COL. BASLIM'S FINAL REPORT.

I KNEW HIM AND ADMIRED HIM VERY MUCH.

THE SECOND IS--I'D LIKE TO GO BACK INTO THE GUARD AND GO *'X' CORPS*.

HEGEMONIC GUARD

SO MR. RUDBEK OF RUDBEK...

I'M GETTING THAT FIXED

A MAN COMES HERE, WE DON'T PROMISE HIM CERTAIN WORK. HE DOES WHAT HE'S TOLD.

WE USUALLY USE HIM UP. OUR CASUALTY RATE IS HIGH.

I'LL DO WHAT I'M TOLD.

I JUST HAPPEN TO BE INTERESTED IN THE SLAVE TRAFFIC. WHY, MOST PEOPLE HERE DON'T SEEM TO KNOW IT EXISTS.

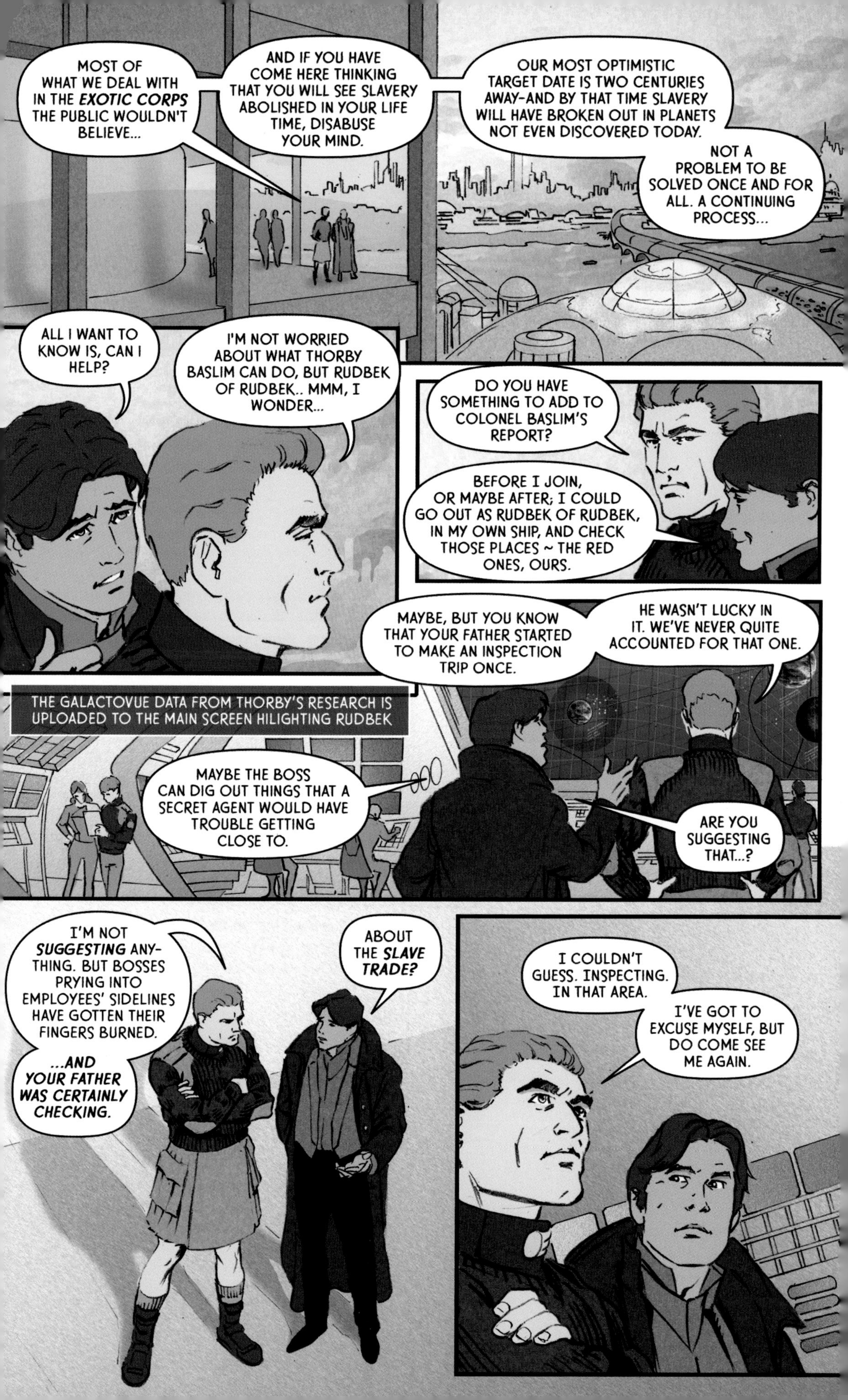
MOST OF WHAT WE DEAL WITH IN THE *EXOTIC CORPS* THE PUBLIC WOULDN'T BELIEVE...
AND IF YOU HAVE COME HERE THINKING THAT YOU WILL SEE SLAVERY ABOLISHED IN YOUR LIFE TIME, DISABUSE YOUR MIND.
OUR MOST OPTIMISTIC TARGET DATE IS TWO CENTURIES AWAY-AND BY THAT TIME SLAVERY WILL HAVE BROKEN OUT IN PLANETS NOT EVEN DISCOVERED TODAY.
NOT A PROBLEM TO BE SOLVED ONCE AND FOR ALL. A CONTINUING PROCESS...
ALL I WANT TO KNOW IS, CAN I HELP?
I'M NOT WORRIED ABOUT WHAT THORBY BASLIM CAN DO, BUT RUDBEK OF RUDBEK.. MMM, I WONDER...
DO YOU HAVE SOMETHING TO ADD TO COLONEL BASLIM'S REPORT?
BEFORE I JOIN, OR MAYBE AFTER; I COULD GO OUT AS RUDBEK OF RUDBEK, IN MY OWN SHIP, AND CHECK THOSE PLACES ~ THE RED ONES, OURS.
MAYBE, BUT YOU KNOW THAT YOUR FATHER STARTED TO MAKE AN INSPECTION TRIP ONCE.
HE WASN'T LUCKY IN IT. WE'VE NEVER QUITE ACCOUNTED FOR THAT ONE.
THE GALACTOVUE DATA FROM THORBY'S RESEARCH IS UPLOADED TO THE MAIN SCREEN HILIGHTING RUDBEK
MAYBE THE BOSS CAN DIG OUT THINGS THAT A SECRET AGENT WOULD HAVE TROUBLE GETTING CLOSE TO.
ARE YOU SUGGESTING THAT...?
I'M NOT *SUGGESTING* ANY-THING. BUT BOSSES PRYING INTO EMPLOYEES' SIDELINES HAVE GOTTEN THEIR FINGERS BURNED.
...AND YOUR FATHER WAS CERTAINLY CHECKING.
ABOUT THE *SLAVE TRADE?*
I COULDN'T GUESS. INSPECTING. IN THAT AREA.
I'VE GOT TO EXCUSE MYSELF, BUT DO COME SEE ME AGAIN.

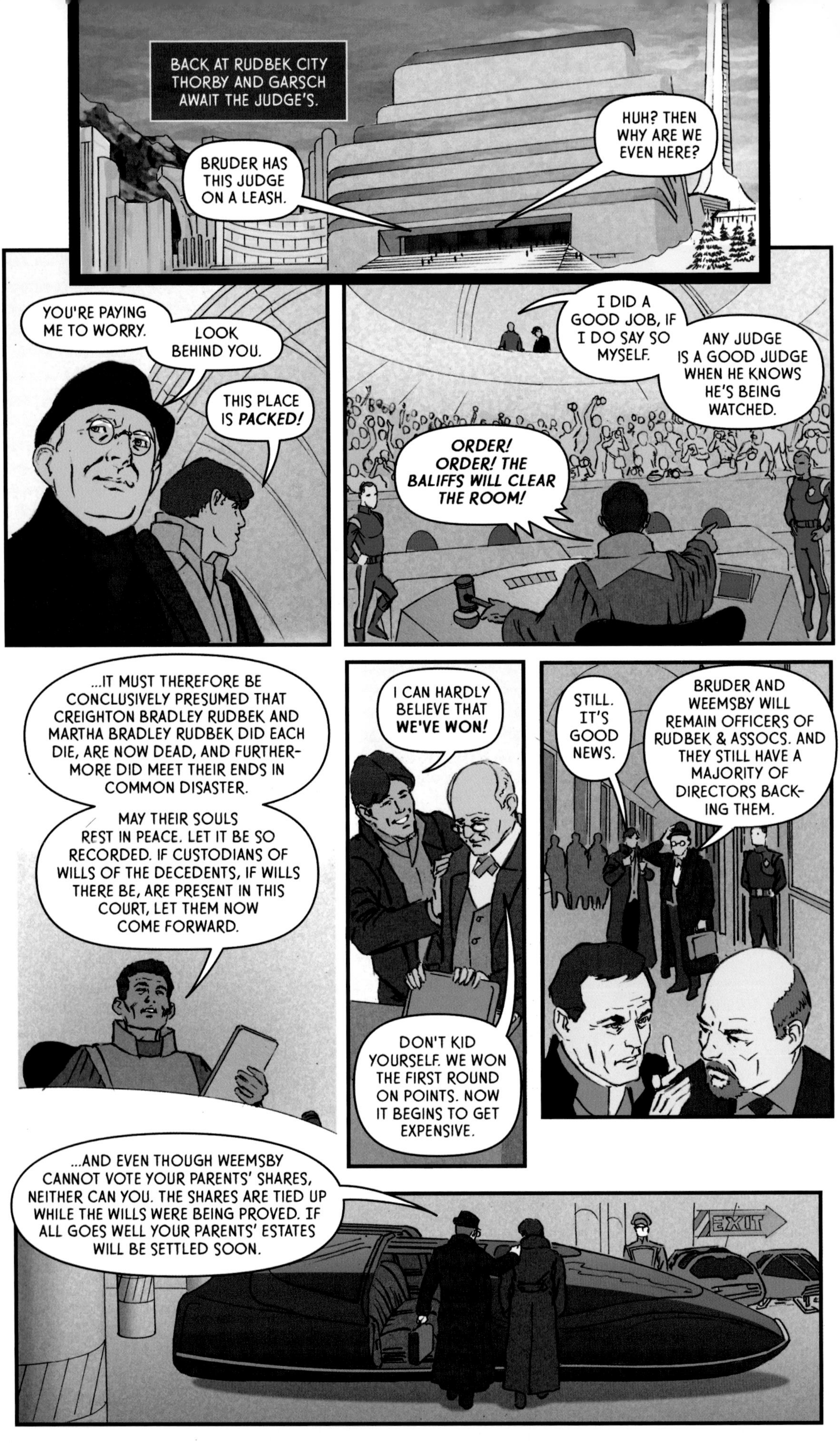
BACK AT RUDBEK CITY THORBY AND GARSCH AWAIT THE JUDGE'S.
BRUDER HAS THIS JUDGE ON A LEASH.
HUH? THEN WHY ARE WE EVEN HERE?
YOU'RE PAYING ME TO WORRY.
LOOK BEHIND YOU.
THIS PLACE IS PACKED!
I DID A GOOD JOB, IF I DO SAY SO MYSELF.
ANY JUDGE IS A GOOD JUDGE WHEN HE KNOWS HE'S BEING WATCHED.
ORDER! ORDER! THE BALIFFS WILL CLEAR THE ROOM!
...IT MUST THEREFORE BE CONCLUSIVELY PRESUMED THAT CREIGHTON BRADLEY RUDBEK AND MARTHA BRADLEY RUDBEK DID EACH DIE, ARE NOW DEAD, AND FURTHERMORE DID MEET THEIR ENDS IN COMMON DISASTER.
MAY THEIR SOULS REST IN PEACE. LET IT BE SO RECORDED. IF CUSTODIANS OF WILLS OF THE DECEDENTS, IF WILLS THERE BE, ARE PRESENT IN THIS COURT, LET THEM NOW COME FORWARD.
I CAN HARDLY BELIEVE THAT WE'VE WON!
DON'T KID YOURSELF. WE WON THE FIRST ROUND ON POINTS. NOW IT BEGINS TO GET EXPENSIVE.
STILL. IT'S GOOD NEWS.
BRUDER AND WEEMSBY WILL REMAIN OFFICERS OF RUDBEK & ASSOCS. AND THEY STILL HAVE A MAJORITY OF DIRECTORS BACKING THEM.
...AND EVEN THOUGH WEEMSBY CANNOT VOTE YOUR PARENTS' SHARES, NEITHER CAN YOU. THE SHARES ARE TIED UP WHILE THE WILLS WERE BEING PROVED. IF ALL GOES WELL YOUR PARENTS' ESTATES WILL BE SETTLED SOON.
EXIT

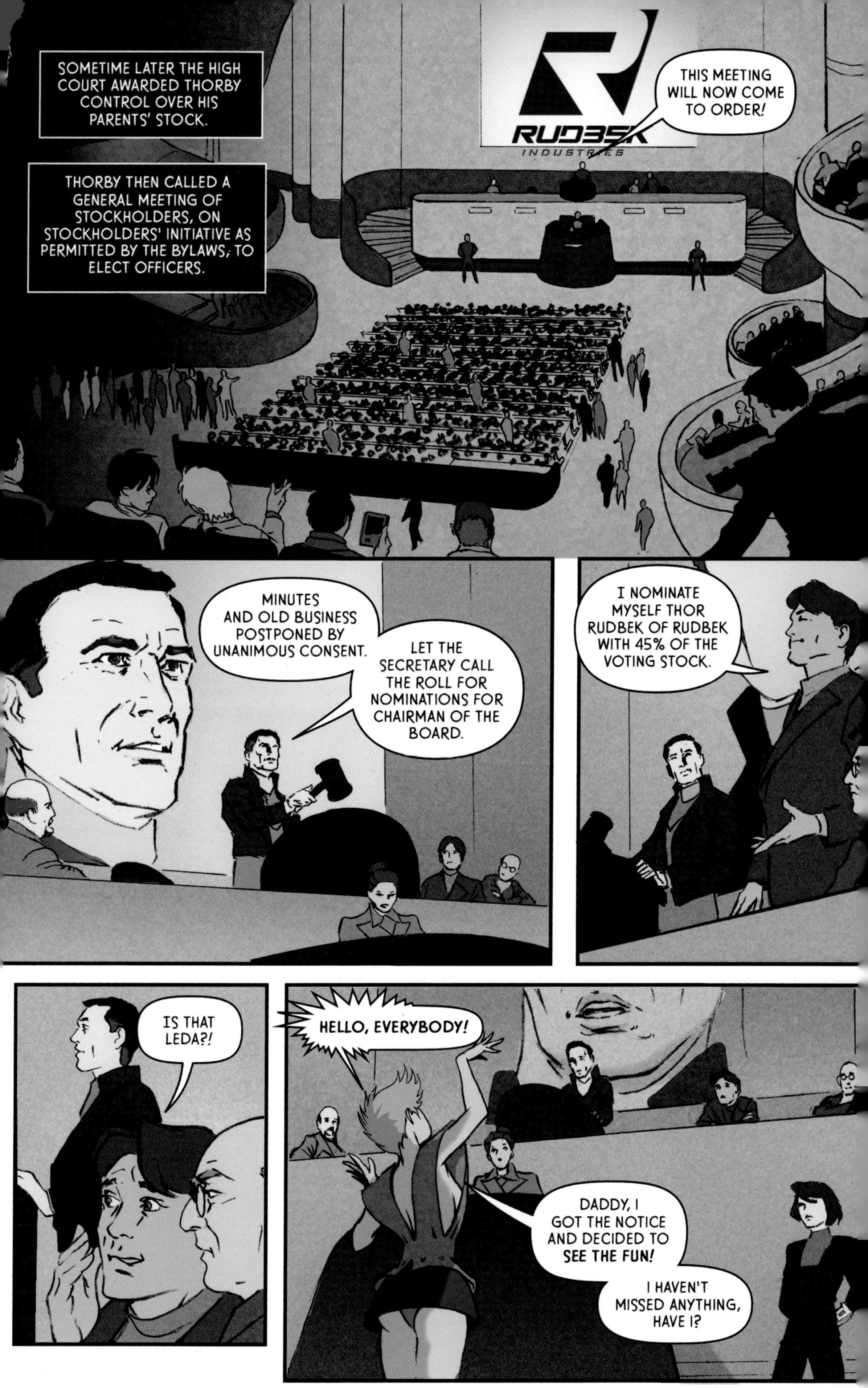

SOMETIME LATER THE HIGH COURT AWARDED THORBY CONTROL OVER HIS PARENTS' STOCK.
THORBY THEN CALLED A GENERAL MEETING OF STOCKHOLDERS, ON STOCKHOLDERS' INITIATIVE AS PERMITTED BY THE BYLAWS, TO ELECT OFFICERS.
RUDBEK INDUSTRIES
THIS MEETING WILL NOW COME TO ORDER!
MINUTES AND OLD BUSINESS POSTPONED BY UNANIMOUS CONSENT.
LET THE SECRETARY CALL THE ROLL FOR NOMINATIONS FOR CHAIRMAN OF THE BOARD.
I NOMINATE MYSELF THOR RUDBEK OF RUDBEK WITH 45% OF THE VOTING STOCK.
IS THAT LEDA?!
HELLO, EVERYBODY!
DADDY, I GOT THE NOTICE AND DECIDED TO SEE THE FUN!
I HAVEN'T MISSED ANYTHING, HAVE I?

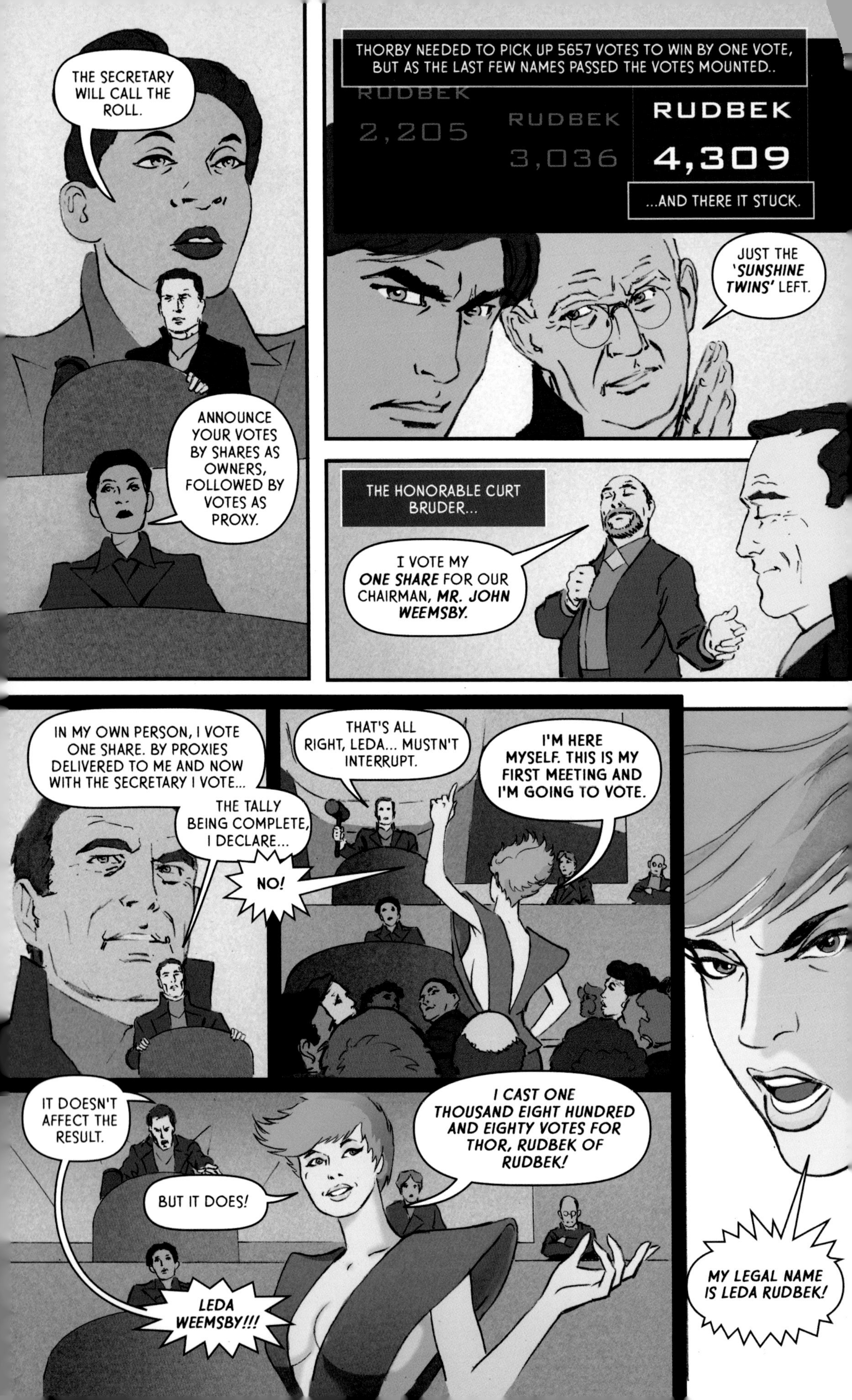
THE SECRETARY WILL CALL THE ROLL.
ANNOUNCE YOUR VOTES BY SHARES AS OWNERS, FOLLOWED BY VOTES AS PROXY.
THORBY NEEDED TO PICK UP 5657 VOTES TO WIN BY ONE VOTE, BUT AS THE LAST FEW NAMES PASSED THE VOTES MOUNTED..
RUDBEK
2,205
RUDBEK
3,036
RUDBEK
4,309
...AND THERE IT STUCK.
JUST THE 'SUNSHINE TWINS' LEFT.
THE HONORABLE CURT BRUDER...
I VOTE MY ONE SHARE FOR OUR CHAIRMAN, MR. JOHN WEEMSBY.
IN MY OWN PERSON, I VOTE ONE SHARE. BY PROXIES DELIVERED TO ME AND NOW WITH THE SECRETARY I VOTE...
THE TALLY BEING COMPLETE, I DECLARE...
NO!
THAT'S ALL RIGHT, LEDA... MUSTN'T INTERRUPT.
I'M HERE MYSELF. THIS IS MY FIRST MEETING AND I'M GOING TO VOTE.
IT DOESN'T AFFECT THE RESULT.
BUT IT DOES!
I CAST ONE THOUSAND EIGHT HUNDRED AND EIGHTY VOTES FOR THOR, RUDBEK OF RUDBEK!
LEDA WEEMSBY!!!
MY LEGAL NAME IS LEDA RUDBEK!

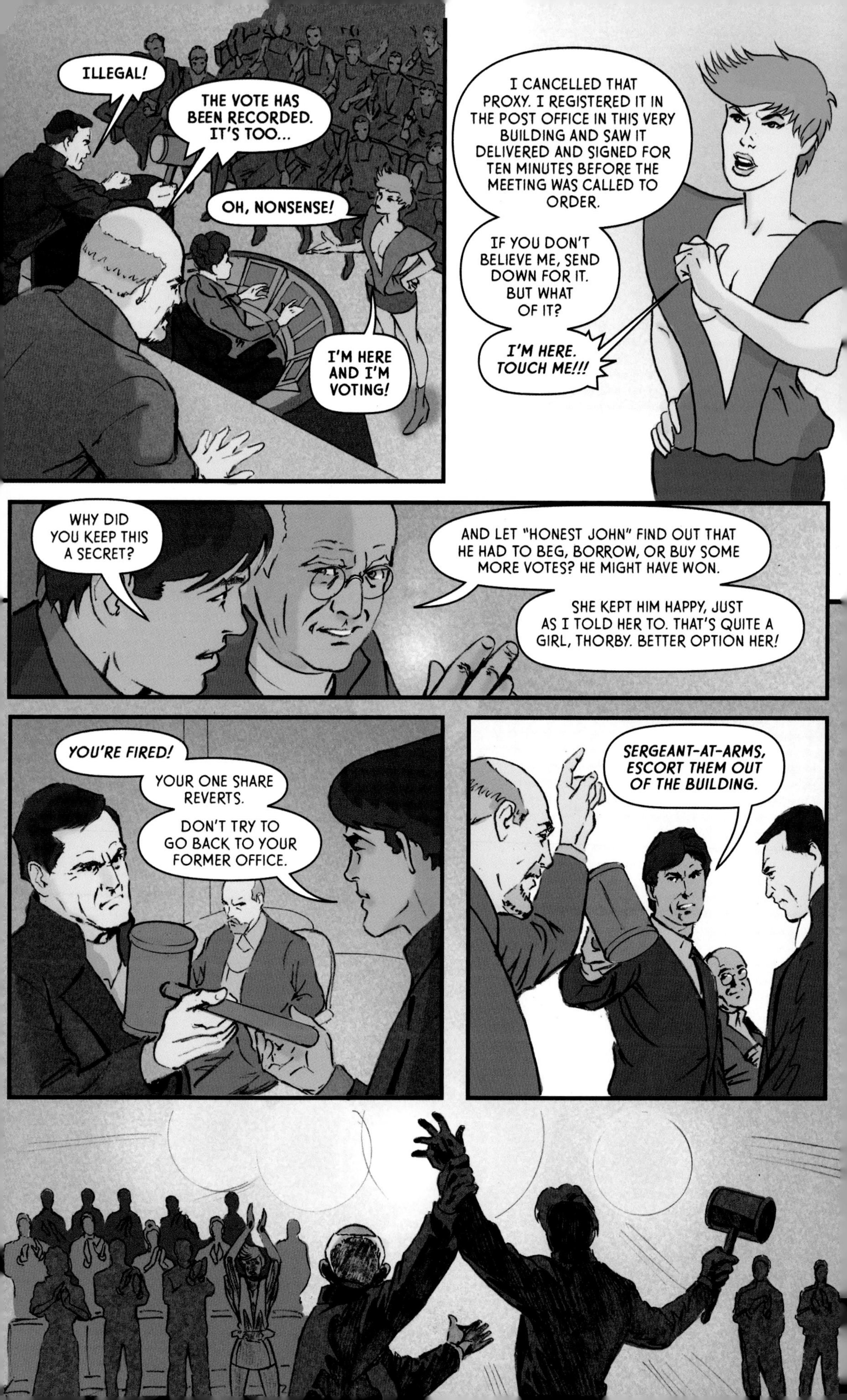
ILLEGAL!
THE VOTE HAS BEEN RECORDED. IT'S TOO...
OH, NONSENSE!
I'M HERE AND I'M VOTING!
I CANCELLED THAT PROXY. I REGISTERED IT IN THE POST OFFICE IN THIS VERY BUILDING AND SAW IT DELIVERED AND SIGNED FOR TEN MINUTES BEFORE THE MEETING WAS CALLED TO ORDER.
IF YOU DON'T BELIEVE ME, SEND DOWN FOR IT. BUT WHAT OF IT?
I'M HERE. TOUCH ME!!!
WHY DID YOU KEEP THIS A SECRET?
AND LET "HONEST JOHN" FIND OUT THAT HE HAD TO BEG, BORROW, OR BUY SOME MORE VOTES? HE MIGHT HAVE WON.
SHE KEPT HIM HAPPY, JUST AS I TOLD HER TO. THAT'S QUITE A GIRL, THORBY. BETTER OPTION HER!
YOU'RE FIRED!
YOUR ONE SHARE REVERTS.
DON'T TRY TO GO BACK TO YOUR FORMER OFFICE.
SERGEANT-AT-ARMS, ESCORT THEM OUT OF THE BUILDING.

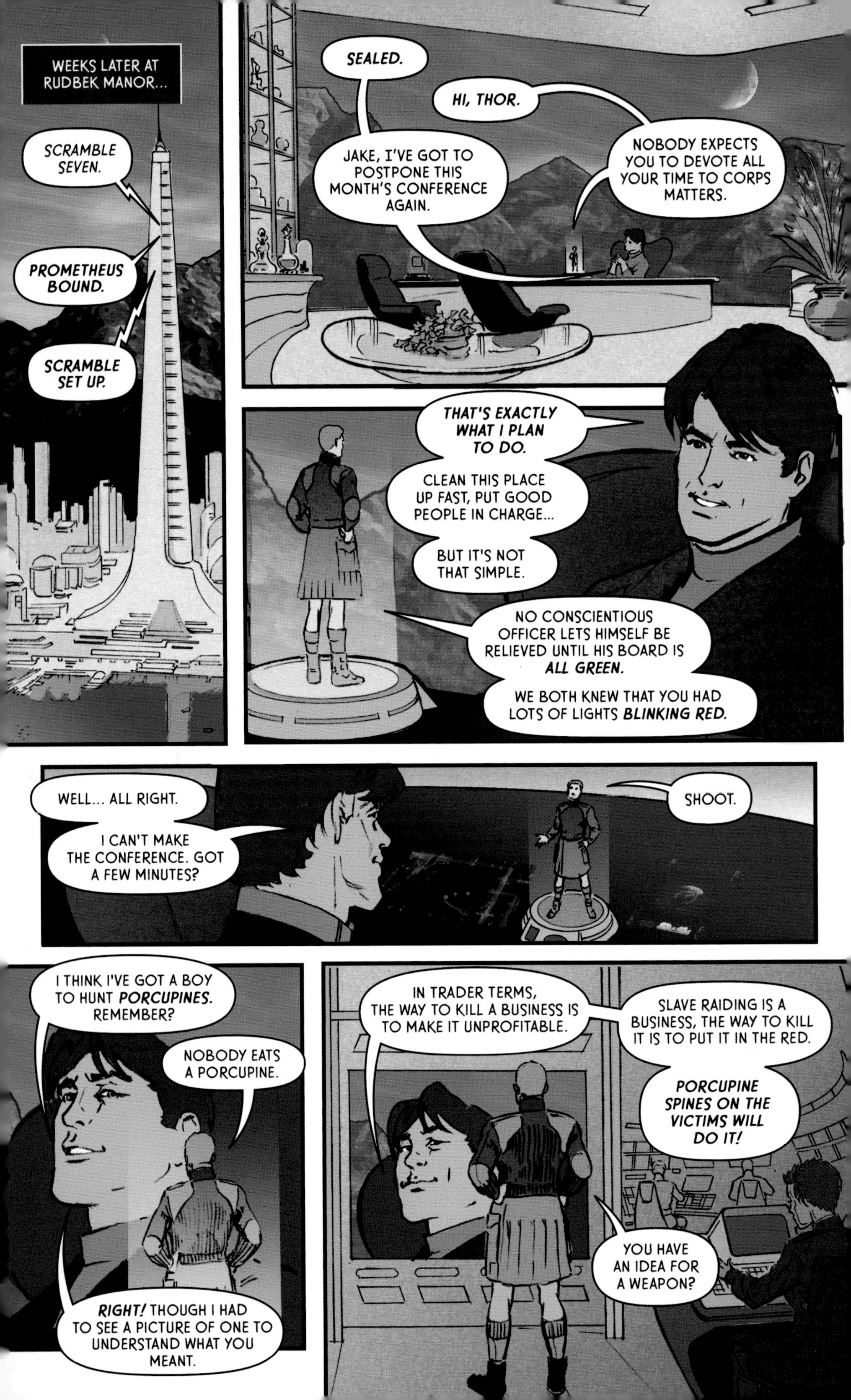
WEEKS LATER AT RUDBEK MANOR...
SCRAMBLE SEVEN.
PROMETHEUS BOUND.
SCRAMBLE SET UP.
SEALED.
HI, THOR.
JAKE, I'VE GOT TO POSTPONE THIS MONTH'S CONFERENCE AGAIN.
NOBODY EXPECTS YOU TO DEVOTE ALL YOUR TIME TO CORPS MATTERS.
THAT'S EXACTLY WHAT I PLAN TO DO.
CLEAN THIS PLACE UP FAST, PUT GOOD PEOPLE IN CHARGE...
BUT IT'S NOT THAT SIMPLE.
NO CONSCIENTIOUS OFFICER LETS HIMSELF BE RELIEVED UNTIL HIS BOARD IS ALL GREEN.
WE BOTH KNEW THAT YOU HAD LOTS OF LIGHTS BLINKING RED.
WELL... ALL RIGHT.
I CAN'T MAKE THE CONFERENCE. GOT A FEW MINUTES?
SHOOT.
I THINK I'VE GOT A BOY TO HUNT PORCUPINES. REMEMBER?
NOBODY EATS A PORCUPINE.
RIGHT! THOUGH I HAD TO SEE A PICTURE OF ONE TO UNDERSTAND WHAT YOU MEANT.
IN TRADER TERMS, THE WAY TO KILL A BUSINESS IS TO MAKE IT UNPROFITABLE.
SLAVE RAIDING IS A BUSINESS, THE WAY TO KILL IT IS TO PUT IT IN THE RED.
PORCUPINE SPINES ON THE VICTIMS WILL DO IT!
YOU HAVE AN IDEA FOR A WEAPON?

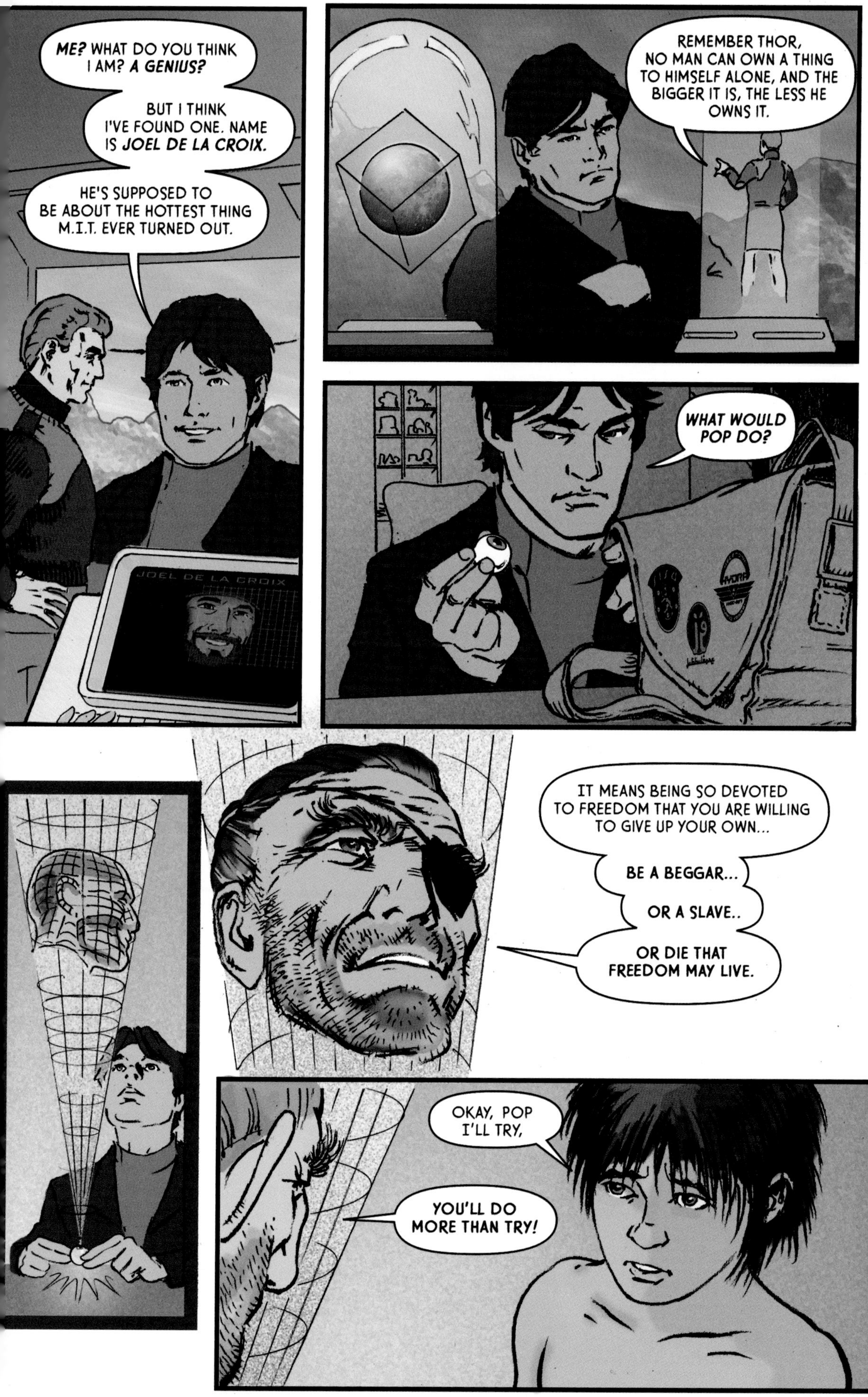
ME? WHAT DO YOU THINK I AM? A GENIUS?
BUT I THINK I'VE FOUND ONE. NAME IS JOEL DE LA CROIX.
HE'S SUPPOSED TO BE ABOUT THE HOTTEST THING M.I.T. EVER TURNED OUT.
JOEL DE LA CROIX
REMEMBER THOR, NO MAN CAN OWN A THING TO HIMSELF ALONE, AND THE BIGGER IT IS, THE LESS HE OWNS IT.
WHAT WOULD POP DO?
IT MEANS BEING SO DEVOTED TO FREEDOM THAT YOU ARE WILLING TO GIVE UP YOUR OWN...
BE A BEGGAR...
OR A SLAVE..
OR DIE THAT FREEDOM MAY LIVE.
OKAY, POP I'LL TRY,
YOU'LL DO MORE THAN TRY!

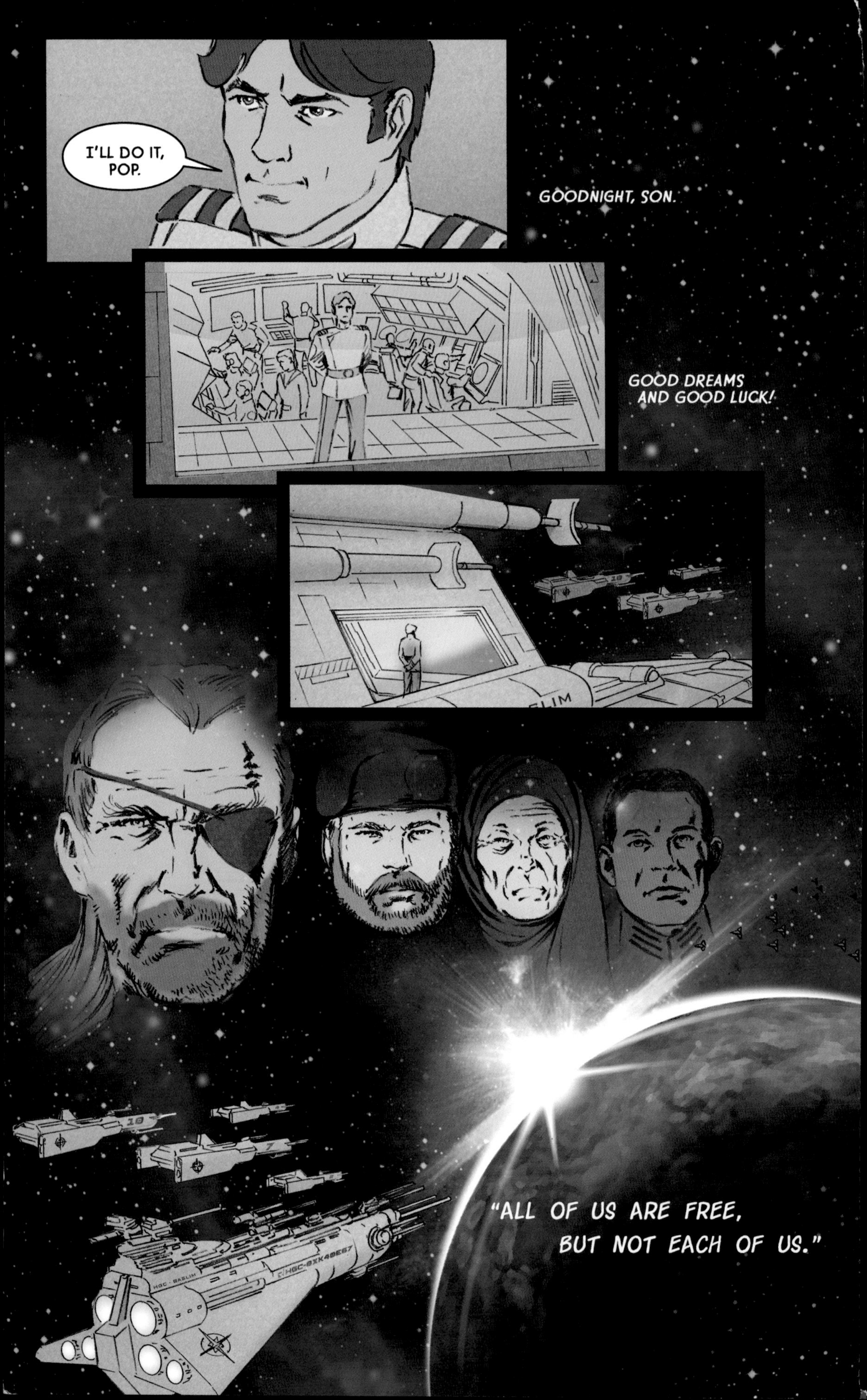
I'LL DO IT, POP.
GOODNIGHT, SON.
GOOD DREAMS AND GOOD LUCK!
"ALL OF US ARE FREE, BUT NOT EACH OF US."

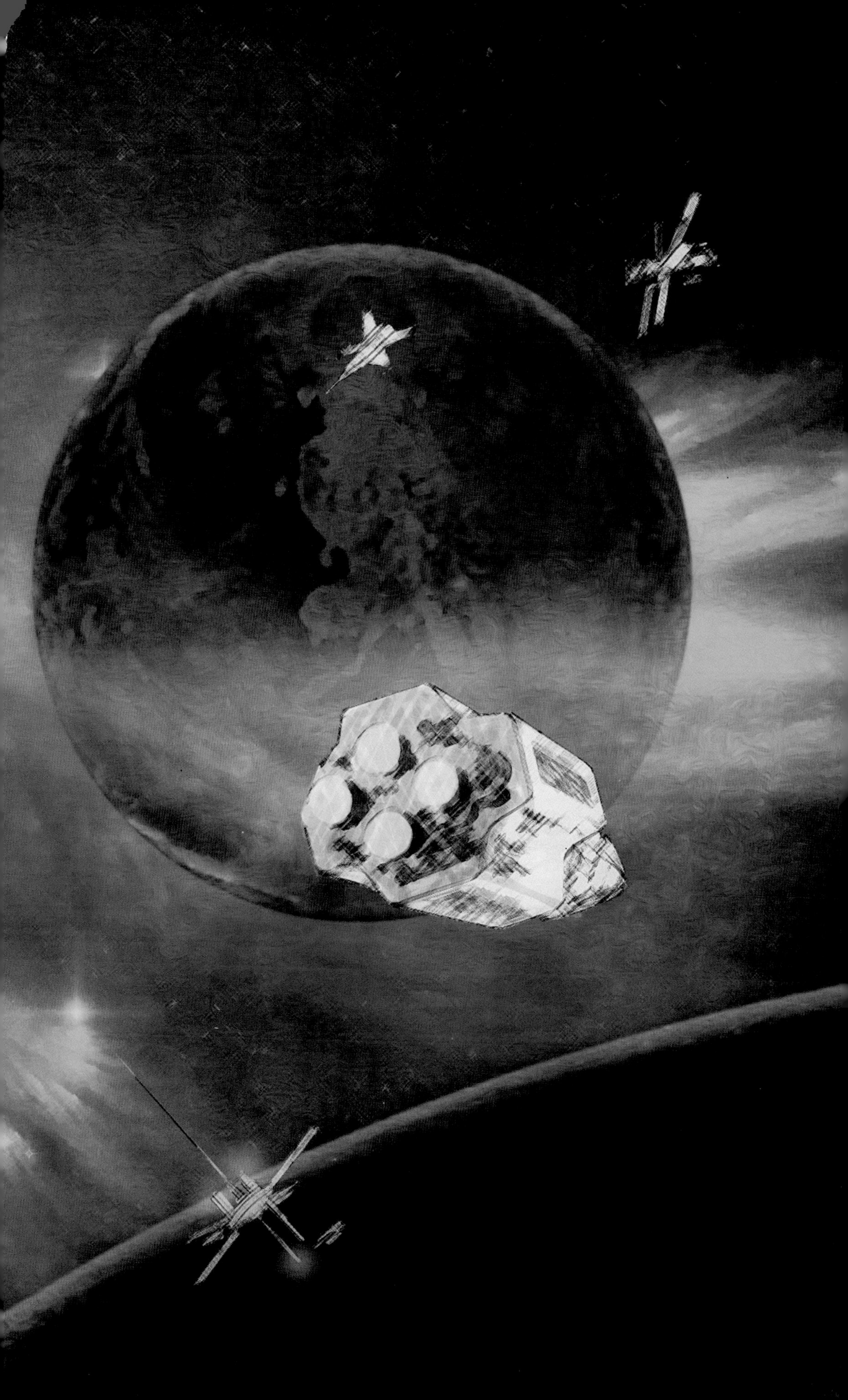

Art by STEVE ERWIN Inks & Colors by ERIC GIGNAC

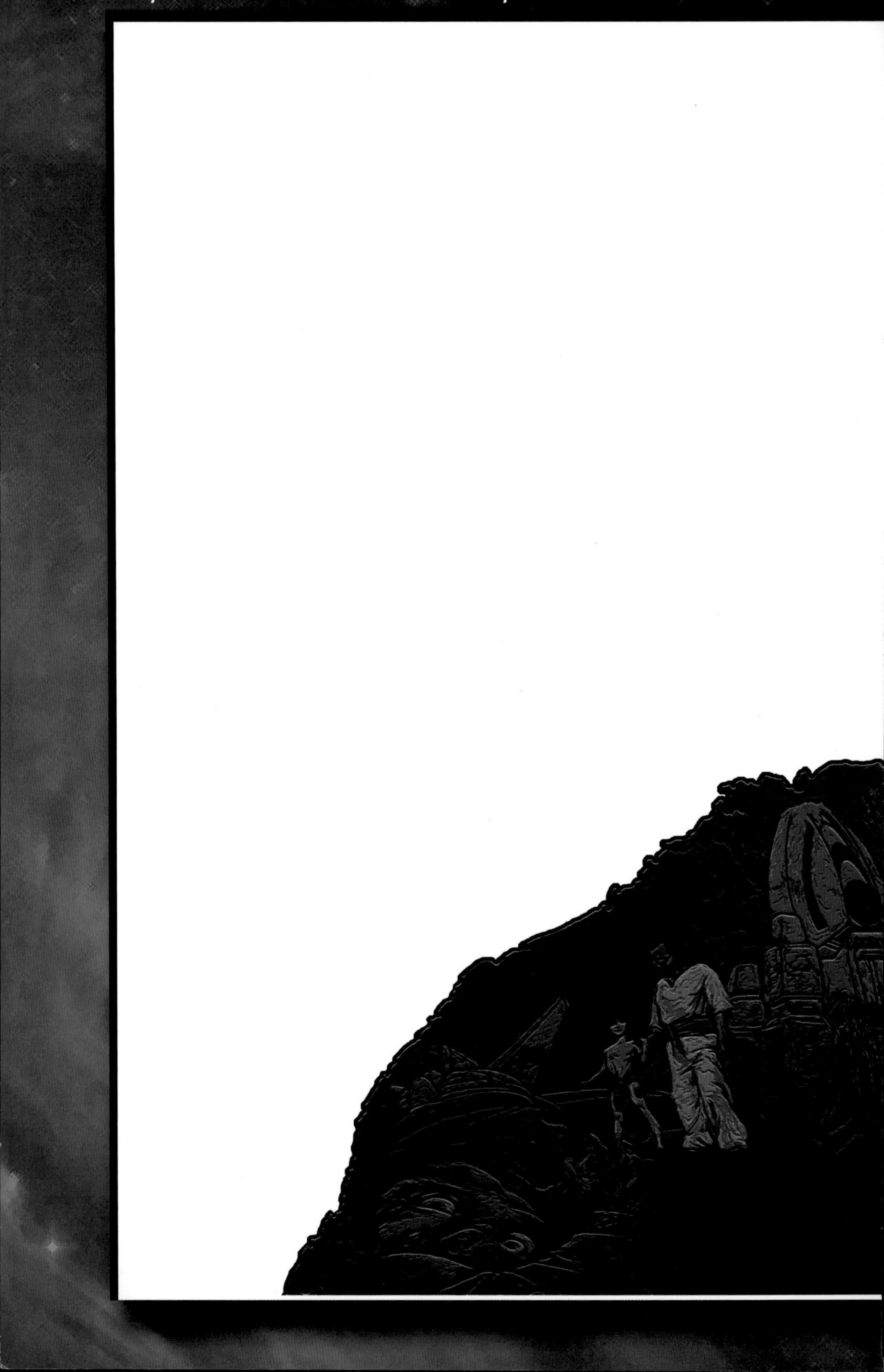

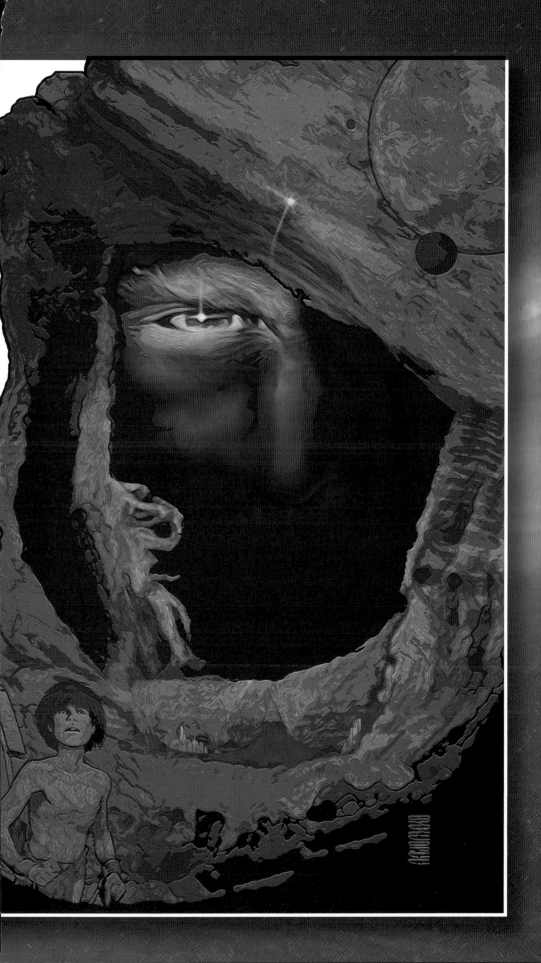

Art by **STEVE ERWIN** Inks & Colors by **ERIC GIGNAC**

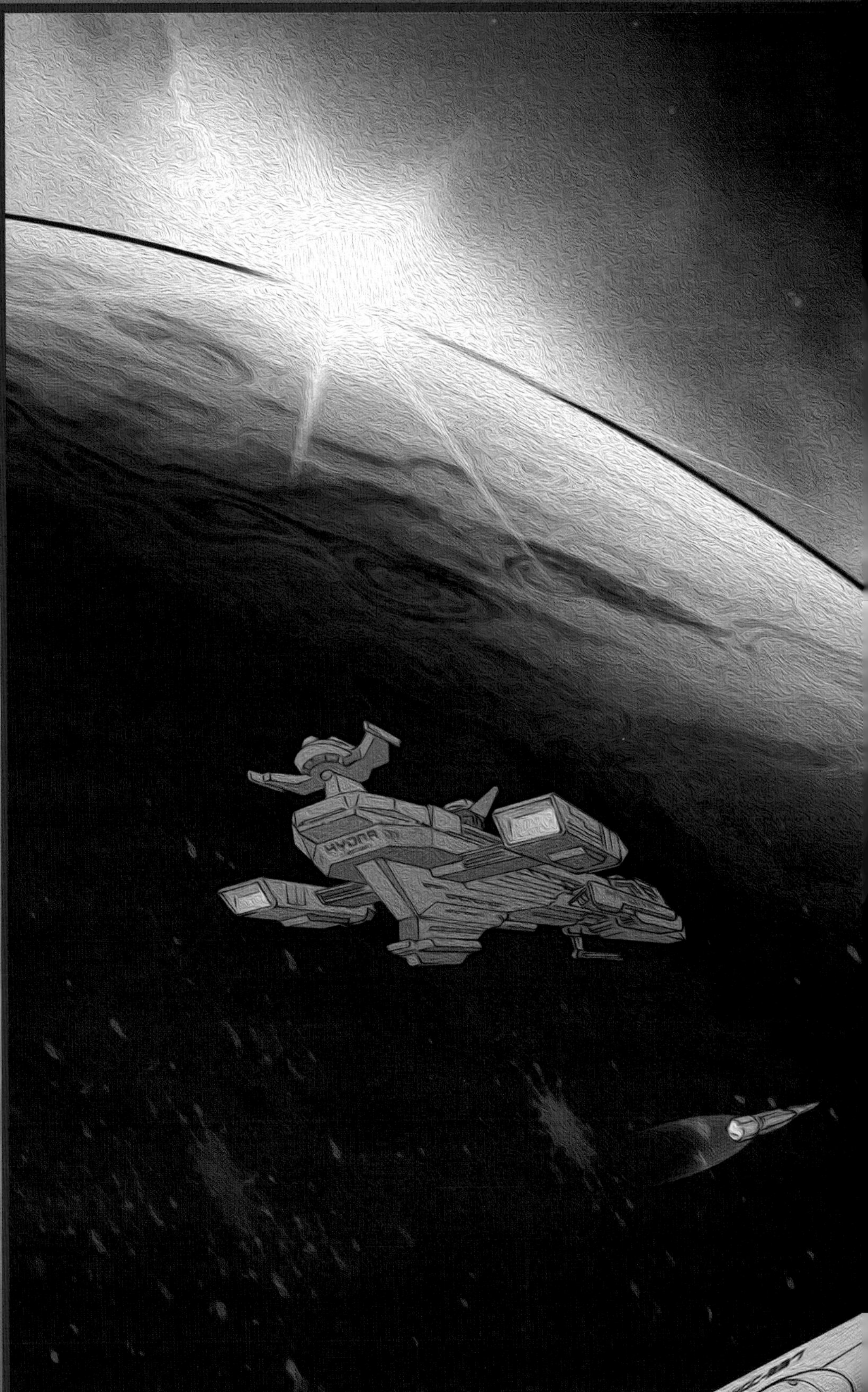

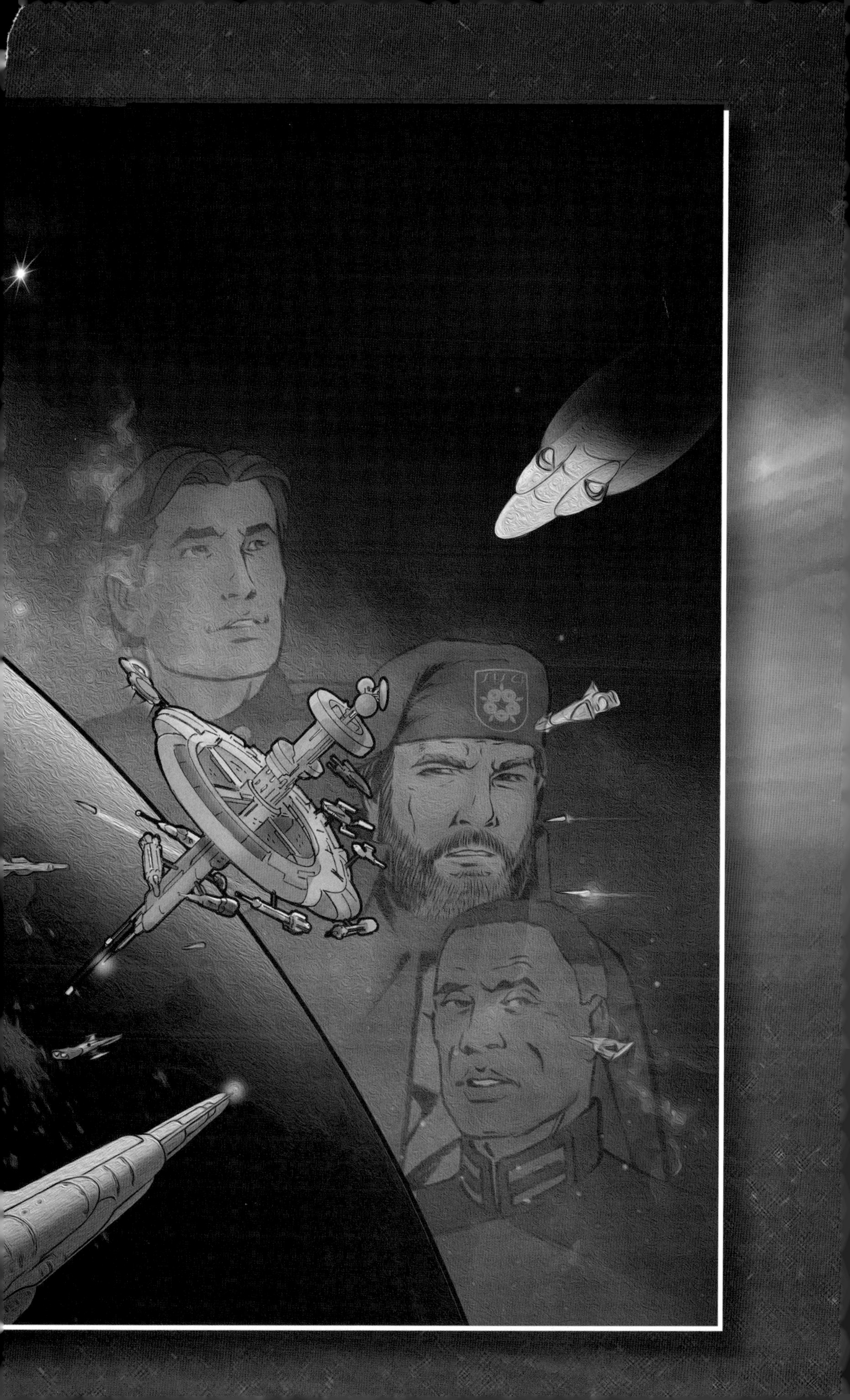

Art by STEVE ERWIN Inks & Colors by ERIC GIGNAC

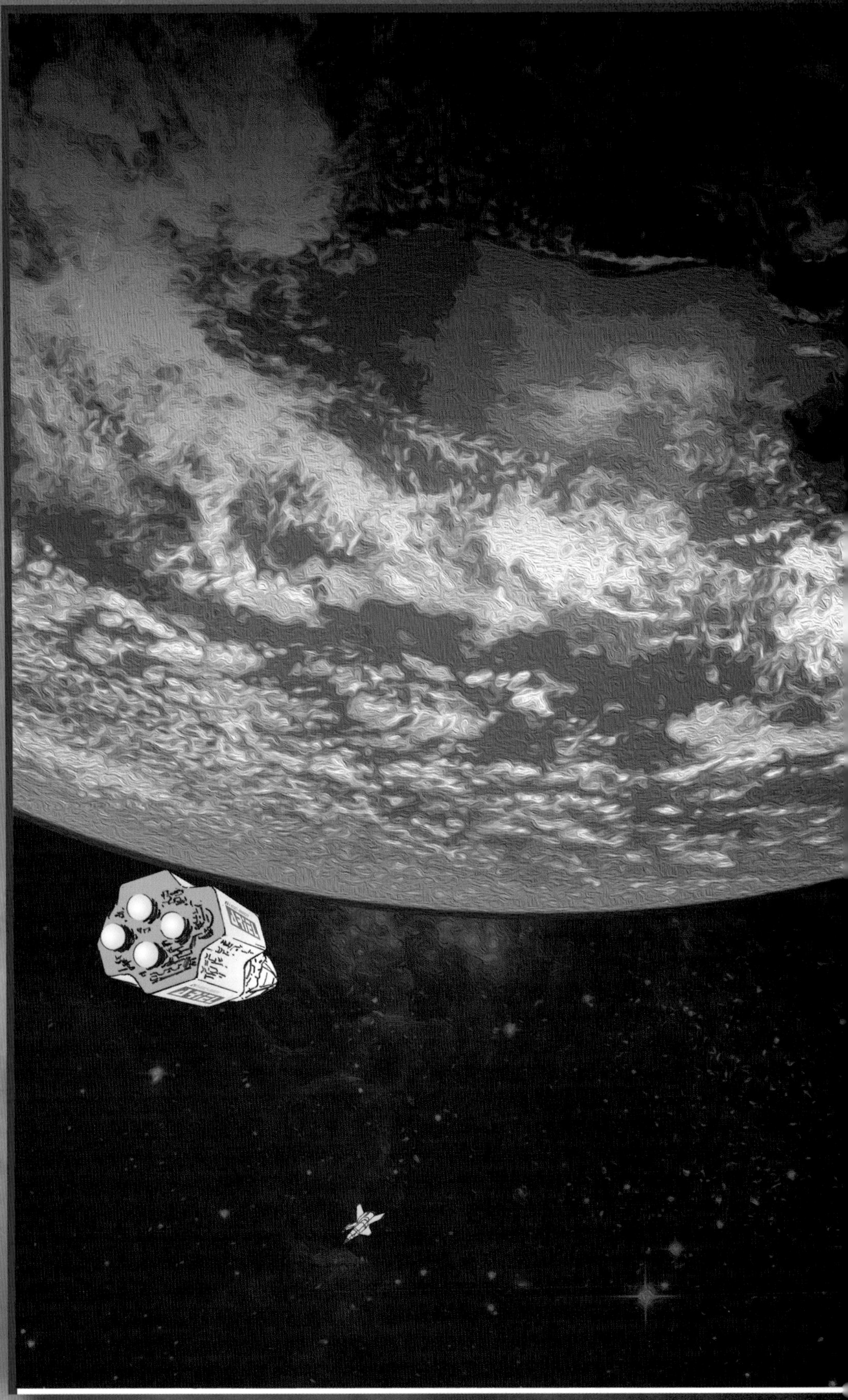

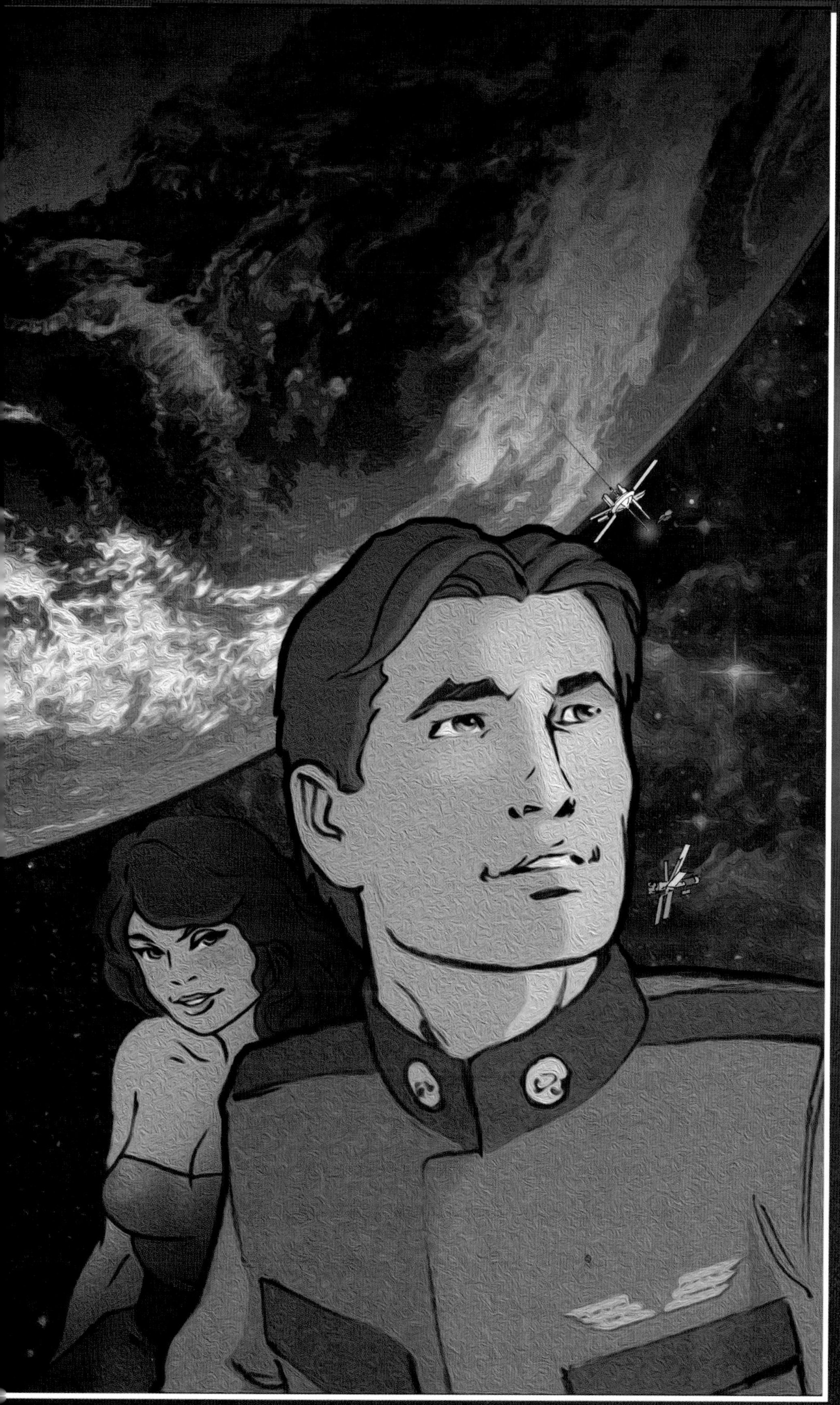

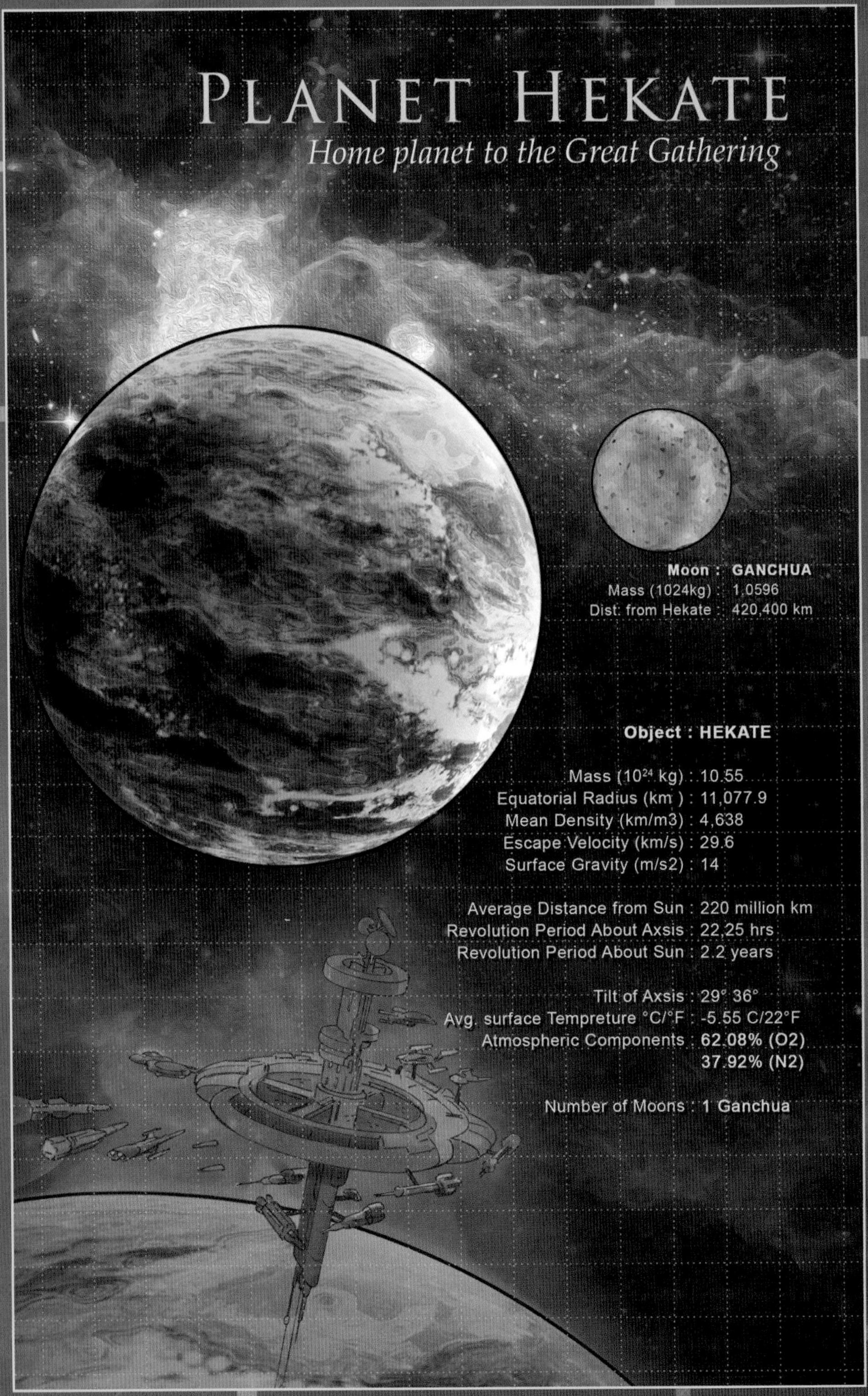
PLANET HEKATE
Home planet to the Great Gathering
Moon : GANCHUA
Mass (1024kg) : 1,0596
Dist. from Hekate : 420,400 km
Object : HEKATE
Mass (10^{24} kg) : 10.55
Equatorial Radius (km) : 11,077.9
Mean Density (km/m3) : 4,638
Escape Velocity (km/s) : 29.6
Surface Gravity (m/s2) : 14
Average Distance from Sun : 220 million km
Revolution Period About Axsis : 22,25 hrs
Revolution Period About Sun : 2.2 years
Tilt of Axsis : 29° 36°
Avg. surface Tempreture °C/°F : -5.55 C/22°F
Atmospheric Components : 62.08% (O2)
37.92% (N2)
Number of Moons : 1 Ganchua

PLANET JUBBUL

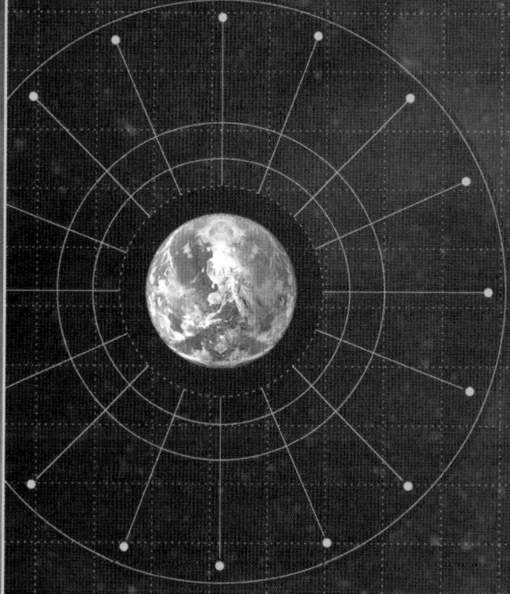

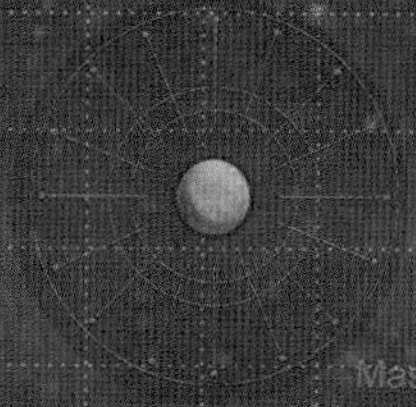

Moon 1	:	LYPTO
Mass (10^{24} kg)	:	0.06342
Volume (10^{10} km3)	:	1.59

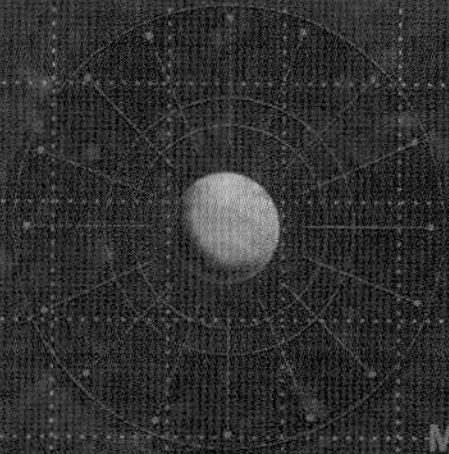

Moon 2	:	ZANITH
Mass (10^{24} kg)	:	0.80275
Volume (10^{10} km3)	:	2.79

Object	:	**JUBBUL**
Mass (10^{24} kg)	:	6.15
Equatorial radius (km)	:	6678.4
Mean density (kg/m3)	:	5432
Escape velocity (km/s)	:	12.2
Surface gravity (m/s2)	:	9.90
Average distance from Sun 1	:	152 million km
Average distance from Sun 2	:	220 million km
Revolution period (days)	:	22.3217
Revolution period (years)	:	1.9
Spin axis tilt (degrees)	:	32.73
Orbit inclination (degrees)	:	2.25
Orbit eccentricity	:	0.0167
Average surface tempreture °C/°F)	:	283 K to 293 K (10 to 20 C)
Atmospheric components	:	68.08% Nitrogen (N_2), 30.95% Oxygen (O_2)
Number of Moons	:	2 (Lypto, Zanith)

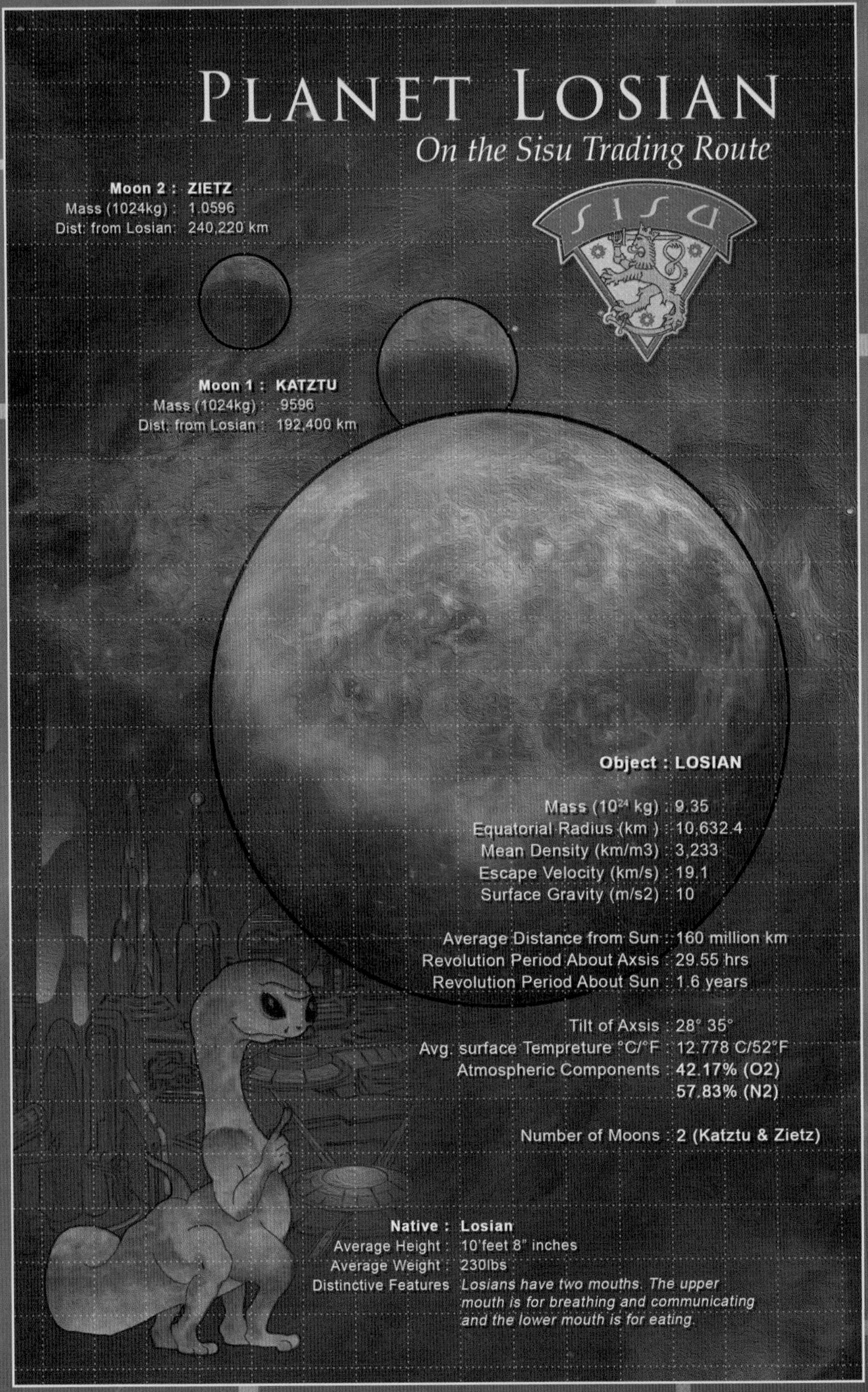

PLANET LOSIAN
On the Sisu Trading Route
SISU
Moon 2 : ZIETZ
Mass (1024kg) : 1.0596
Dist. from Losian : 240,220 km
Moon 1 : KATZTU
Mass (1024kg) : .9596
Dist. from Losian : 192,400 km
Object : LOSIAN
Mass (10^24 kg) : 9.35
Equatorial Radius (km) : 10,632.4
Mean Density (km/m3) : 3,233
Escape Velocity (km/s) : 19.1
Surface Gravity (m/s2) : 10
Average Distance from Sun : 160 million km
Revolution Period About Axsis : 29.55 hrs
Revolution Period About Sun : 1.6 years
Tilt of Axsis : 28° 35°
Avg. surface Tempreture °C/°F : 12.778 C/52°F
Atmospheric Components : 42.17% (O2)
57.83% (N2)
Number of Moons : 2 (Katztu & Zietz)
Native : Losian
Average Height : 10'feet 8" inches
Average Weight : 230lbs
Distinctive Features : Losians have two mouths. The upper mouth is for breathing and communicating and the lower mouth is for eating.

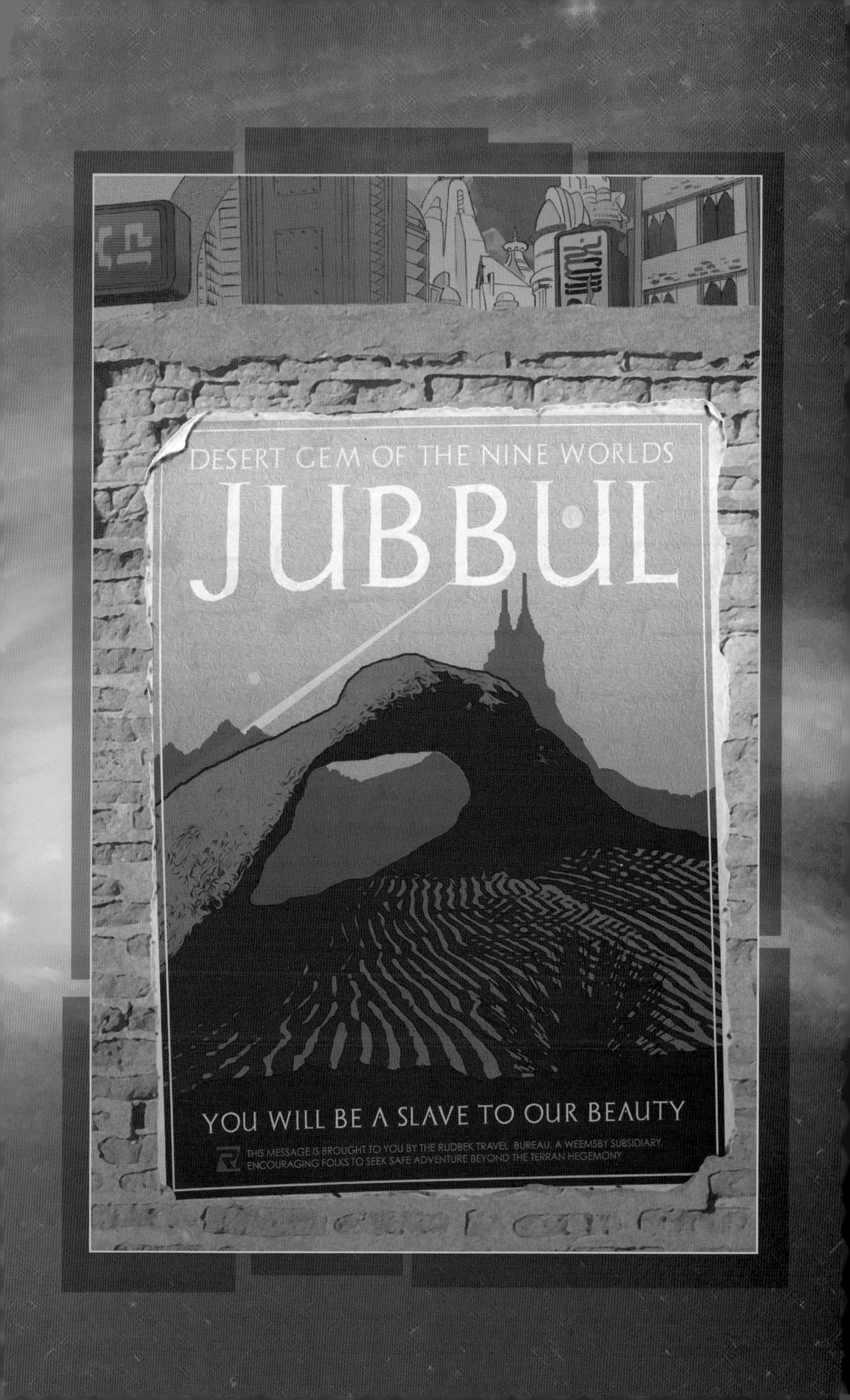
DESERT GEM OF THE NINE WORLDS
JUBBUL
YOU WILL BE A SLAVE TO OUR BEAUTY
THIS MESSAGE IS BROUGHT TO YOU BY THE RUDBEK TRAVEL BUREAU, A WEEMSBY SUBSIDIARY.
ENCOURAGING FOLKS TO SEEK SAFE ADVENTURE BEYOND THE TERRAN HEGEMONY

The following four pages contain rough layouts for a scene we eventually had to cut for brevity.

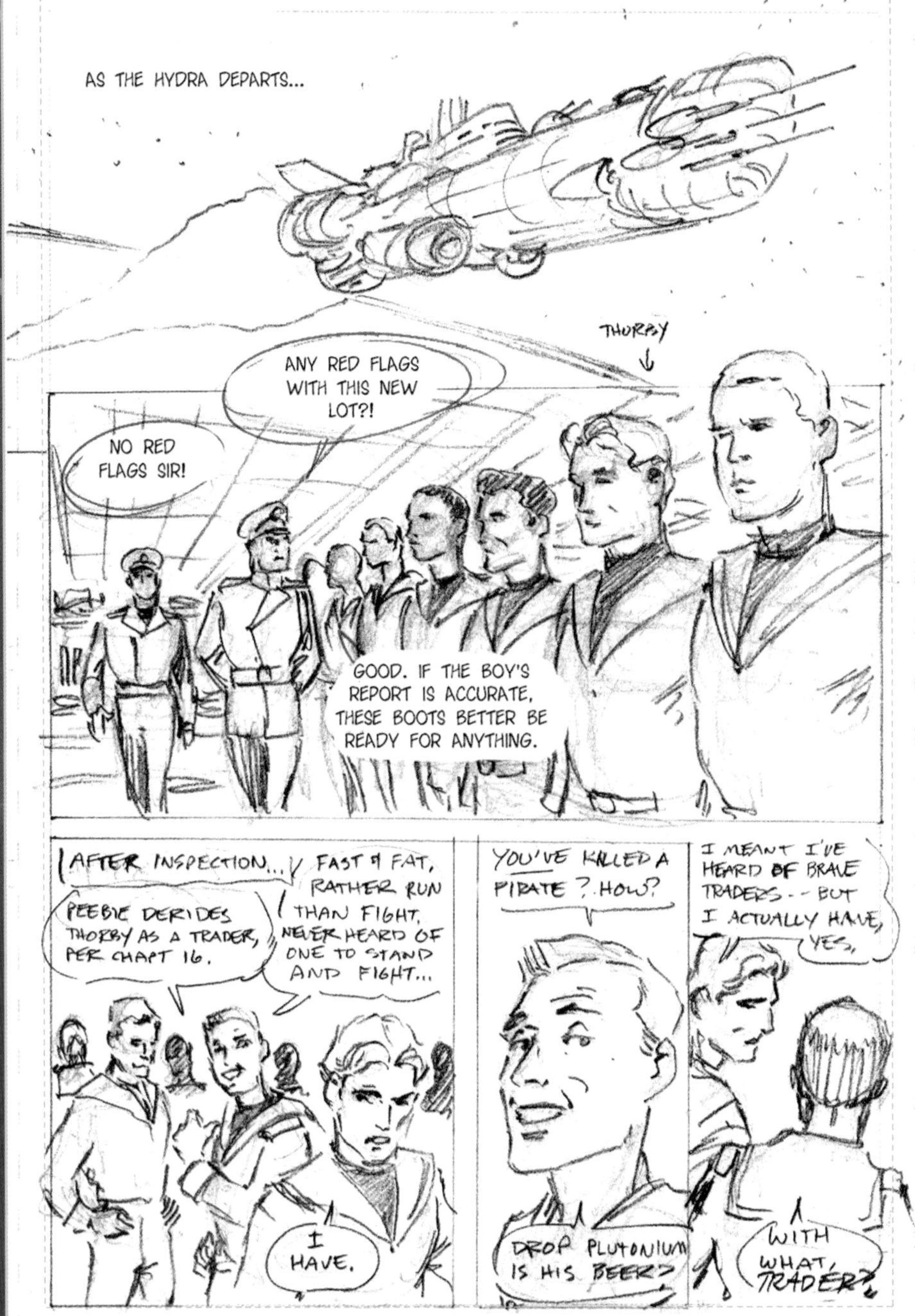
AS THE HYDRA DEPARTS...
THORBY
ANY RED FLAGS WITH THIS NEW LOT?!
NO RED FLAGS SIR!
GOOD. IF THE BOY'S REPORT IS ACCURATE, THESE BOOTS BETTER BE READY FOR ANYTHING.
AFTER INSPECTION...
PEEBIE DERIDES THORBY AS A TRADER, PER CHAPT 16.
FAST & FAT, RATHER RUN THAN FIGHT, NEVER HEARD OF ONE TO STAND AND FIGHT...
I HAVE.
YOU'VE KILLED A PIRATE? HOW?
DROP PLUTONIUM IS HIS BEER?
I MEANT I'VE HEARD OF BRAVE TRADERS -- BUT I ACTUALLY HAVE, YES,
WITH WHAT, TRADER?

APPROXIMATE DIALOGUE PER CHAPTER 16--

IT WAS A MARK XIX ONE-STAGE TARGET-SEEKER MADE BY... ETC ETC, "DECIBEL,"
SILENT PANEL
...
WHERE DID YOU READ THAT?
I READ IT ON THE MANUFACTURER'S MANUAL AS PART OF MY STUDIES AS SENIOR FIRE CONTROLMAN OF THE TRADESHIP SISU.
CHIEF PETTY
THORBY.
YOU NEED TO COME WITH ME. NOW.
HYDRA MAIN FIRE CONTROL (OR WHATEVER)
SO WHAT DO YOU THINK? CAN YOU HANDLE THIS SET UP?
IT'S MUCH MORE... ADVANCED... THAN SISU'S SYSTEMS. I'VE NEVER SEEN SUCH CONTROLS.
WHAT IS SISU OUTFITTED WITH?
DELL/H-P HYBRID POS 3000 WITH A MS WINDOWS XP TARGETING PLATFORM
IF YOU CAN HIT A MOVING TARGET WITH THAT CRAP THIS IS YOUR NEW JOB!

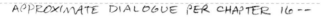

THORBY INSIDE FIRE CONTROL CONTRAPTION

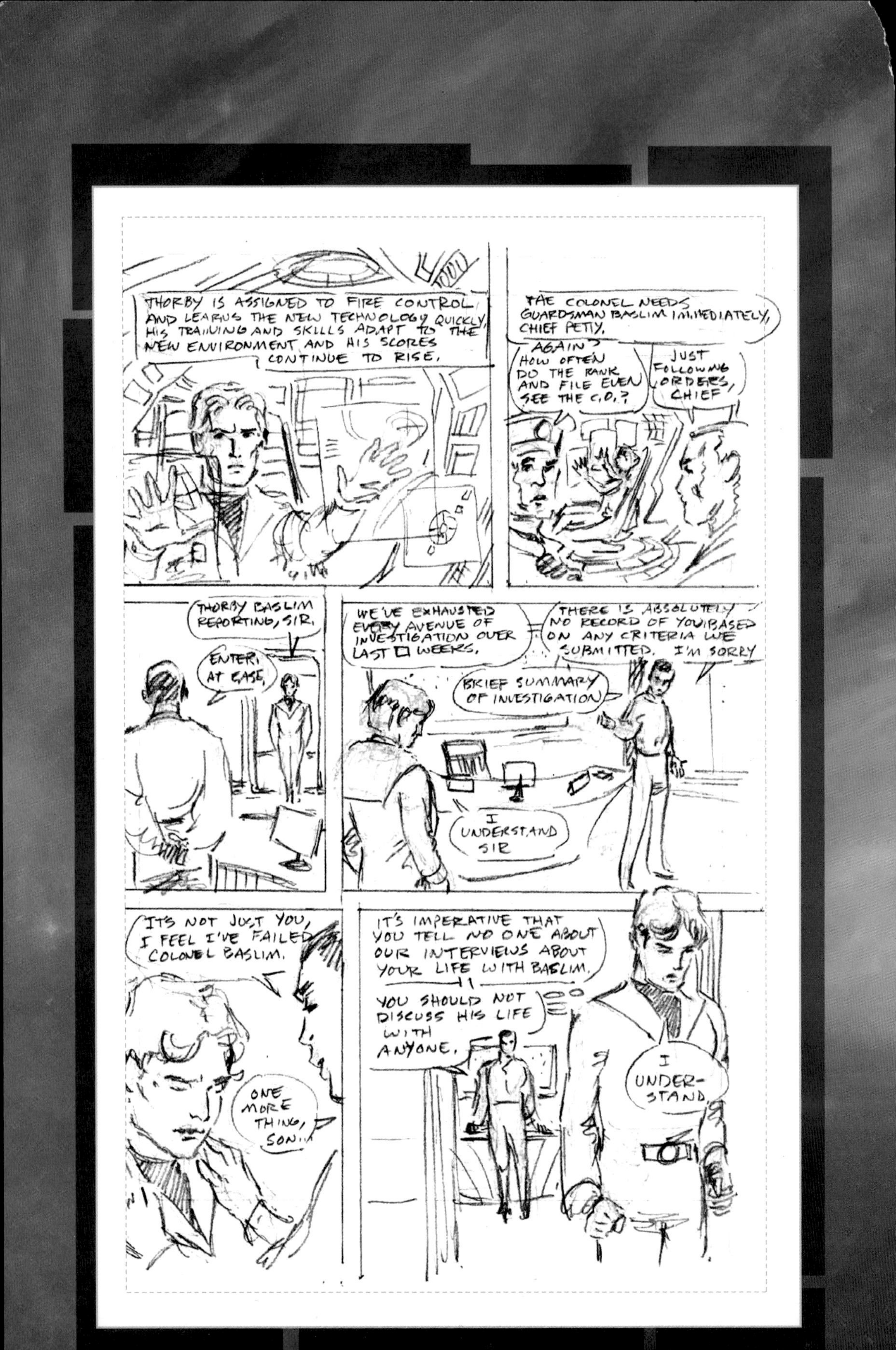
THORBY IS ASSIGNED TO FIRE CONTROL AND LEARNS THE NEW TECHNOLOGY QUICKLY, HIS TRAINING AND SKILLS ADAPT TO THE NEW ENVIRONMENT AND HIS SCORES CONTINUE TO RISE.
THE COLONEL NEEDS GUARDSMAN BASLIM IMMEDIATELY, CHIEF PETTY.
AGAIN? HOW OFTEN DO THE RANK AND FILE EVEN SEE THE C.O.?
JUST FOLLOWING ORDERS, CHIEF
THORBY BASLIM REPORTING, SIR.
ENTER, AT EASE.
WE'VE EXHAUSTED EVERY AVENUE OF INVESTIGATION OVER LAST ☐ WEEKS.
THERE IS ABSOLUTELY NO RECORD OF YOU BASED ON ANY CRITERIA WE SUBMITTED. I'M SORRY
BRIEF SUMMARY OF INVESTIGATION
I UNDERSTAND SIR
IT'S NOT JUST YOU, I FEEL I'VE FAILED COLONEL BASLIM.
ONE MORE THING, SON...
IT'S IMPERATIVE THAT YOU TELL NO ONE ABOUT OUR INTERVIEWS ABOUT YOUR LIFE WITH BASLIM.
YOU SHOULD NOT DISCUSS HIS LIFE WITH ANYONE.
I UNDERSTAND.

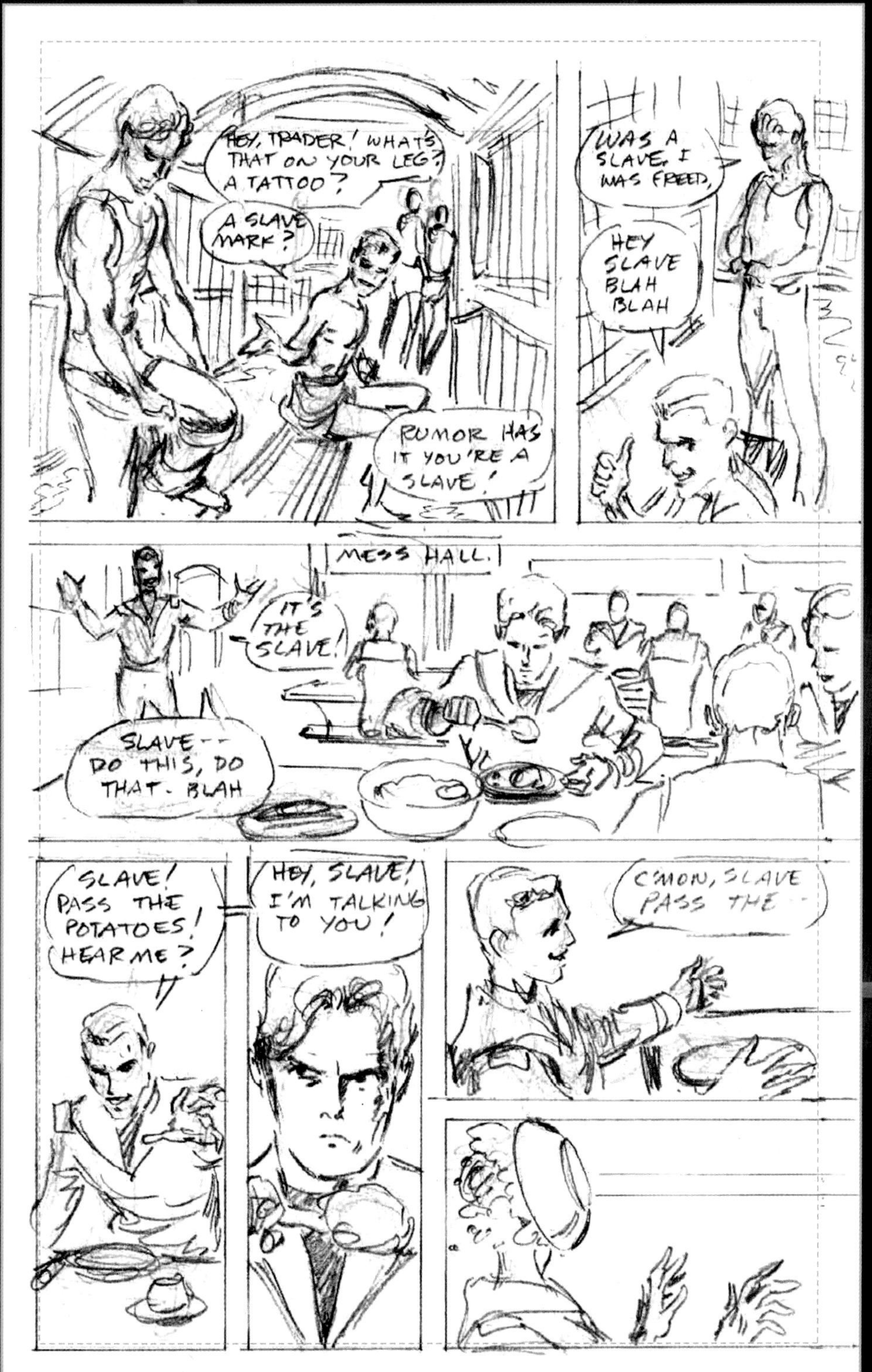
HEY, TRADER! WHAT'S THAT ON YOUR LEG? A TATTOO?
A SLAVE MARK?
RUMOR HAS IT YOU'RE A SLAVE!
WAS A SLAVE, I WAS FREED.
HEY SLAVE BLAH BLAH
MESS HALL.
IT'S THE SLAVE!
SLAVE-- DO THIS, DO THAT. BLAH
SLAVE! PASS THE POTATOES! HEAR ME?
HEY, SLAVE! I'M TALKING TO YOU!
C'MON, SLAVE PASS THE--

This page was almost final. We wanted to introduce the word 'Fraki' earlier then it was introduced in the book and give it a visual. In the end we opted to go with the way the term was introduced in the book.

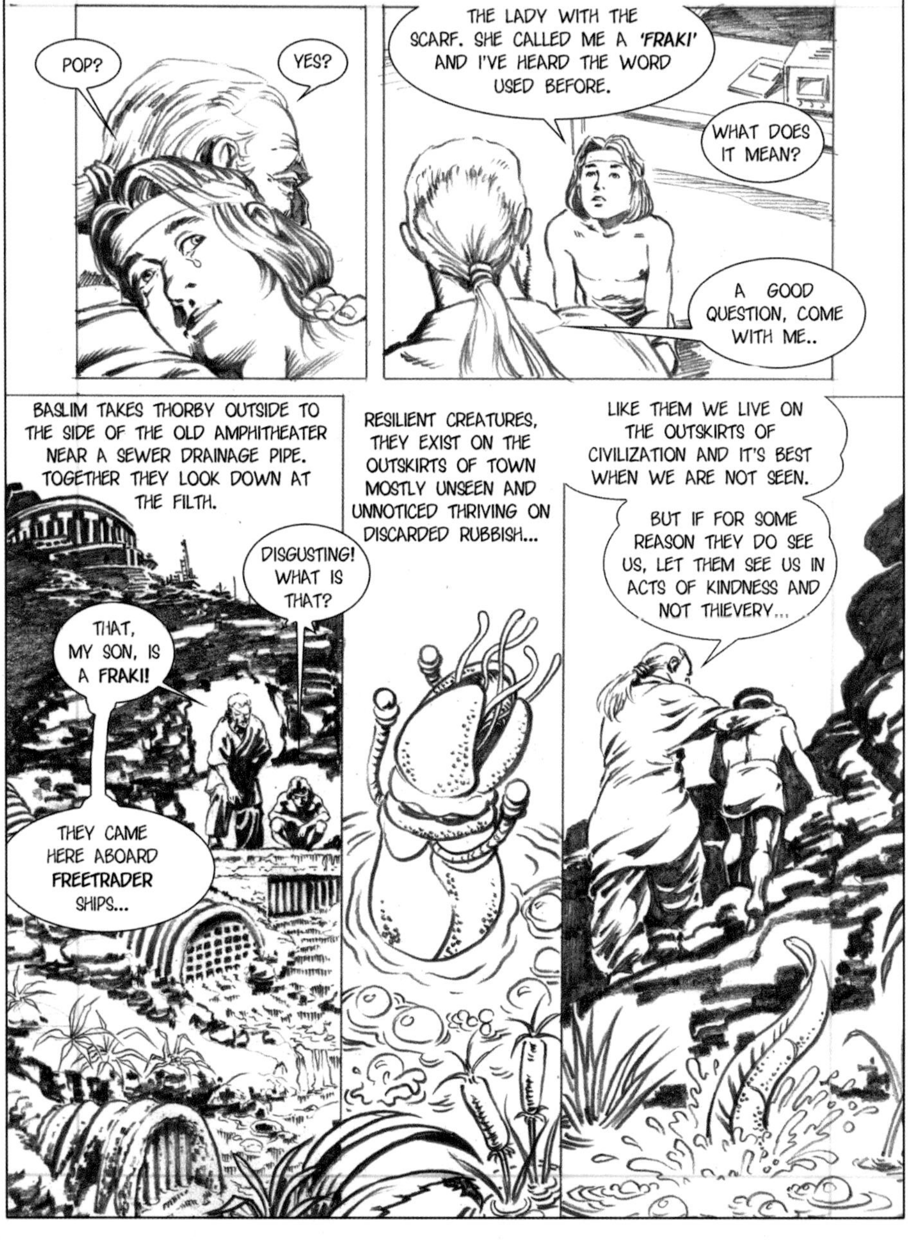

POP?
YES?
THE LADY WITH THE SCARF. SHE CALLED ME A 'FRAKI' AND I'VE HEARD THE WORD USED BEFORE.
WHAT DOES IT MEAN?
A GOOD QUESTION, COME WITH ME..
BASLIM TAKES THORBY OUTSIDE TO THE SIDE OF THE OLD AMPHITHEATER NEAR A SEWER DRAINAGE PIPE. TOGETHER THEY LOOK DOWN AT THE FILTH.
DISGUSTING! WHAT IS THAT?
THAT, MY SON, IS A FRAKI!
THEY CAME HERE ABOARD FREETRADER SHIPS...
RESILIENT CREATURES, THEY EXIST ON THE OUTSKIRTS OF TOWN MOSTLY UNSEEN AND UNNOTICED THRIVING ON DISCARDED RUBBISH...
LIKE THEM WE LIVE ON THE OUTSKIRTS OF CIVILIZATION AND IT'S BEST WHEN WE ARE NOT SEEN.
BUT IF FOR SOME REASON THEY DO SEE US, LET THEM SEE US IN ACTS OF KINDNESS AND NOT THIEVERY...

BIOGRAPHIES

Steve Erwin - Penciler

Steve studied commercial art at Oklahoma State University–Okmulgee. His first published comic book work appeared in *Grimjack* #18 (Jan. 1986) published by First Comics. During the 1980s and 1990s, he worked primarily for DC Comics, his first story for that publisher appearing in *The Vigilante* #48 (Dec. 1987). Erwin co-created the title *Checkmate!* with writer Paul Kupperberg. In August 1991, Erwin and Marv Wolfman launched the *Deathstroke The Terminator* title (now a popular character on the hit CW series Arrow), a series which Erwin would draw from 1991 to 1994. Erwin drew the comics adaptation of *Batman Returns* as well as *Star Trek: The Next Generation Shadowheart,* and the graphic novel adaptation of *The Ashes of Eden.*

Eric R. Gignac - Adaptation/Colors & Layout

Eric graduated from the Art Institute of Houston in 1986 and has worked in the aerospace industry for over 25 years as a graphic artist and concept illustrator. He has worked at Lockheed Martin, Barrios Technologies, Space Services and Excalibur Almaz. He's even designed a few NASA mission patches. Currently Eric works for the Virginia Edition Publishing co. promoting the first and most complete set of writings by the award winning author Robert A. Heinlein. Through his work with the Virginia Edition Eric was granted the first ever rights to produce a Robert A. Heinlein story as a graphic novel... *Citizen of the Galaxy.*

Robert Lazaro PhD. - Adaptation

Rob is a military veteran with more than 15 years of experience in the aerospace industry. He has worked at NASA, Excalibur Almaz Aerospace, and the U.S. Air Force. Shortly after the start of the War on Terrorism, he was one of the first military journalists to cover stories from the frontline. He is a graduate of the University of Texas, El Paso where he earned a Bachelor's degree in Communications, the University of Nebraska, Lincoln where he earned a Master's degree in Journalism, and Northwestern University where he earned a Master's degree in Management. Most recently, he completed a Doctorate in Business Administration at the University of Phoenix. Rob lives in Clear Lake, TX with his wife Kristy and son Christian who is his toughest critic as well as biggest fan.

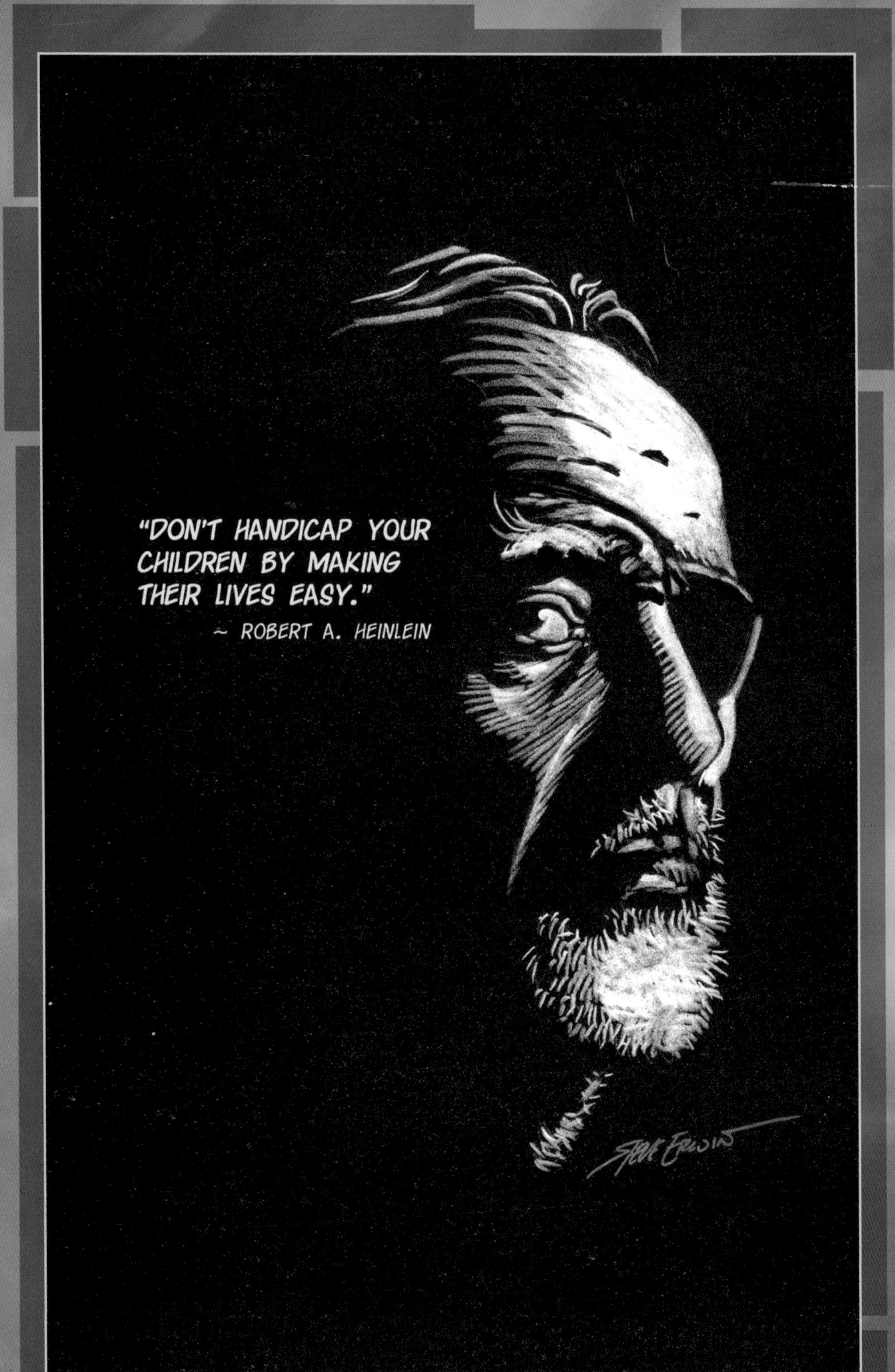
"DON'T HANDICAP YOUR CHILDREN BY MAKING THEIR LIVES EASY."
~ ROBERT A. HEINLEIN